J. ROSS BROWNE: *Confidential Agent in Old California*

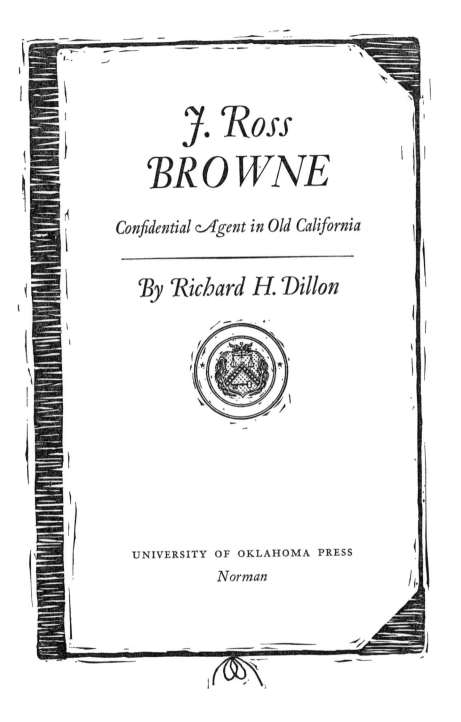

J. Ross
BROWNE

Confidential Agent in Old California

By Richard H. Dillon

UNIVERSITY OF OKLAHOMA PRESS

Norman

BY RICHARD H. DILLON

Bully Waterman (San Francisco, 1956)

Crusoes of Pitcairn Island (Los Angeles, 1957)

Conduct of the Modoc War (Los Angeles, 1959)

Embarcadero (New York, 1959)

(Editor) *The Gila Trail: The Texas Argonauts and the California Gold Rush,* by Benjamin Butler Harris (Norman, 1960)

Shanghaiing Days (New York, 1961)

California Trail Herd (Georgetown, California, 1961)

The Hatchet Men (New York, 1962)

Meriwether Lewis: A Biography (New York, 1965)

J. Ross Browne: Confidential Agent in Old California (Norman, 1965)

LIBRARY OF CONGRESS CATALOG CARD NUMBER: 65-11243

TO ALLAN R. OTTLEY

Preface

IN THE LAST THIRTY YEARS OR SO, much gold—literary gold— has been rediscovered in California. It was in 1937 that George Stewart exhumed George Horatio Derby, alias John Phoenix, alias Squibob, the presumed founding father of the whole Western frontier school of American humor of which both J. Ross Browne and Mark Twain were members. In recent years much prospecting of Browne's old pen-and-ink tailings has been done by latter-day literary Argonauts. The "sooner" of this group was Reverend Francis J. Rock of San Francisco, whose biographical dissertation of 1929 was the foundation stone upon which all recent studies of J. Ross Browne have been built. But others have helped to restore Browne to a more prominent place in American literary and (particularly) regional history, among them Jane Grabhorn, Arthur Lites, George Chambers, Horace Parker, and myself.

Ten years after Father Rock's biobibliographical study, Franklin Walker in his delightful yet definitive work, *San Francisco's Literary Frontier,* gave Browne another push back toward the limelight he had once enjoyed as a page-one contributor to *Harper's New Monthly Magazine.* The WPA, too, did more than lean on its pencils where Browne was concerned. The Sutro Library Project, a WPA Writer's Program group, brought out a reprint edition of Browne's *Washoe Revisited* in 1939.

But the tide did not begin to flood until the 1940's and 1950's. In 1944, Jane Grabhorn, mistress of San Francisco's Colt Press, published her limited-edition, fine-press version of Browne's *Indians of California*. By 1950, Duncan Emrich of the Library of Congress had selected Browne (*A Peep at Washoe*) as the lead-off man for his compilation titled *Comstock Bonanza,* and Lindley (Pink) Bynum had edited a collection of letters written by Browne to his wife, Lucy, when he was reporter-recorder of the California Constitutional Convention of 1849. Bynum's work appeared as a publication of the Book Club of California, titled *Muleback to the Convention.* The third volume on Browne to appear in 1950 was a handsome reprint of his work *A Dangerous Journey,* published by Arthur Lites at his press in Palo Alto, California, in an edition of one thousand copies.

The following year George F. Chambers, publisher of Southwestern regional history under the Arizona Silhouettes imprint, brought out *Adventures in the Apache Country* but retitled it *A Tour Through Arizona, 1864* for modern consumption. During the next year Chambers republished Browne's *Explorations in Lower California,* originally a *Harper's* article. In 1957 one of Joseph Sullivan's Biobooks out of Oakland, California, was a reprint edition of *Washoe Revisited,* and during the subsequent year Oscar Lewis excerpted some of the Irishman's travel writing in his *Autobiography of the West,* as did Charles Neider in his book, *The Great West.*

Another devotee of J. Ross Browne made his public appearance in 1959. Dr. Horace Parker of Balboa Island, California, and his Paisano Press became as busy as a pair of road runners in the pursuit and capture of Browniana. If ever a deceased writer had a counselor pleading his case for him in the courts of American literary and regional history, it was J. Ross Browne, defended by Horace Parker from the sentence-fate of obscurity. Parker's first Browne title was *The Coast Rangers,* a charming but little-known work which had first appeared as a series of articles in Volumes XXIII and XXIV of *Harper's New Monthly Magazine* for June, July, August, October, and December, 1861, and February, 1862.

Dr. Parker asked me to compose an Introduction to *The Coast Rangers* and in so doing infected me with an apparently incurable case of Brownitis. This contagious affection for the man and his work led to the writing of *J. Ross Browne: Confidential Agent in Old California.*

But Doc Parker was not yet content. From his Paisano Press there came, again in 1959, a double-barreled item, *A Peep at Washoe and Washoe Revisited,* and, finally, in 1961, a collection of Browne's scattered articles on Western mines and miners titled *J. Ross Browne's Illustrated Mining Adventures.*

These disciples have made Browne's observations, both serious and comic, available to new generations of readers. But one period of his life remains rather obscure still—the period covered approximately by the years 1854–57, that is, between his return from his first trip to Europe and his setting out on his now oft-recalled adventures in Nevada's Washoe and Comstock Lode. Browne touched on these years in a section, "Observations in Office," of that curious hodgepodge of a book, *Crusoe's Island,* and in several of his magazine articles. But only one segment of his "Observations" has been given much attention—"The Indians of California," which was also a *Harper's* article as part of the Coast Rangers series; which was a chapter in W. W. Beach's compendium of 1877, *The Indian Miscellany,* though retitled "The Indian Reservations of California"; which was reprinted as a now-rare pamphlet in 1923 with the extended title *The California Indians, A Clever Satire on the Government's Dealing with Its Indian Wards*; and which was finally done by Jane Grabhorn as Number Two of the Colt Press's Series of California Classics.

J. Ross Browne: Confidential Agent in Old California attempts to illuminate this "lost" chapter of Browne's life. The reader will follow Browne, in his role of confidential government agent of the Treasury Department and quasi minister without portfolio of both the General Land Office and the Office of Indian Affairs, on his tours of inspection through Uncle Sam's farthest-flung bureaucracy, that of the Western frontier.

This book, and the documents upon which it is based, serve to reveal for the first time that J. Ross Browne was not only ordered to survey customs houses and mints for "irregularities," smugglers and smuggling, and government featherbedding, but that he was also charged with an investigation of the trail-herding of cattle into California. It is very likely that Browne's repeated, strong urgings that Mexican cattle be made duty free led to the act of Congress which abolished the duty on imported livestock. This book, thus, adds at least a tidbit to our scant knowledge of cattle in post–Gold Rush California. Many, such as J. Evetts Haley, have lamented the fact that of all the cattle-trade areas of the nineteenth century, none is as little known or little written about today as California.

Browne was the ideal man for the job of efficiency expert, muckraker, and inspector general. He was a hard-nosed Diogenes. He could smell out fraud and sloth as a ferret can detect rats. Browne was incessantly hard working, honest, and dogged of purpose. As a bonus, he gave the government the use of one of the most talented and observant minds ever to see the Far West, an area which he covered from Galveston to San Francisco to Seattle. He was a more mobile Frank Marryat, a more prolific Bayard Taylor.

His view of the rawness of the frontier is not surprising. But Browne's scathing appraisal of the cupidity of our romanticized and eulogized pioneer forebears will come as a shock to many readers. It is not likely to win any friends for Browne among the membership of native-son societies whose nervous and defensive jokes about skeletal horse thieves in the closet may now ring altogether too true. Nowhere in the annals of Western Americana will you find so thoroughgoing and explicit a study of the blacklegs and ante bellum carpetbaggers of the West. Some of their actions would turn the bronze stomach of the Pioneer Mother in Golden Gate Park and give the vapors to the Madonna of the Plains in Lamar, Colorado. This field of the speculators and swindlers who flocked to El Dorado is virtually terra incognita, and Browne's observations are most illuminating. In the tours of inspection which he made in 1854–57, which are documented in this volume, the seeds of Browne's searing satire were sown.

J. Ross Browne was proud of his efforts to make the West a better place in which to settle, just as he was proud of his efforts to make government work of those pre–civil service days a more respectable and efficient employment. In a printed, undated *Letter from J. Ross Browne in Relation to the State Geological Survey* he said: "It has always been my chief aim to promote to the best of my ability the development of our material resources and however I may have fallen short of the objects of my ambition, none will deny that I have labored long and faithfully in an honorable cause." His labors in behalf of the West's human resources were equally long and honorable.

As a humorist per se, Browne was small caliber in comparison with the Big Gun from Hannibal. But J. Ross Browne does deserve to be remembered. He was more than just a Pacific Slope do-gooder for hire. He was a skillful writer, a keen and witty observer and reporter. He was a builder of the West and a reformer, above all. His recommendations as a reformer were heeded in Washington (for a time—until they hurt too much to be politically bearable) and, thanks to his efforts on the Coast, the Augean mew which was San Francisco in the 1850's was cleaned up to a considerable extent.

Fifteen years after he closed out his tour of duty as a special agent, J. Ross Browne looked back on his experiences and with irony reminisced about them in an essay titled "My Official Experiences":

> There is something very fascinating in public office. The dignity of the position touches our noblest sympathies and makes heroes and patriots of the most commonplace men. . . .
>
> The consideration of a per-diem allowance could not be wholly discarded but, I assure you, upon the veracity of a public officer, it had not the slightest influence upon me when I accepted the responsible position of Inspector General of Public Depositories. The Secretary of the Treasury—a gentleman in whom I had great confidence—required my services. I was unwilling, of course, to stand in the way of an efficient administration of the affairs of his department. The fact is, I had great personal respect for him and was anxious to afford him all the assistance in my power. I do not pretend to say that the appointment of inspector general was destitute of attractions in itself, but they were not of a pecuniary character. The title had a sonorous and authoritative ring about it altogether different from the groveling jingle of filthy lucre—something that vibrated upon the higher chords of the soul. . . .

To make a short story of it, I was obliged to accept the position. The party in power stood in need of my services. I could not refuse without great detriment to the country. This was many years since, and I beg to say that there is nothing in my journal of experiences bearing upon the present state of affairs. At great pecuniary sacrifice (that is to say, in a prospective sense, for I hadn't a dime in the world), I announced myself as ready to proceed to duty. In his letter of instructions the Secretary of the Treasury was pleased to direct me to the Pacific Coast and carefully examine into the condition of the revenue service in that remote region. I was to see that the accounts of the collectors were properly kept and rendered; that the revenue laws were faithfully administered; that the valuation of imports was uniform throughout the various districts; whether any reductions could be made in the number of inspectors and aids to the revenue stationed within their limits, with a view to a more economical administration of the laws; whether the public moneys were kept in the manner prescribed by the Independent Treasury Act of August 6th, 1846; and what additional measures, if any, were necessary for the prevention of smuggling and other frauds upon the revenue, all of which I was to report, with such views as might be suggested in the course of the investigation for the promotion of the public interest.

These were but a few of the important subjects of official inquiry upon which I was to enlighten the Department. I frankly confess that, when I read the instructions and pondered over their massive proportions and severe tone of gravity, I was appalled at the immensity of the interests committed to my charge. A somewhat versatile career, during which I had served before the mast on a whaler, studied medicine, hunted squirrels in the backwoods, followed the occupation of ferry-keeper, flatboat hand and shorthand writer, had not fitted me particularly for this sort of business. What did I know about the forms of accounts current, drawbacks, permits, entries, appraisements, licenses, enrollments, and abstracts of imports and exports? What reliable or definite information was I prepared to give to collectors of customs in reference to schedules and sliding scales? What hope was there that I could ever get to the bottom of a fraud upon the revenue service when I had but a glimmering notion of the difference between fabrics of which the component parts were two thirds wool and fabrics composed in whole or in part of sheet iron, leather, or gutta percha?

As for inspectors of customs, how in the world was an agent to find out how many inspectors were needed except by asking the collector of the district, who ought to know more about it than a stranger? But if the collector had half a dozen brothers, cousins, or friends in office as inspectors, would it not be expecting a little too much of human nature to suppose he would say there were too many in his district? I reflected over the idea of asking one of these gentlemen to inform me confidentially if he thought he could dispense with a dozen or so of his relatives and friends without detriment to the public service, but abandoned it as chimerical. Then, to go outside and question any disinterested member of the community seemed equally absurd. Who could be said to be disinterested when only a few offices were to be filled and a great many people wished to fill them? I would be pretty sure to stumble upon some disappointed applicant for an inspectorship or, worse still, upon a smuggler. . . .

There was another serious duty imposed upon me—to ascertain the character and standing of all the public employees, their general reputation for sobriety, industry, and honesty and to report accordingly. . . . I did not much relish the notion of placing any man's personal infirmities upon the official records. If a public officer drank too much whisky, it was certainly a very injurious practice, alike prejudicial to his health and morals; but where was to be the gauge between too much and only just enough? No man likes to have his predilection for stimulating beverages made a matter of public question, and the gradations between temperance and intemperance are so arbitrary in different communities that it would be a very difficult matter to report upon. I have seen men "sociable" in New Orleans who would be considered "elevated" in Boston, and men "a little shot" in Texas who would be regarded as "drunk" in Maine. . . . With respect to honesty, that was an equally delicate matter. What might be considered honest among politicians might be very questionable in ordinary life. . . .

The Department furnished me with a penknife, pencil, several quires of paper, and a copy of Gordon's Digest of the Revenue Laws. This was my outfit. It was not equal to the outfit of a minister plenipotentiary but there was a certain dignity in its very simplicity. To be the owner of a fine Congressional penknife, a genuine English lead-pencil, paper *ad libitum* and Gordon's Digest was no trifling advance in my practical resources. I looked into the Digest, read many of the laws and became satisfied that the Creator had not gifted me with any capacity for understanding that species of writing. For Mr. Gordon, who had digested those Laws, I felt a very profound admiration. His powers of digestion were certainly better than mine. I would much rather have undertaken to digest a keg of spike nails. The Act of March 2, 1799, upon which most of the others were based, was evidently drawn with great ability and covered the whole subject. Like a Boeotian fog, however, it covered it up so deep that I don't think the author ever saw it again after he got through writing the law. Whenever there was a tangible point to be found, it was either abolished or so obscured by some other law made in conformity with the progress of the times that it became no point at all; so that, after perusing pretty much the whole book, and referring to Mayo's Compendium of Circulars and Treasury Regulations, I am free to confess the effect was very decided. I knew a great deal less than before, for I was utterly unable to determine who was right—Congress, Gordon, Mayo, or myself.

Under these circumstances, it will hardly be a matter of surprise that serious doubts as to my capacity for this service entered my mind. . . . The position was highly responsible; the duties were of a very grave and important character, bordering on the metaphysical. . . .

Had I been appointed to succeed Sancho Panza in the government of Nantucket (which I verily believe was the island referred to by Cervantes), I could have had no misgivings of success. But this awful thing of abstracts and accounts current; this subtile mystery of appraisements, appeals, drawbacks, bonds and bonded warehouses; this terrible demon of manifests, invoices, registers, enrollments and licenses; this hateful abomination of circulars on refined sugar and fabrics composed in whole or in part of wool; this miserable subterfuge of triplicate vouchers and abstracts of disbursements, combined to cast a gloom over my mind almost akin to despair.[1]

Bewildered, assailed by doubts and confusion, J. Ross Browne nevertheless kept his mind fixed on the per diem and the honor of the post, or so he said, and succumbed to Secretary Guthrie's solicitation. His efforts and those of Confidential Agent William M. Gouge, in the East, made it possible for Guthrie to report to the Congress in glowing terms on the renaissance in the Treasury Department on December 4, 1854:

The Department has caused the collectors' offices in all the ports to be examined within the year, with but few exceptions, by agents of the Department, in order to ascertain how their books and accounts were kept and, by

[1] J. Ross Browne, *Crusoe's Island* (New York, Harper Brothers, 1867) 249–55.

personal inspection, how the official corps discharged their duties. These examinations have enabled this Department to correct errors and omissions and to see that the official corps devote themselves, in person, to the duties confided to them, and have resulted in securing greater vigilance and a more faithful application of the revenue laws.[2]

Guthrie concluded his message to Congress on a hopeful note, optimistic of continued improvement in the Department thanks to the exertions of such agents as Gouge and J. Ross Browne. He said:

The important interests confided to this Department require that the clerical force should be not only capable but trustworthy in all respects. I find there has been great improvement in that force. In most cases the best of those found in office were retained and under the system of classification when vacancies occurred a rule was established to promote for capacity and efficiency from the lower to the higher classes, whilst the required examinations have secured more capable clerks for the first class. The rules of the office are strictly enforced and there exists commendable industry, capacity, efficiency and, it is believed, integrity in the corps employed. The Department is being brought into good condition.[3]

Three volumes of J. Ross Browne's confidential reports from the Far West have survived the years and are to be found today in the National Archives in Washington. They have recently been microfilmed, and the individual communiqués assigned serial numbers, beginning with 82 and ending with 408. It was discovered that the missing documents of the group preceded the existing reports chronologically and were apparently 1–81. Browne, as a secret agent, reported regularly on his itineraries and investigations, forwarding to Washington such supporting material as maps, charts, newspaper clippings, statistics, tables, and so forth, along with his formal reports. Since his investigations were made basically to cure irregularities and to improve the efficiency of the Customs Service, some of his reports resulted in rather sweeping reforms, disciplinary actions, and reduction or replacement of personnel.

[2] *Appendix to the Congressional Globe* (December 4, 1854), 33 Cong., 2 sess. Senate and House of Representatives, Report of the Secretary of the Treasury (Washington, John C. Rives, 1855), New Series, XXXI, 8.
[3] *Ibid.*, 10.

Browne's hitherto unpublished reports throw a great deal of light on a zone of Western Americana long obscured by haze and shadow. The Gold Rush has been much documented; the Graft Rush which followed has hardly been studied at all. Con men, quacks, and thimbleriggers were not given to bragging over their reprehensible conduct. They preferred to operate under cover. They have not yet been "discovered" by the popular historians who have made famous their colleagues in the more open outlawry of murder and road agentry. No one has yet attempted to make them into Robin Hoods of the Wild, Wild West. But one day it will be found that the carpetbaggers of the noisome spoils system of nineteenth-century American politics did not wait for Reconstruction to head for the provinces; there were easy pickings in California in the 1850's. If it is true, as the bawdy ballad suggests, that "the miners came in '49, the whores in '51," then the carpetbaggers were in San Francisco by '52.

It is unfortunate that so many—eighty-one—of Browne's documents, most of which presumably dealt with Texas, have been lost to us. But his habit of recapitulating in subsequent letters—a habit born of a marked mistrust of the mails of that period and of that frontier—allows us to see in brief, at least, what struck him most in his tours of inspection of Texas as well as of the Pacific Coast.

RICHARD H. DILLON

Mill Valley, California
March 13, 1965

Contents

Illustrations

J. ROSS BROWNE: *Confidential Agent in Old California*

CHAPTER ONE

A-Roving

ON FEBRUARY 11, 1821, a boy was born[1] to Thomas Egerton Browne and his wife in the Dublin suburb of Beggar's Bush.[2] "Like father, like son," goes the old saw and it was thus with the Brownes. The elder Irishman was a cultured journalist in whose veins coursed as much ink as gore. His young son, John Ross Browne, would prove to be but a later edition of the parent. It is likely, too, that J. Ross Browne, as the boy came to call himself, inherited his hatred of sham and dishonesty from the fighting Wesleyan Irishman who was his father. Thomas Browne's weapons were pen and ink, type and newsprint. Although he was a poet, Thomas Browne won fame—notoriety, in government eyes—in the field of journalism. He wrote under such pseudonyms as Jonathan Buckthorn, "J.G.," and Fondriangle, as well as

---

[1] Various sources give various dates of birth for Browne. *Appleton's Cyclopedia of American Biography* gives the year 1817; in J. D. B. Stillman's *Seeking the Golden Fleece* a list of passengers has Browne's age in 1849 as twenty-seven years. February 11, 1821, appears to be the most likely birth date in view of both family tradition and the research of Browne's biographer, Rev. Francis J. Rock.

[2] However, when Browne wrote his wife in 1862 from Edinburgh that he would like to run over to Ireland to see his old home, he located it at "Ballykilkaran." Lindley Bynum (ed.), *Muleback to the Convention: Letters of J. Ross Browne* (San Francisco, Book Club of California, 1950), i. (Hereinafter cited as *Muleback*.)

3

under his own proper name.[3] By 1831 he was editing three Dublin papers, the *Comet,* the *Valentine Post Bag,* and the *Parson's Horn Book.* Sometimes called "the Irish Cobbett," like that Anglo-American Porcupine he had a knack of prickling and irritating those in authority. As a result of his attacks on the British system of tithes, he became *persona non grata* in Dublin and was sentenced to a fine of one hundred pounds and a year's imprisonment. The fine being remitted, perhaps on condition that he emigrate, Browne was released from gaol after three months' detention[4] and allowed to sail to America with his family. And thus it was that William Makepeace Thackery lost a friend in the Irish poet-journalist whom some called the "Knight of Innishowan" but more called the "Irish Whisky Drinker."

The *émigré* and his family landed in America virtually destitute but made their way to what was then the West, settling in Louisville, Kentucky, where the couple opened a private school for girls in 1833. Little is known of J. Ross Browne, the youngster, except that he developed a love of reading and of travel, both of which would last him a lifetime. Defoe's *Robinson Crusoe* was his favorite book. It formed in the lad a never-to-be quenched wanderlust and curiosity about far places.

Browne's well-educated parents tutored him, but he rebelled against their insistence that he master the classics. Crusoe, Gil Blas, and Don Quixote were much more his cup of tea than Greco-Roman orators or phalanxes. The boy dabbled in art and music in the congenial cultural climate in which he found himself. In later years he became an accomplished humorous artist as well as a fair-to-middling flutist. After a few part-time jobs as a tailor's errand boy and as a clerk, J. Ross Browne had a go at medical school but found it not at all to his liking.

The year in which it becomes possible to follow the spoor of J. Ross Browne, thanks to Father Rock's bibliographic detective work, is 1838. That was the year in which he hired out as a deck hand on a flatboat.

---

[3] All biographical details on Browne and his family, unless otherwise noted, are from Rev. Francis J. Rock, *J. Ross Browne: A Biography* (Washington, D.C., Catholic University Press, 1929).

[4] Lina Fergusson Browne, J. Ross Browne's granddaughter-in-law, has given the length of his incarceration as eleven months, as opposed to Father Rock's three months, in her unsigned biographical introduction to *Muleback, i.*

For a year Browne cruised the Ohio and Mississippi rivers, from Louisville to New Orleans. His tutor, like Sam Clemens', was the Father of Waters. Browne also traveled over parts of Texas as well as in areas of several Eastern states by shank's mare, in the manner of future Western writers Stephen Powers, John Muir, and Charles Lummis. When he was but twenty years old, he found that he had covered 2,200 miles of the United States, of which 1,600 miles had been by flatboat and 600 on foot.

Like so many adventurous youths of his day, Browne yearned to travel around the world. He wanted to go first cabin, to do it in style. In his own words, he wished to roam the world as a "gentleman of leisure." He would eventually see his dream of world travel come true, but Browne was never one to overindulge in leisure. Usually, when he traveled he worked hard, if only at writing. In any case, there would be long years of hard, bone-wearying travel on horseback, muleback, or shank's mare before he would see Europe in the style to which he hoped to become accustomed.

Since he had no means, Browne decided to create a demand for his services, a demand which would see him called to distant parts for employment. His choice of study was fortunate. He took up stenography and shorthand, or "business and commercial hieroglyphics" as they were popularly called at the time. To most Americans the various shorthand systems which Browne mastered—Taylor's, Gurney's, and Gould's—were truly hieroglyphs, and few were the Champollions in the 1840's who could master them. He became expert in stenography and shorthand while working as a police reporter on the Louisville *Advertiser*.

In what time he could spare from his duties with the fourth estate, Browne made his first attempt at creative writing. He drew on his brief fling at medical school for inspiration and background material. The result of his short hitch in the Louisville Medical Institute was a little book called *The Confessions of a Quack; The Autobiography of a Modern Aesculapian*. There survives today but one known copy of this work, and it is an imperfect one. Father Francis J. Rock found the thirty-two-page volume in the Library of Congress while he was in the process of compiling his Ph.D. thesis on Browne. The little collection of tales marked a start for Browne the writer, but it was a false start. No child prodigy, it was Browne's fate to have to work and work, write and write, before he became a skilled craftsman with the pen. *The Confessions of a Quack* was completely unlike his later writing. It was verbose, pompous, stilted, humorless, and—worse—unoriginal. But Father Rock did see in it one emerging indication of the adult Browne—a hatred of sham and fraud. The entire book was intended as a satire on quackery, and while Browne did not return to the attack in the field of medicine again, quacks of all ilks would be his targets for the rest of his writing and reporting life. Loafers, frauds, and charlatans loomed large in his surveys in behalf of the government, the documents upon which this present book is based.

About this same time, according to family tradition, Browne received encouragement from Edgar Allan Poe by having some of his minor works accepted and published in Poe's journal, *Graham's Magazine.*[5]

In 1841, J. Ross Browne accompanied his father to Washington, D.C. There he was fortunate enough to secure a position on the *Globe,* the ancestor of our *Congressional Record,* as a reporter of debates. He was thus privy to all of the goings-on, public and private, of Capitol Hill. As might be expected, this was a period of disillusionment, for the idealistic and romantic youth found that many of his political heroes had feet of clay. Political jobbing and trickery sickened him.[6] Before the end of the session he was eager to be away. He was sure that the long-sought glories of Europe would be balm for his wounded spirit. With a young Ohioan

---

[5] Poe, who edited *Graham's Lady's and Gentleman's Magazine* from January, 1841, until May, 1842, upped the circulation of the journal from 8,000 to 40,000 subscribers, made it the most popular magazine in either Europe or America and, indeed, the first mass-appeal magazine of history. *Dictionary of American Biography* (New York. Charles Scribner's Sons, 1935), VIII, 24.

[6] Many years later (in 1866), when circumstances forced him to work as a lobbyist in Washington for Western wine and mining interests, Browne wrote his wife: "The truckling to men in office, the trivial details of official intrigues, worry and disgust me. Washington stinks of it; the houses stink of it; the people stink of it. I want to go back to California." *Muleback*, xvii. Not that California was politically pristine; earlier Browne had written of his situation in his adopted state: "Thank God I have no ambition in that way (politics), as I can safely say that it is not in the power of mortal men to make me believe wrong is right." *Ibid.*, viii.

friend whom he identified only as "W——," he spent hours in the Library of Congress, studying the lands which he hoped to visit—France, Italy, Turkey, and Egypt. The two youths would meet in the Capitol gardens on pleasant Washington evenings to explore ways of winning fame and fortune—and, perchance, a pair of Arabian princesses, dark of eye—before returning home from their travels to the admiration of all America. Their target date for sailing, July 5, 1842, came and went. The grand tour proved to be quite beyond them. Instead of the six to eight hundred dollars which they each needed, they could muster, between them, a mere forty dollars.[7] The two boys then decided to abandon their first-class plans but not to give up the idea of travel. They determined to work their way around the globe. Accordingly, after blowing their minute bankroll in a three-day spree in New York, they signed on a New Bedford whaler as sailors before the mast.

Browne was tough spirited and wiry, though in later life in the West he complained of ill health. He was able to put up with a bucko captain on the whaler, whose name Browne never mentioned but which he aptly renamed the "*Styx*." His friend's constitution, however, could not hold up under the hard work, hazing, and cruelty which passed for shipboard discipline in the American merchant navy in the 1840's.[8] The boy from Ohio had to be put ashore at Fayal in the Portuguese Azores. Browne missed his comrade but kept his mind occupied by studying navigation and hungrily reading anything he could lay his hands on. At Majunga, on the northwest coast of Madagascar, where the Betsiboka River empties into the Mozambique Channel, Browne went ashore from the anchored whaleship to treat the amused natives to their first taste of such exotic tunes as *Old Zip Coon* on his flute.

---

[7] Like many creative people, Browne was no money manager. Only once did he make a "killing" on his writing ability, and that was in the publication of the debates of California's first constitutional convention. He never let money bother him excessively. He once wrote: "What is money? I am rich, for I have enough. And who else in the world has enough? . . . Sometimes in the enthusiasm of the moment I am carried away with splendid visions of wealth, but it is only the excitement of action that governs me. I care nothing about the result." *Ibid.*, xxi.

[8] For a history of buckoism in the American merchant marine, see Richard H. Dillon, *Shanghaiing Days* (New York, Coward-McCann, 1961).

7

By this time the flautist-whaleman of Beggar's Bush, along with most of the crew, was ready to jump ship at the drop of a watch cap. Anything would serve better than the hellship in which Browne found himself virtually imprisoned. At Zanzibar the crew began to desert, so the captain forbade shore leave. Browne was so completely fed up with the whaleman's life that he determined to buy his freedom from the greedy captain, even if he had to impoverish himself. The Captain drove a hard bargain but finally released Browne for ten dollars in cash, his entire sea chest of clothes, and a man to take his place. Browne found a South Carolina quadroon on the beach in Zanzibar who was so eager to go home that even the blood-boat "*Styx*" looked good to him.

After he had signed off, Browne was taken in tow by the American Consul. Although he had little more than the clothes on his back, and his flute, his stay on the island was pleasant enough. The young Yankee explored N'Googo (Unguja) practically foot by foot and was able to eke out a living by sketching and writing. He was a keen and interested observer of the Arabic-African civilization he found on the spice isle. But the misery and wretchedness of the Imam of Muscat's subjects destroyed completely his romanticized and fanciful dreams of the Old World. He welcomed the chance to get home when the *Rolla* called at Zanzibar. She proved to be a happy ship, as different from the "*Styx*" as wine from bile. Browne was more of a passenger than a hand, though he was called on to stand watch with the crew. After visiting St. Helena, where Browne saw Napoleon's tomb and, thus, had what might be considered his first brush with Europe, the *Rolla* sailed to Massachussetts. She arrived in New Bedford in November, 1843. Browne did not tarry in New England but hurried south to the capital and, luckily, on November 8 was given a job as reporter in the Senate.

In 1844, J. Ross Browne married Lucy Ann Mitchell, daughter of a Dr. Spencer Cochrane Mitchell, a physician of Washington and a one-time surgeon in the Royal Navy. Devotion to his wife became one of the four absorbing passions in Browne's life, along with travel, writing, and reform. In 1845 he began what was to become a long though not continuous career in government service. He became first a clerk in the

Treasury Department, but, shortly, Robert J. Walker,[9] Secretary of the Treasury (1845–50) in President James K. Polk's cabinet, selected J. Ross Browne as his personal secretary. He remained in this position until the end of 1848. During this period of federal employment he saw to press his first successful book. In 1846, Harper Brothers published his *Etchings of a Whaling Cruise, with Notes of a Sojourn on the Island of Zanzibar.* This was a romanticized account of his life as a whaler and as a high-class beachcomber of Zanzibar. As he would often do in the future, Browne based his account on fact and personal experience but did a great deal of dramatizing and embroidering to fit public taste. It was creative writing but it was still nonfiction which he produced in *Etchings, A Dangerous Journey*, and *Coast Rangers*, all refined from the raw material of his experiences, diaries, and reports.

Publication of this book was important to Browne. It seemed to indicate that, perhaps, the life of which he dreamed was possible. Moreover, the book was well received. It was read and reviewed by men like Herman Melville, and Melville, of course, was influenced by it in the writing of his American classic, *Moby Dick*. The *Edinburgh Review* compared Browne favorably with Richard Henry Dana of *Two Years before the Mast*. Browne, like Dana and Melville, hoped to awaken public sympathy for the sorry plight of the sailor by means of his book and, thereby, to secure an improvement in the jack-tar's lot. But, again like the other two writers, he saw little success of this nature as a result of his efforts. The merchant sailors of America would have to throw off their bonds of servitude and near-slavery themselves.[10]

J. Ross Browne's lasting association with the American Far West began just one year after the discovery of placer gold in John Sutter's Coloma millrace by Jim Marshall. On January 22, 1849, Browne sailed

---

[9] Walker is described by biographical directories as an indefatigable worker who handled the financing of the Mexican War, revised the tariff, and established the lasting warehouse system of the Customs Service. He was also mainly responsible for the creation of the Department of the Interior. *Dictionary of American Biography*, X, 356. A lifelong friendship grew between the two men, and Browne spoke of Walker as "one of the ablest statesmen who ever presided over the Treasury Department since the days of Alexander Hamilton." J. Ross Browne, "A Quarter of a Century," *Overland Monthly*, Vol. XV, No. 4 (October, 1875), 353.

[10] Dillon, *Shanghaiing Days*.

from New York for San Francisco on the *Pacific*, leaving his wife and two children in Washington. The *Pacific*, as it lay in the harbor, was a confused jumble of lumber and water casks piled all over the deck, higher than a man's head. Through this maze of cargo ran narrow passageways. Everything was covered with six inches of new snow, and, since there were no fires aboard, almost all of the passengers speedily took to their bunks in hopes of getting warm. One of the shivering passengers who hunkered down under his blankets was destined to make his mark in the West—thirty-five-year-old Mark Hopkins. The master of the *Pacific* did not lose any time in setting the tone of the voyage. When a passenger lost a bag overboard and called out, "Please, Captain, won't you lower a boat and get my bag?" Captain Tibbitt's reply was a roaring "Go to hell with your luggage!"[11]

But Browne would not let a snarling captain spoil the excitement of his adventure. Just prior to sailing, he wrote his wife: "I am in such a whirl of excitement about California, I am too darned crazy to write."[12] He had just met and visited the Collector of Customs of New York, and rumors were flying all over the ship as a result. As he told Lucy: "The news got out from the Customs House that I am going out on important public business and everybody wants to know what it is. Of course, I have to answer all questions with discretion.[13] The New York papers are making a great noise about my trip to California. They insist upon it that I am going out under secret instructions for the Government, on business connected with the gold mines."[14] Actually, Browne bore in his pocket only an appointment as Third Lieutenant, United States Revenue Service, from Secretary of the Treasury Walker. His job was to assemble information on how best to prevent the mass desertion of sailors to the gold fields from ships in San Francisco Bay. (This would prove a job too big even for a man of Browne's caliber; there simply was no solution.)

Browne soon found that his passage to San Francisco would be no pleasure cruise. Captain Tibbitts was cut of the same sailcloth as the

---

11 J. D. B. Stillman, *Seeking the Golden Fleece* (San Francisco, A. Roman, 1877), 36.
12 *Muleback*, 1.
13 *Ibid.*, 2.
14 *Ibid.*, 3.

bucko who had commanded the *"Styx."* Passengers and crew alike were soon sick of the poop-deck tyrant, to the point of mutiny. One of Browne's fellow passengers, Dr. J. D. B. Stillman, wrote in his journal when only five days out that "the Captain is an old Turk. He tells us to go to hell if we can't eat raw mush and 'old junk' [beef]."[15] On February 2 the passengers held a meeting to consider the captain's treatment of them. The committee of J. Ross Browne, N. D. Morgan, and Hiram Bingham (not the Hiram Bingham of Hawaii fame), chosen by the passengers, presented their grievances to Tibbitts. The Captain responded by abusing them, promising to fire the magazine and blow them all to hell together if he had any more trouble with them, and then posting a notice which read, "Any person interfering with the Captain of this ship will be put in irons during the pleasure of the Captain."[16] When the passengers remonstrated with First Mate Douglass' tyranny over the forecastle hands, that bucko just sneered at them and said, "Damn them! I had to serve an apprenticeship at it!"[17] If this was James Douglass, he would have his comeuppance in just two years. In the *Challenge* case of 1851, Captain Bully Waterman and Mate Douglass had to flee Embarcadero mobs in San Francisco until the Vigilantes restored order, as a result of the public indignation over their brutalization of the clipper's crew.[18]

By the time the *Pacific* reached Rio de Janeiro, crew and passengers were in a mutinous condition. Browne's committee quickly contacted Lt. Bartlett of the *Ewing*,[19] Consul Gorham Parks, and the United States Minister to Brazil, David Tod.[20] They received a hearing. The Captain changed his chantey markedly once the *Pacific*'s anchor had slammed

---

[15] Stillman, *Seeking the Golden Fleece*, 37.

[16] *Ibid.*, 40.

[17] *Ibid.*, 52.

[18] Dillon, *Shanghaiing Days*, 66–126.

[19] Lt. Washington Allen Bartlett, U.S.N., was active in the Coast Survey, but, normally, the Survey ship *Ewing* should have been under the command of Lt. James Alden. Bartlett served as the first alcalde of San Francisco after the American conquest, largely because of his command of Spanish, acquired in Latin-American duty posts. *Appleton's Cyclopedia of American Biography* (New York, D. Appleton and Company, 1888), I, 185.

[20] The Ohio Democrat, Tod, was appointed minister to Brazil in 1847, and he served in that capacity until 1851 with tact and common sense, managing to ease some of the misunderstandings of long duration between the two countries. His own efforts to stop the

home on the bottom of Guanabara Bay. He was the personification of humility, contrition, and solicitude. But Browne learned that his change of heart was all a sham and that he was secretly preparing his ship to sail for Valparaiso, having cleared at customs without mentioning it to his irksome passengers. His excuse to the Brazilians for his hasty sailing was that he had to go to Valparaiso to replenish his water supply. The committee alerted Consul Parks who, luckily, was a Jacksonian Democrat who was not afraid to take the responsibility of halting the ship. The Consul sat down that night and wrote a note to the chamberlain of the Emperor of Brazil. The terse message read: "Stop the ship if you have to blow her out of the water." The two forts in the harbor stopped the *Pacific* from sailing.[21]

Consul Parks placed Tibbitts on trial and, on March 24, relieved him of his command. Browne had championed the passengers' cause so well that he was offered the command of the ship, but he wisely declined. He had acquired little knowledge of command aboard the "*Styx*," although he had picked up navigation. Moreover, as he noted later in a letter to his wife, Lucy: "I determined on reflection not to accept it inasmuch as it would immediately be said that I had labored to have Captain Tibbitts deposed that I might become master of the vessel myself."[22]

A real salt, Captain George T. Eastabrook, was secured to replace Tibbitts. He took command and skippered the *Pacific* on to California via the rocky maze of the Straits of Magellan and up the coast of South America. He proved completely satisfactory to the passengers. Indeed, when they arrived at San Francisco they wrote a letter of thanks to Eastabrook for his kindness, humanity, and seamanship. Browne signed the document "J. Ross Browne, U.S.R. [United States Revenue

---

slave trade in Africans to Brazil failed because of his government's refusal to take action. During the Civil War he became governor of Ohio, and President Lincoln offered him the post of Secretary of the Treasury in 1864, upon Salmon P. Chase's resignation. However, he declined for reasons of ill health. He died in 1868. *Dictionary of American Biography*, IX, 567–68.

21 Stillman, *Seeking the Golden Fleece*, 58.

22 *Ibid.*, 4.

Service]." It was published in the major paper of San Francisco, the *Alta California.*[23]

The voyage from Rio to California was uneventful except for Browne's foolhardy small-boat expedition to his "Crusoe's Island"—Juan Fernández, off the coast of Chile. He successfully negotiated the stormy seas to the site of Alexander Selkirk's stranding and led his party in tramping over the island at the same time that Sam Brannan and his Mormon colony of the *Brooklyn* were breaking their voyage to San Francisco there. At Callao, too, Browne went ashore with a few others to make the strenuous hike to Lima. The only other major event during the northward passage was the celebration of the Fourth of July on board the *Pacific.* Browne was appointed Poet of the Day, but he caused more than a little anger in addition to mirth. His personalized satire on the voyage so nettled his fellow passengers that he was interrupted in his oratory. This was a surprise, since his earlier literary efforts on the *Pacific*— publication of a manuscript ship's newspaper, the *Daily Pacific Journal* —had been popular. Dr. Stillman said, "It gave us much amusement and an opportunity to vent ourselves against each other and the ship without stint."[24]

On August 5, 1849, Browne saw the plunging brown hills of the Golden Gate's headlands sliding aft over the rail. He wrote Lucy: "I have reached the land of promise at last!"[25] Here was a land worth exploring! The sea passage, for all its vexations, had restored his health, which had not been of the best in Washington. Browne found himself filled with a zest to see the new El Dorado, although he was, at first, disappointed. Shortly after landing, he wrote: "As for San Francisco, it is about the most miserable spot I have seen in all my travels. The climate is cold, damp, foggy and windy. The town is filled with dust during the greater part of the day."[26] But later he would write: "I slept upon those hills, breathed the invigorating air, and felt the inspiration of California life."[27]

[23] August 23, 1849, p. 2, col. 5.
[24] Stillman, *Seeking the Golden Fleece*, 52.
[25] *Muleback*, 10.
[26] *Ibid.*, 27.
[27] J. Ross Browne, *Coast Rangers* (Balboa Island, Calif., Paisano Press, 1959), 16.

At the moment, Browne considered himself to be just a sojourner in California, on his way to the Old World. He did not yet dream that he would set down his roots in the tough adobe of *Alta California*. He planned only to "see the Elephant," then press on to Asia and Europe. He was still pampering his wanderlust, still yearning for a true Continental *Wanderjahr*. The last sentence in a letter which he wrote to his wife made this clear "I am so inspired with the prevailing spirit of adventure that I dream night and day of being the bright particular star of these young heroes. Visions of adventure that span the whole world haunt me. I feel within me a spirit just burst from the bondage of office, panting to explore the great wilderness of land and ocean. . . . California is but a step."[28]

However, although he did not yet realize it, from August 5, 1849, on, J. Ross Browne would be identified primarily with California and secondarily with Nevada, Arizona, Washington, and Oregon. He had become a Westerner. His career henceforth would be entangled with the problems and progress of the farthest western states of the continent.

Browne found that the revenue cutter *C. W. Lawrence* had been dismasted and would be delayed in making San Francisco. This circumstance made it necessary for him to postpone the Treasury task for which he had been assigned the post in San Francisco. So, he accepted a temporary commission from a Colonel Allen, special agent of the Post Office Department, whom he met through an old acquaintance, Dr. William M. Gwin. The latter, who became California's first Senator, was the first man whom Browne met on the Embarcadero as he landed. Gwin, who would secure the establishment of the United States Mint in San Francisco as well as the hydrographic-topographic survey of the Pacific Coast, was a powerful figure. No one dreamed in 1849 that eclipse would come in 1861, for disloyalty (secession).[29] It was the luck of the Irish that Browne ran into him when he did. Post offices were not yet functioning in the hinterland so Browne accepted the job of survey-

---

28 *Muleback*, 3.

29 Dr. Gwin eventually returned to California, and to favor after the Civil War and several abortive attempts to found colonies of Southerners in Sonora during Maximilian's reign in Mexico. *Appleton's Cyclopedia of American Biography*, III, 19–20.

ing the postal route from San Francisco south along the coast to San Luis Obispo, and the establishing of post offices along the route. He was given letters to John C. Frémont and to other important military and civic functionaries. An extra reason for Browne's eagerness to take the job was the reported wreck of a French ship near San Luis Obispo. The story was that its cargo of goods was being taken off with no duty paid on it. He wanted to investigate the matter for the Secretary of the Treasury.

Browne set up only one post office, San Jose, but his lonely ride through the Salinas and Santa Margarita valleys—the heart of California's *bandido* country—delighted him, with its grizzlies, desperadoes, fandangos, stabbings, and so forth. The wild, free life of California intoxicated him. Browne was able, at least, to take care of the customs matter at San Luis Obispo—the shipwreck. He turned over $10,000 to the Collector of Customs in San Francisco, either Collector James Collier or his predecessor, Acting Collector Edward H. Harrison, after having completed his customs business at San Luis Obispo.[30]

On August 27, Browne wrote to his wife from Monterey that he had seen a copy of the *National Intelligencer*. The paper listed the names of officers and cutters of the Revenue Service which were being dropped from the Service by the Secretary of the Treasury. His name was on the list. But instead of being disappointed, Browne was delighted. "This rather pleases me," he wrote Lucy, "than otherwise, as it relieves me from all embarrassment in regard to keeping my commission while attending to my own business. . . . As to any effect my course in the affair of Captain Tibbitts may have produced at headquarters, I care nothing about it. I feel conscious of the rectitude of my motives, and would do precisely the same thing over again under similar circumstances if it were to cost me the friendship of every man upon the face of the earth, much less a paltry salary which a California Indian would scorn to receive."[31]

The business of his own which he hoped to attend to was the California Constitutional Convention. He turned back from San Luis Obispo and retraced his steps to Monterey and the Convention which General

[30] J. Ross Browne, *Crusoe's Island*, 246.
[31] *Muleback*, 31.

Bennett Riley had called. Browne had been given an inside track to the job of recording secretary by Dr. Gwin, although there were other rivals for the post—a reporter from the *Herald* and one from the New Orleans *Picayune*. He wrote Lucy on August 8, 1849, almost a month before the convening of the constitutional assembly at Colton Hall: "He [Gwin] says I *must* be elected Stenographer to the Convention, at any price.... Dr. Gwin says I may rest easy, retain my commission and be fully satisfied that my fortune is made on the spot and my position established in California." Apparently, the happy turn of events was beginning to change Browne's mind about pulling out of California. His letter describing his plans for the inspection of the postal route to San Luis Obispo already had suggested as much to Lucy: "We [he and a shipmate from the *Pacific,* J. W. Allen] anticipate a romantic and delightful ride of a thousand miles through the finest portion of California. I have a *carte blanche* to do what I please, go where I please, and cost what I please. We are to sleep under trees, light a fire, cook our meat, and live in real Indian style. Won't it be glorious? I am crazy with enthusiasm. I look forward to my career in California as a series of triumphs. It is a horrible place for women but for a man of enterprise, it is just the thing."[32]

As Recording Secretary of the Convention, Browne displayed a sudden and atypical flash of business brilliance. He secured the rights to publish the record. His *Report of the Debates in the Convention of California,* published in Washington in 1850, was a best seller. There was even a Spanish-language edition, *Relación de los debates....* His volume sold like flapjacks, both in the West and in the East. The entire country was dying of curiosity about the fabled land of El Dorado. It had developed an enormous appetite for anything in print regarding California. Congress alone bought several thousand copies of the *Report,* and if the book did not make him rich overnight, it certainly made him well fixed for 1850, to the tune of $10,000.

The Recording Secretary, once his work in Monterey was finished, lost no time in resigning his temporary postal commission and returned to his family via Panama. He left San Francisco on November 2, 1849,

[32] *Ibid.,* 13–14.

and on the passage home polished the manuscript of the *Report* for publication. Upon his arrival, he busied himself with plans for his first trip to Europe. Browne took his wife and three children to Italy in March, 1851, settling them in Florence while he acted as wandering correspondent for the *National Intelligencer* in the Mediterranean area. When Browne returned to the United States in 1852, he gathered together many of the humorous travel sketches which he had contributed to the *National Intelligencer* and to *Harper's* and published them as a book called *Yusef, a Journey among the Frangi; Or, a Crusade in the East.* This was destined to become his best-known book, going through at least seven dated editions. It was a forerunner of Mark Twain's *Innocents Abroad* and a whole school of humorous, satirizing travel accounts by Yankees at large in the world. Joaquin Miller made the debt of Twain to Browne plain by saying, "It is clear to the most casual reader that if there had been no *Yusef* there would have been no *Innocents Abroad.*"[33] Browne himself once wrote from London, without bitterness; "I met Mark Twain a day or two ago at Judge Turner's. He is just the same dry, quaint old Twain we knew in Washington. I believe he is writing a book over here. He made plenty of money on his other books—some of it on mine."[34]

The mid-1850's were among the most active—almost frenetic—years of Browne's life. Yet they are the least known. This is because he functioned as a secret government agent at this time. His reports were confidential. Only one or two were ever published. But his reports were important. They were in great measure responsible for the reputation which his chief, Secretary of the Treasury James Guthrie, received. (The *Dictionary of American Biography* saluted the latter in these words: "He showed himself a ruthless reformer, overhauling the treasury regulations, curbing extravagance, reducing the debt, and weeding out incompetence.") Unfortunately, most of Browne's unpublished and confidential reports have vanished in the century and more which has elapsed since he filed them. That they were important to him is clear from the letter which he wrote to the editors of *Harper's New Monthly Magazine* from Europe

33 *Ibid.*, vii.
34 *Ibid.*, vii.

in 1860 or 1861. They wished to delete from his Coast Rangers sketches the scorching criticism of the Revenue and Indian Services, based on his governmental reports. Browne wrote: "To cut out the part on the Indian Reservations and the Revenue Service would be manslaughter in the first degree.... I must say, therefore, that poor as I am, I would rather return the money than have my jolly party of Rangers struck in the umbilical."[35] The passages remained.

This period, of which Browne's scanty biographical sketches tell little, was a decisive one for him. He removed his family and himself to the Far West, for good. These years also supplied him with the raw material for some of his best writing, including "The Indians of California," "Observations in Office," "The Great Port Townsend Controversy," "Coast Rangers," "The Indian Wars of Oregon and Washington," "Old Texan Days," and "A Ride on the Texas Frontier."

Browne's best biographer, Father Rock, did not miss the importance of these formative years of Browne's in the West as a government agent. Rock wrote:

> This [1854–57 tour of duty] is an example of Browne's wonderful powers of endurance but what is more to the point, it is an illustration of the intimate way in which he got his knowledge of the American frontier and of the American frontiersman. Working in the Federal service, he got, also, an insight into the problems confronting the nation during the era of rapid expansion. Browne's removal to California in 1855, however, as a Customs official, made the Pacific frontier a special subject of his study for the rest of his days.[36]

After returning to Washington in 1853, J. Ross Browne was appointed confidential agent of the Treasury Department. He was charged primarily with the investigation of customs house operations on the Minnesota, Texas, and Pacific Coast frontiers, but he was not restricted to that province of the federal service. Browne attacked the new challenge with his customary zeal and diligence.

[35] *Ibid.*, xiii.
[36] *J. Ross Browne: A Biography*, 33.

CHAPTER TWO

Port of Gold

NOWHERE WOULD J. ROSS BROWNE'S TASK of investigating and reforming prove to be easy. But San Francisco was the worst problem he would have to face. There was more poetry, alas, than truth in the proud boast which San Franciscans liked to make in regard to themselves—"The cowards never started, and the weak ones died by the way." For knight-errant Browne would find himself battling a spoils-system Hydra whose heads represented graft, cupidity, sloth, vapidity, and five other similarly classifiable vices. San Francisco had just "growed," like Topsy, and overnight, from a sleepy Mexican village to a world port. The sky was the limit, there was little or no law west of the Pecos, and "Frisco" was 1,500 miles west of the Pecos.

California had become a part of the United States by the Treaty of Guadalupe Hidalgo, on February 2, 1848. This was just six years before Browne was given his investigating commission. But it was not until March 3, 1849, with the Gold Rush in full flood, that Congress saw to it that the revenue laws of the United States were extended to California. A single collection district—San Francisco—was set up, with the city the port of entry and San Diego and Monterey the only ports of delivery. The Secretary of the Treasury was asked to designate a third port of entry somewhere near the Gulf of California and the Gila and Colorado rivers. By 1855 there were two, Fort Yuma and Colorado City, the latter now a ghost town. The collector was charged with the selection and appointment of deputy collectors to head these branch offices of his San Francisco headquarters.

Browne himself explained the complicated and chaotic customs situation in California to his wife long before he became personally involved and, in fact, before James Collier arrived to take office as collector. Writing from Monterey on September 30, 1849, Browne told Lucy:

> There has been great confusion here for some time in regard to the political affairs of California. It appears that after the treaty of peace between the United States and Mexico, and while the territory of California was under military law, the American military commandant collected about seven hundred thousand dollars in imposts on foreign merchandise. There was no revenue law then in existence on the Pacific Coast, except at Astoria, Oregon. Consequently, no foreign vessels could discharge their cargoes at any other port. But in consideration of the great inconvenience resulting . . . the military commandant assumed the responsibility of permitting foreign vessels to enter their cargoes at San Francisco under the existing tariff laws of the United States. The duties collected in this way were not considered as in the Treasury of the United States because no monies can go into or out of the Treasury except by law. Congress having failed to make any disposition of the fund thus collected, at its last session, the Executive issued instructions to the Civil Governor of California to defray out of that fund all the necessary expenses of civil government. General [Bennett] Riley, an old military officer entirely ignorant of political affairs, was placed at the head of the government of California in consequence of having greatly distinguished himself in the Mexican War. The merchants who paid the duties have made a strong effort to get them back, on the plea that they were illegally collected. General [Persifer] Smith, who is commander of the military forces in California, assumed the authority of Governor; but the military being subordinate to the civil powers, General Riley is recognized as, and in fact is, the only governor. A quarrel has sprung up between them, General Smith claiming the right to the fund in dispute.[1]

[1] *Muleback*, 39.

The President of the United States had the duty of appointing the collector of San Francisco, who would receive a salary of $1,500 per year plus fees and commissions of 3 per cent on all money received as duties on imports. However, this was not an open-ended largesse. The government limited these fringe benefits. Fee income was not to exceed $3,000 in any given year, and the collector was allowed a top of only $400 per annum from other duties which he might perform. Since California was not yet a state and did not even have a system of courts, the collector was advised that violations of the revenue laws were to be prosecuted in the nearest available courts—the District Court of Louisiana and the Supreme Court of Oregon.[2]

On March 15, 1849, President Zachary Taylor appointed James Collier of Litchfield, Connecticut, to the post of collector of customs for San Francisco. Collier made a hazardous and exhausting overland trip to California, arriving on November 12. He took immediate possession of his office that day and wrote his first report to Secretary of the Treasury William M. Meredith[3] on the following day. Collier's first words were these: "I am perfectly astounded at the amount of business in this office." He found that between April 1 and November 13, 1849, 697 vessels had arrived in San Francisco Bay, including 401 bottoms of American registry. On November 10, tonnage of ships in the harbor totaled 120,000. Some 87,494 tons of this shipping were American.[4]

The Collector continued his report: "Desirous as I am of conforming to the instructions from the Treasury Department"—Meredith had sent him the usual instructions to hire personnel at a certain scale of pay, to enter and to clear vessels, to collect customs, to secure warehouses, and to act as a depository for public monies—"yet you will see from what follows that, so far as the salaries are concerned, it will be wholly im-

[2] Grant Foreman, *Adventures of James Collier, First Collector of the Port of San Francisco* (Chicago, Black Cat Press, 1937), 7–8.

[3] William M. Meredith was not only eminent, he was one of those men fabled in song and story—a great Philadelphia lawyer. After serving in the Pennsylvania House of Representatives, he was appointed Treasury secretary by President Taylor and served from March, 1849, until Taylor's death, in July, 1850. Joseph Thomas, *Universal Pronouncing Dictionary of Biography* (Philadelphia, J. B. Lippincott Co., 1901), II, 1708.

[4] Foreman, *Adventures of James Collier*, 30.

21

possible." (Clerks in San Francisco were getting from $1,000 to $3,000 a year, when they could be found to take a job. Positions were going begging.) "It is impossible to retain clerks or other officers without the payment of salaries corresponding with the expense of living."[5]

But Collier wasted no time bemoaning his situation. He made a series of recommendations in his very first report to the Department. First, a customs house simply had to be built or, at least, a prefab structure would have to be sent around the Horn to San Francisco. Collier thought that the new cast-iron type might do the trick. The business of the port, he assured Meredith, would more than justify the cost. He added that he was afraid to rent a decent building in San Francisco after having had one offered to him at a rent of a mere $2,400 per month. For the moment, he would have to continue using the tumble-down old Mexican customs house and nineteen storeships in the Bay. The latter solution to the storage problem—using as warehouses some of the great dead fleet of hulks stranded in the mud flats—was not well thought of by the Collector. He felt that their use was "a hazardous and most inconvenient practice, and it opens a broad door for smuggling."[6]

Collier was highly unimpressed with his headquarters. He wrote:

> I am occupying what was the old Mexican Customs House, constructed of unburnt brick. It is a long, dark one-story building in miserable condition. The roof leaks so badly that during a rain our papers are liable to be wet. The doors are, some of them, off their hinges and all are insecure. I have no vault for safekeeping of the public money. . . . The walls are so dilapidated by time and the rats as to render them liable to be crushed by the heavy roof. . . . A person so disposed could, with a knife, make such a breech in the wall as to enter the room in twenty minutes.[7]

The new Collector must have had remarkable powers of persuasion. Somehow, he got Andrew Randall[8] to accept the post of deputy collector at Monterey, although the $1,000 salary did not even cover his

---

[5] *Ibid.*, 40.
[6] *Ibid.*, 41.
[7] *Ibid.*, 42.
[8] Randall was very likely the "Dr." Andrew Randall, onetime gunner of the U.S.S. *Portsmouth* and self-anointed medic who was a state assemblyman in the second legislative session. He was murdered in 1856 by Joseph Hetherington, and the latter was lynched for

board. The Collector begged Meredith to increase the salary of the deputy collectors to $2,000 a year although, even at that figure, he was anything but sanguine about attracting good men to the Customs Service.[9]

Collier could do nothing about the major problem of the harbor, the abandonment of vessels by their crews. Few ships left the bay in relation to the number which arrived. The great majority were left to rot offshore. Seamen, gold hungry, were deserting by the hundreds every month. There was absolutely nothing that Collier could do. He could not even enlist the aid of Captain Alexander V. Fraser of the revenue cutter *C. W. Lawrence,* which supposedly lay at his disposal in the bay. Actually, most of the *Lawrence*'s crew had jumped ship too, and Fraser was only able to keep a skeletal complement aboard by raising their wages, on his own, to $35 a month and pampering them in every way possible in order to prevent their desertion.[10]

Collier's instructions were general, not detailed. He had a great deal of leeway in the application of them, and in many areas he had to steer his own course, since he was too far from Washington to check constantly on policy and procedure. His strict "rule" over the harbor came as a decided jolt to merchants and shippers used to a wide-open, *laissez faire* laxity of regulation on the Embarcadero. Complaints began to mount, especially from a Mr. Robinson and from Colonel John B. Weller.[11] Colonel Weller ranted against Collier: "The people ought to take possession of the Customs House—seize the money that is in the custody of the Collector and collect the duties themselves. . . . If California is admitted to the Union, they can account with the Government. If California is not admitted, the money belongs to them."[12]

the foul deed by the Vigilantes. Hubert H. Bancroft, *Popular Tribunals* (San Francisco, the History Co., 1887), II, 489–90.

[9] Foreman, *Adventures of James Collier,* 39.

[10] *Ibid.,* 40.

[11] Weller, an Ohioan, was a Democratic Congressman, a lieutenant-colonel in the Mexican War, and a commissioner to Mexico under the Treaty of Guadalupe Hidalgo. He was United States Senator from California from 1852 until 1857; governor of California in 1858–60; and minister to Mexico in 1860–61. He died in 1875. Thomas, *Universal Pronouncing Dictionary of Biography,* VI, 426.

[12] Foreman, *Adventures of James Collier,* 45.

By September 28, 1850, California *was* in the Union, however, and the wind was taken out of Weller's sails. But just when Collier felt he could rest a bit more easily, the ax fell. Congress passed new legislation to set up six collection districts to replace the single San Francisco District in California. President Millard Fillmore nominated Collier for collector of the new San Francisco District, but the nomination failed of confirmation in the Senate. Thomas Butler King,[13] of Georgia, was confirmed in the post instead of Collier on February 27, 1851.[14]

James Collier had been a diligent worker—perhaps too much so. There was no gentle transition period from chaos to the rule of law on the waterfront. He found a lot of commerce—and a lot of smuggling. (This was a time-honored old California custom.) He sent an inspector south to check on commerce at San Pedro and Santa Barbara and to put a stop to contrabanding there.

Much was accomplished during Collier's term of office. He suggested that San Pedro and Santa Barbara be made ports of delivery, and they were. He asked for a second cutter in order to put a stop to smuggling on the Pacific Coast, and it finally came. Since he found the Embarcadero fairly crawling with sick and destitute seamen, he requested that a United States Marine Hospital be built in San Francisco. This, too, was done.[15]

Collier got much, even most, of what he asked for, but friction increased during his term of appointment. He countermanded the decision of his predecessor, Acting Collector Edward H. Harrison, who had allowed vessels flying foreign flags to enter the river and bay trade because of the scarcity of American bottoms. Collier insisted upon the law's being carried out. He therefore forbade foreign ships from engaging in purely domestic traffic. The old practice had been countenanced by shippers, by the public, by the Customs, and even by Captain Thomas Ap Catesby Jones of the Navy. When Collier put a stop to it his enemies increased.[16]

---

[13] King's interest in trade presumably grew from his attentions to naval affairs and oceanic steam navigation while a Congressman. *Appleton's Cyclopedia*, III, 546.

[14] Foreman, *Adventures of James Collier*, 46.

[15] *Ibid.*, 32–33.

[16] *Ibid.*, 36–37.

Finally, there were so many complaints about Collier that a Special Agent was sent by the Treasury Department to conduct an official and confidential inquiry, much as J. Ross Browne did three years later. The man chosen for the task was a clerk in the Secretary's own office. Gilbert Rodman. He was not of the caliber of Browne, by any means, and he tended to act as a blotter to rumor rather than as a filter of it. At least, he was hard working. But he accepted all charges against Collier as gospel. Rodman thus carried East tales that Collier had misapplied the proceeds of sales of ships confiscated for violation of revenue laws; that his son, John A. Collier, was collecting rents on government land for his own use; that John was part-owner of a bonded storeship in the harbor; that the Collector made deals to sell storeship merchandise for a slice of the profits; that a banking house, Wells & Company, paid him 5 per cent per month on all deposits of government money. Some, or all, of these charges may have been true. For one thing, Confidential Agent Rodman was not contradicted when he asserted that Collier had $130,000 in his personal bank account by April, 1850. But many of the charges were based on a single affidavit, that of Edward Byrne, a Customs House worker. And Byrne, in the final analysis, refused to sign the affidavit. Nevertheless, Rodman took the information back East where it doubtless had much to do with the defeat of Collier's nomination. When Collier found himself involved in government suits, he filed countersuits and in 1859 finally enjoyed some sort of vindication when the legal tangle was abandoned and Congress paid him $9,580.27.[17]

Collier's term of office was important to J. Ross Browne for many reasons. For one thing, the Collector's pleas for higher salaries and his reports on inflated prices and wages remained long in Department minds, long after the inflationary boom had subsided. They were an invitation to graft, and they plagued Browne during his investigation. The name-calling and accusations of the Collier collectorship also, unfortunately, set a precedent for backbiting which would be continued during the terms of his successors. The bickering of the early administrations suggested that things were not always on the up-and-up in the San Francisco Customs House. Worse, this was more often true than

[17] *Ibid.*, 51.

not. There were splendid opportunities for profiteering, plunder, and quasi-legal piracy in the Customs House, and they were not overlooked by certain of the more predatory pioneers. Whatever the degree of Collier's guilt or innocence on the charges against him, Browne would find that his successors, at all levels, were tempted to do their prospecting in the offices and halls of the Customs House rather than in the ravines and hills of the Mother Lode. The smell of graft came to hang over the building. When it became obvious that there was something rotten in Frisco, the Treasury Department dispatched a man to clean up the mess. The man was J. Ross Browne.

Until a Division of Special Agents was created in the Office of the Secretary of the Treasury in the late 1860's, it was the Secretary himself who supervised the flying squad of trouble shooters called "Secret Inspectors of Customs." After 1849, with the establishment of the position of Commissioner of Customs, the Secretary had the assistance of that officeholder in the supervision of his confidential agents in the field. These men were the Department's chief means of ferreting out frauds, thimblerigging of all kinds, and what were euphemized as "irregularities" in Treasury Department affairs about the country, particularly by importers and collectors of customs.

An act of March 2, 1799, authorized the appointment of the secret operatives who, in eighteenth- and early nineteenth-century parlance were termed "Aides to the Revenue." This team of primordial T-Men constituted the only detective force in the Treasury Department until the Secret Service was created in 1865. The Confidential Agents, or Special Agents, therefore, should be considered to be the godparents, at least, of the T-Men and Secret Service Men who protect government interests today. The Confidential Agents like J. Ross Browne, however, were not charged either with guarding the President's person or with detecting or arresting counterfeiters.

Browne explained his own interpretation of his duties to Secretary of the Treasury James Guthrie in a letter of January 19, 1856: "To examine into every branch of public business connected with the collection of the revenue and the disbursement of the public moneys."[18]

[18] Manuscript 330 of National Archives Microcopy 177, Roll 1 (J. Ross Browne), "Letters

If the majority of Treasury agents of the 1850's were anywhere near Browne in quality, Secretary Guthrie was fortunate. In an era of rampant skulduggery and scalawaggery, especially on the remote Pacific Coast, Browne stood out like one of his Department's lighthouses, towering over the men he investigated. He was that *plus rara avis,* an honest man in government employ on the farthest-flung frontier of the 1850's. The duties of Browne and his colleagues were varied and seldom spelled out in detail, as Browne's statement above indicated. But, for the most part, they were to investigate United States mints and their depositories of money; customs houses and their subordinate offices; United States marine hospitals; and, occasionally at least, the activities of federal agencies other than the Department of the Treasury. Browne tried to implement his reforms quietly, without antagonizing either public servants or the public itself whenever possible. He was not always successful, but he was able to write to his wife that "I have never yet seen a man I could not conciliate when I set my mind to it. I have even conciliated women."[19]

No more honest or candid employee ever accepted Uncle Sam's meager pay, and few, if any, were more intelligent or more devoted to duty. San Francisco would not see such a reformer again until Francis Heney, Fremont Older, Hiram Johnson, and Rudolph Spreckels took on city boss Abe Ruef and his gang of grafters in a cleanup drive coincident with the great 1906 earthquake and fire. After Browne's funeral in 1875, Reverend Hamilton said of him: "If our Government had no officials less honest and true, I think we should begin to believe in the millenium."[20]

& Reports Rec'd. Secy. of Treasury From Special Agents, 1854–1861." (The designation, henceforth, of this item and its fellow manuscripts will be in this fashion: N. A. 177-1-330.)

[19] *Muleback,* iv.

[20] *Ibid.,* xix.

CHAPTER THREE

The Lone-Star State

O
N JANUARY 26, 1854, J. Ross Browne wrote Secretary of the Treasury James Guthrie from Austin, Texas. He reported that he had finished his Galveston business and was en route to the Rio Grande via San Antonio to visit all revenue stations on that border between Eagle Pass and Point Isabel.[1]

The summer previous he had examined the United States border in the Minnesota lakes area, and this trip had prepared the insatiably curious rover to accept with pleasure his government's next assignment—the Lone-Star State of Texas. Browne looked forward with pleasure to his West Texas tour of inspection for a number of reasons. The country through which he would travel was entirely different in its climate and topography from any which he had yet visited. Moreover, West Texas was interesting to Browne because of the "romantic and eventful character of its history. Some of the most sanguinary battles recorded in the annals of border warfare had taken place in those wild stretches of prairie laying between the Nueces and the Rio Grande,"[2] through which his route lay.

---

[1] N. A. 177–1–83.
[2] J. Ross Browne, "A Ride on the Texan Frontier," *Overland Monthly*, Vol. I, No. 2 (August, 1868), 157.

Browne landed in Galveston in early March to find the weather of Gulf Coast Texas soft, balmy, and tropical. The aspect of the town charmed him, with its agave hedges, its groves of "alianthus" (oleander), and its streets paved with shining sand or sea shells. He hiked through its streets past white frame cottages, dodging out of the way of half-wild horses ridden by half-wild Texans. The *embarcadero* he found to be a few rusty-looking warehouses and wharves. The latter were piled high with bales of cotton atop which Negroes lay asleep. Three or four small sailing vessels and a few river steamers were in port.

By midday, Browne found the Galveston sun to be, to his thinking, hot enough to give him brain fever. But everything else he liked. He found Texans to be a hard-smoking and hard-drinking lot, but he felt that "it would be difficult to find in any part of the world a more stalwart set of men. With their determined expression of eye, tall, athletic forms, dark hair and sunburnt features, their self-possessed manners and courteous address, their broad-brimmed palmetto hats and easy, careless style of costume—a mixture of the ranger and the planter—they certainly present as fine a type of the Southerner as the traveler could well meet with."[3]

Browne examined the books and accounts of the Galveston Customs House and found them all in good order. Such was not the case with the former Collector, however. He was, in fact, in quite pronounced *mal odeur*.[4] He was, according to Browne, a defaulter to the amount of $21,000. Browne hoped that Smith's prosecution would be speedily pressed, and he wrote Washington to that effect. He could not verify the rumor that Smith had paid the money in question to the Assistant Treasurer in New Orleans. Owing to what he described in his reports as "the total inefficiency" of the United States District Attorney there, Browne had to hire an able lawyer to aid the District Attorney in the prosecution of Smith and other grafters.[5] The Californian secured John

---

[3] *Ibid.*, 158.

[4] The former collector was Robert Bolyn Smith. The collector was Hamilton Stuart, three-time mayor of Galveston. Appointed collector in January, 1853, he served until March, 1861, when Texas seceded from the Union. *Appleton's Cyclopedia*, V, 730.

[5] N. A. 177–1–84.

Woods Harris, former attorney general of the Republic of Texas, and a man of unquestioned integrity.[6]

After concluding his Galveston business, Browne took passage on the steamer which ran from Galveston to Buffalo Creek and Houston. The reckless reputation of its captain, together with the excessive amount of steam he was wont to carry, plus the vibrations ("convulsions," Browne termed them) of the craft, "accompanied by strong smells of grease, whiskey and machinery," did not enhance the agent's expectations of the trip. But his years on the Ohio and Mississippi rivers had prepared him for *any* steamboat. "One can even get used to being blown up," he said.[7]

The thoughtful clerk gave Browne a berth right over the boilers—where it was nice and warm, he said, for the nights tended to be cool. (Also, there was no other bunk available.) When he saw the worried look on Browne's face, he tried to soothe the government agent. "It won't make any difference, if she blows up. We'll all go to where we belong together. Them that sleeps over the boilers 'll get thar first—that's all."[8]

While the steamer was not another "*Styx*" or *Pacific*, it was no pleasure cruiser to Browne, either. Up the narrow creek she crept, all night long. From time to time she jammed herself into mudbanks, jarring to a dead stop. All hands, laughing uproariously on such occasions, would then jump into the mud and water and attempt to push her off the shoal. Then she would careen into the opposite bank, stagger in a drunken carom back to the shore she had just left, and crash into the overhanging tree limbs. After a few uneasy hours of sleep, the night finally inched its way into oblivion, and J. Ross Browne found himself and the steamboat lying safely alongside the creek bank at Houston. "Not much need be said of Houston," reported the agent. "It is a pretty little country town situated on the edge of a prairie, with a few stores, a great many barrooms, one or two indifferent taverns, a jail and a church,

[6] Walter Prescott Webb (ed.), *The Handbook of Texas* (2 vols., Austin, Texas State Historical Association, 1952), I, 775.

[7] "Texan Frontier," *loc. cit.*, 158.

[8] *Ibid.*

some pretty gardens in the outskirts, and a scattering population of idle-looking gentlemen, mules and blackbirds."[9]

To his dismay, Browne found that the stage for Austin had already left. No seats were to be had for a week, thanks to the pressure placed on the Lone-Star State's transportation resources by the legislature's going into session. Forced to seek other means of reaching West Texas and the Rio Grande, Browne joined three men heading west. One was a Yankee trader, one an old Texan doctor, and the third a hunter named Johnson who had left his horse on the Rio Grande. They hired a light wagon, actually an ambulance, and a team of horses for $100. This was a steep enough price to pay, but Browne felt that, under the circumstances, he had to put up with it. The trio won over their cantankerous driver—typical of the whole genus *jehu*—with cigars and an occasional pull at the medic's flask. The good M.D. kept a bottle with him at all times to forestall fainting spells and to throw off the effects of the bites of rattle-snakes. Their driver, Colonel Washington, or "Mustang," for he answered to either go-by, led them off after a good jolt of medicinal redeye.

Washington took them through parklike country of meadowlands dotted with open groves of oak, pine, and sycamore. The grass was lush and water was abundant. Wild flowers brightened every vista. Browne observed great masses of honeysuckle enveloping—smothering—tree trunks and branches and perfuming the air for miles. Wild horses, cattle, deer, antelope, and wild turkey soon made their appearance. The hunter, Johnson, frequently brought down game for himself and his comrades, and once killed a buck with a quick shot from over two hundred yards. Browne was much impressed with Texas frontiersmen. Of the hunter he wrote: "Johnson was always ready with his rifle. He seemed to have a natural propensity for killing something; it mattered little what, though he said he preferred Indians, 'on general principles' "[10]

As the horses jogged along the well-marked road of beaten-down white gravel, with a vast greensward on every side, Browne felt an enormous sense of well-being. He relaxed and enjoyed the Texas country-side. The wild and free prairie delighted him much as California pleased him. As he later recalled:

[9] *Ibid.*   [10] *Ibid.*, 159.

Whether it was the pleasant motion of the ambulance, the balminess of the air, or the exemption from all the petty vexations of civilization that gave such a charm to our journey, I certainly enjoyed it very much. There was something approaching a primeval condition of happiness in the sensation of ease and luxury one experienced in rolling along without trouble, almost without thought, through this enchanting country. To lie back in the open ambulance, the smoke of a genuine Havana curling lazily up, to forget the cares of office and the frivolous vexations of city life, to feel no concern about the busy world, to lose all morbid curiosity about the news, to enjoy a perpetual feast of beautiful scenery without the least personal exertion, were surely enough to afford pleasure to any man not naturally hard to please.[11]

One warm evening, as they took their ease under a clear sky, Johnson surprised Browne by suggesting that he put on his coat and prepare for the norther that was coming. Puzzled, Browne asked him why he thought a norther was on the way. "Don't you see that band of cattle in the distance?" asked the hunter, pointing toward the horizon. "Observe how they switch their tails in the air and make for the woodland. They already feel it." Browne could hardly believe that the balmy night was hiding a norther, but he had little time to spare for the luxury of disbelief in the Nimrod of the party. Only a few minutes after Johnson had called his attention to the tail-switching longhorns, Browne noticed little whirls of dust beginning to rise from bare patches on the prairie. Next, the temperature fell sharply. A chill invaded the air as the dust-devils danced like dervishes.

Suddenly, the norther was upon them. Browne recalled:

Before we could get our coats from underneath the seats, the first blast of wind struck us, like a shower bath. It was almost incredible—the sharpness and suddenness of the change. We were about four miles from the nearest timber. The wind blew in quick sharp blasts, growing colder and colder each moment till it became actually scathing. Neither the covering of the ambulance nor the protection of thick clothing could baffle the fierce gusts that beset us with such surprising force and rapidity. Colonel Washington whipped up his horses and professed to feel a faintness which, of

11 *Ibid.*, 159–60.

course, the doctor was obliged to relieve. In something less than half an hour, so intensely penetrating became the cold that I began to entertain some fear of being frozen and jumped out to take a run alongside the ambulance. The wind had a full sweep across the prairie, and soon increased almost to a hurricane, shivering the canvas cover of our wagon so that the shreds cracked like a running fire of pistols. The horses, naturally wild, were stricken with a panic; the reins broke in the struggle to hold them and away they dashed with frantic speed toward the woodland. I was soon left behind, notwithstanding I was a tolerably good runner. The wind bore against me with terrific force, sometimes sweeping me clear off the road, almost lifting me up bodily. Incredibly as it may seem, I had to watch the chances and lean against it as against a solid wall. Fortunately, at this time we were not over a mile from the timber. By dint of hard struggling I got there in time to see the horses run against a tree, capsize the ambulance, break the tongue and tumble over, tangled up in the harness. Upon reaching the scene of the disaster, I found the Yankee trader badly frightened but uninjured; the doctor somewhat painfully bruised; the driver knocked senseless; and Johnson sitting on the ground bewailing his ruined rifle, which was smashed beyond redemption.

The most serious case seemed to be that of the driver. He was apparently very badly injured. Upon examination, we could find no wound. The injury was, doubtless, internal. The poor fellow breathed heavily, occasionally gasping as if for air. Badly as the doctor was bruised, he forgot his own injuries and manifested the greatest concern about the unfortunate driver— "Gentlemen," he said, "I'll have to bleed him, or he'll die," and forthwith he pulled out his lancet and began to bare the man's arm. "Doctor," whispered the driver in a faint voice, and slowly opening his eyes, "don't bleed me. I'll be all right, presently. Give me—a little—pull at the brandy. It's only a kind of fainting spell—brandy always sets me right." Of course, the medicine was administered. The effect was miraculous. Colonel Washington got up, shook himself, gave a yell to test the strength and purity of his voice, and set to work like a man to clear the wreck and get the horses on their feet again.[12]

The men took shelter in the trees, surrounded by nervous cattle which were lowing in fear as the gale shook the branches. Browne and his companions quickly set to work to mend the wagon tongue as the

[12] *Ibid.*, 160–61.

33

norther increased in violence. They finally gave up the attempt to cross the ten miles of open prairie between their timber and the next and, instead, made camp in a little hollow protected by a high bank. There was no water but the grass was lush so they picketed the horses and let them forage. All that the men had to eat was a portion of a deer killed by Johnson. They built a fire and cooked the venison. Smacking his lips, Browne wrote in his notebook, "I do not remember that I ever relished anything better. Even pepper and salt were not necessary to give an edge to the appetite.[13]

The foursome suffered much from the cold during the night, for they had brought no blankets and the chill cut right through their thick coats. Several times one or another had to climb stiffly to his feet to replenish the wood on the fire to keep them all from freezing. But after a breakfast, they all felt better, and by the time they had the horses hitched it was quite calm and a lovely sunrise greeted them. Again they set out, crossing woodland and prairie redolent of fresh earth, clover, and wild flowers. Browne watched darting swallows and meadow larks and saw literally thousands of rabbits dart across their path. But, best of all, a ten-mile drive brought them to a ranch where they were able to enjoy a second breakfast of ham and eggs, coffee, and bread, while the horses fell to over barley and water. As he ate, Browne mentally compared the Texas norther to California's dry norther and, worse, wet norther. His host told him that many travelers perished from the cold and exposure on the plains when caught by northers, including members of emigrant trains and soldiers driving government teams from one military post to another.[14]

The little party reached the Brazos River and left the plains to descend into the low, narrow strip of densely timbered bottom land, mostly sycamore, cottonwood, hickory, and pecan covered, which clothed the banks of the Brazos. The wetness of the earth along the river made the road almost impassable. While a corduroy road had been laid in the boggiest places, the logs were buried under two feet of mud. The horses often mired themselves up to their bellies in the muck, and the men became as filthy as wart hogs from pulling and hauling on the wagon

[13] *Ibid.*, 161.   [14] *Ibid.*, 162.

wheels to free the ambulance from the mud-traps. They were too dirty and tired to admire the flocks of wild turkeys, parakeets, and "chichilacas" which rose from the riverbank, greeting them with surprised cries and cackles as the men fought their way, foot by slimy foot, to the ferry landing.[15]

The sodden, begrimed men found the ferry, but there was no sign of the boatman. Impatient, they took the ferry and essayed the crossing without him. The current of the Brazos was swift, and, if they crossed near the Towash Village north of Waco, the rapid-flowing stream was 250 yards wide. In any case, the unskilled quartet of travelers quickly found water slopping over the gunwale. The ferry began to fill. The horses panicked and tried to back off. The ambulance was soon hanging half-on and half-off the waterlogged craft, which was still attached to its cable. Suddenly, men and horses were plunged into the water. All four men reached the shore safely and ran downstream to drag the wagon and team ashore.[16]

As they shook themselves like spaniels, Browne happened to look back across the river. He made out a man sitting on the bank like an apparition. He focused his eyes on the newcomer and, as he later recalled, "It was certainly the most uncouth looking object I had ever laid eyes upon—a long, gaunt, sallow man with long yellow hair, a red shirt, big boots with his breeches thrust in them, a long corn cob pipe in his mouth and a long rifle in his hand. His long face was so dreadfully cadaverous and his form so long and lean that he might well be the embodiment of the fevers and agues that are said to lurk in these river bottoms." But the apparition could speak, nasally, it turned out, and did so. "Gentlemen, I'll trouble you for your fare. Just lay it thar on the bank, four bits for the wagon and two bits apiece for the men."

Browne was dumbfounded but Colonel Washington spoke. "Say, Guv'ner, be you the ferry man?"

"I be," answered the bean pole, puffing on his cob.

"And you want a dollar and a half for putting us over?"

"I do."

"Well, then," said the jehu, with the width of the wild Brazos between

---

[15] *Ibid.*   [16] *Ibid.*, 162–63.

the boatman and himself, "just draw a check for it on your own bank. And if you ain't paid by the time I get back," he roared, "I'll settle with you then."

There was no angry shouted answer from the scarecrow on the far bank. He carefully laid down his pipe, straightened up—like a jack-knife being unclasped—and checked the priming of his long rifle. He then raised it, set the hair trigger, aimed at Browne and his friends, and quietly, albeit nasally, said:

"Gentlemen, the first man that ondertakes to leave them premises without a 'payin' of his fare, *I'll drop him sure!*"

There was no mistaking the tone of his voice. While Washington raved, Browne quickly dug into his pockets and came up with a quarter. He held up the two-bits, then put it on a chip on the riverbank. "That's all right, stranger," the boatman called to him. "You're out. Just step o' one side." Nodding his profuse thanks, Browne gingerly but hurriedly did as he was told. The doctor and Johnson quickly followed suit, al-though the latter, as he placed his coin on the bank, muttered dejectedly, "My God! If I *only* had my rifle!"

Finally, it was "Mustang" Washington's turn. He fired a volley of trans-Brazos oaths, but paid up. The gaunt ferryman sat down again, paying no attention to the Colonel's threats of dire revenge upon his return to the Brazos. He just put his rifle aside and slowly took up his pipe again. But he shot a glance across the river to Colonel Washington, red-faced and swearing. Before he primed the pipe to resume his smok-ing, he called to the red-faced driver, "That's all right, stranger. Gen'rally speakin', I'm on hand here."[17]

After taking their leave of the bellicose, businesslike boatman, Browne and his party pushed on west. At the close of one particularly dreary day's journey, in which they had been blasted by another norther, they reached the town of Bastrop on the Colorado River of Texas. Bastrop was quite a town—at least, by Texas standards—in 1854. One of the oldest settlements in the state, it was perched on the left bank of the Colorado at the river crossing of the historic road between Nacogdoches and San Antonio de Béxar. The town was incorporated as early as 1837,

[17] *Ibid.*, 163–64.

when the name was changed from Mina to honor the Baron de Bastrop, Don Felipe E. Neri, alcalde of Béxar and a friend of Stephen Austin. When Browne visited Bastrop in 1854 it boasted a library, opened in 1852, a newspaper called the *Bastrop Advertiser* (formerly the *Colorado Reveille*), and a Methodist school, the Bastrop Academy, which was four years old. The first church in town had been built nineteen years before Browne's visit. Like the Academy, it was of Methodist persuasion. Browne sized up the town in these words:

> There seemed to be no lack of that sort of improvement which marks the progress of Texas civilization—a church, a jail, a court house, and the usual accompaniment of barrooms and billiard saloons. The least important object, as in all the towns I had seen, was a decent inn where we could get even tolerable accommodations. Rooms with six or eight beds, and every bed "double shotted," were the nearest approach to comfort to be had anywhere.[18]

Browne finally put up at a frame shanty with a sagging sign outside which proclaimed that the establishment afforded entertainment for man and horse. In the barroom, around a roaring fire, he found a dozen tough-looking *hombres*. Between drags on their cheroots, they were arguing hotly over a fight—or perhaps a series of fights, for Browne could not determine the exact number—which had occurred that day in Bastrop. A man named Jones had been killed by a Brown, it appeared, and members of both families had been wounded by stabbing. Browne discovered that "These affairs in Texas were about as clannish as the old Scottish feuds, in which whole tribes took part. . . . Not infrequently, they invoked entire neighborhoods and extended over a period of several years. The bitter blood must all be shed before they came to an end."[19]

It became clear to Browne that the angry and articulate seegar smokers were not directly involved in the vendetta; the killings were merely a form of spectator sport to them. He also gathered that Tom Jones was busy ransacking Bastrop, from stem to stern, in search of Jack Brown, who had killed his kin. Suddenly, the door of the barroom was kicked

[18] J. Ross Browne, "Old Texan Days," *Overland Monthly*, Vol. I, No. 4 (October, 1868), 367.

[19] *Ibid.*, 367–68.

open, and there stood the avenging Tom Jones. He looked like a poor choice for anyone to tangle with—"A tall powerful man of dark complexion, prominent features, scarred with old cuts and very deep-set, wicked eyes. . . . He stalked into the room and looked around fiercely at the group of talkers. His belt was garnished with pistols and bowie knives and he carried his right hand in the bosom of his waistcoat."[20]

A deadly, oppressive silence filled the room upon his entering. "Has anyone seen Brown?" he demanded. He shot a glance at each man in the room. "Say, have you seen Brown here?" He swore impatiently as he edged through the group. J. Ross Browne gulped hard and tried to imitate the *sang-froid* of his fellow loungers whose faces showed not the slightest emotion of either fear or even interest. The men just kept puffing away on their Havanas, looking coolly into the angry, insolent face of Tom Jones. To his surprise and consternation, Jones came up to Browne. "Have *you* seen Brown?" he demanded. "What Brown?" quavered the federal agent. "*Jack* Brown." "No. sir. I don't know Jack Brown, sir. Never heard of him before tonight to my knowledge."[21]

The answer apparently satisfied Jones, for he strode out of the building, banging the door behind him, leaving Browne shaking in his boots. It was with a sigh of relief that he heard the supper bell ring and he headed for the dining room. One of the crowd was a half-drunken, seedy-looking fellow who had been asleep in the corner during Tom Jones's visitation but who now aroused himself and advanced hurriedly on the dining room. The landlord met him in the passageway and ordered him back. The two men grappled. The uncouth guest drew a knife and shouted that he would have his dinner or he would have blood. The landlord's response was to strike him on the head with the dinner bell, a very heavy weapon. The knifer fell to the floor, senseless. Snatching up the knife which had fallen from the man's hand, the landlord pitched it out into the street and then dragged the unconscious former guest to the door and kicked him out after his bowie knife. Two or three boarders jumped up to see the fight, but with no real prospect of a spectacle they returned to their seats. The landlord picked up the broken bell, scuffed with his shoe at some ugly blood spots on the floor

[20] *Ibid.*, 368.   [21] *Ibid.*

boards, and remarked to Browne: "When a fellow won't pay his board, he must expect to be roughly handled. No man shall loaf on me, sir. No, sir, it shan't be done. I've boarded such chaps long enough, sir."[22]

Browne sat down at the table near the landlord's wife. He observed to her, "Your husband, madam, seems to have no easy time of it."

"No," she replied, laughing. "I heard him scufflin' with someone in the passage just now. Which whipped?"

"Well, madam," answered Browne, "I don't know exactly when a man is considered whipped in Texas, but I saw your husband knock his opponent down with a bell and then pitch him into the street as limber as a bag of meal."

"Yes," the amused landlady responded, "the Major has to do these things sometimes. He's not slow in a tussle when his dander's up. Won't you have some more tea, sir?"

The Major could not spare a single bed but finally gave Browne a small room after dinner. It contained a double bed, all of two and one-half feet wide. If nobody came during the night, Browne stood a good chance of getting a night's sleep without a bedfellow, or at least without another *human* occupant of the bed. "There was certainly one class of bed-fellows omitted by the Major in his estimate of the chances," observed Browne.[23]

To be on the safe side in the wild frontier town, Browne placed a table and a bureau against the lockless door of his room. The noise of voices, glasses, boots, and dice, plus the attentions of the Texas vermin, kept him awake for a long time, but, eventually, the weary Browne fell asleep. He was jolted awake by a loud pounding on the door and the landlord's voice shouting, "Hello, thar, stranger!"

"Hello," muttered Browne.

"Open the door, if you please. Here's a lodger wants to get in."

"Can't do it, sir. He must find another room."

"Sir, if you don't open the door, I'll have to burst it down," warned the Major.

Browne offered to pay for the two spaces that he was occupying. "That's not the thing, sir," answered Mine Host, "that's not the thing. The man must have a bed to sleep in, and there's no other."

22 *Ibid.*, 369. 23 *Ibid.*

"Well, sir, he can't sleep with me," rejoined Browne. Then, seized with an inspiration, he added, "Or, if he does, he must be prepared for the consequences. I'm troubled with fits."

Through the flimsy wall Browne could hear the would-be lodger backing off. "Never mind," the latter said to the hosteler, "let him be." I don't hanker after a bed-fellow with fits. Let's try it somewhere else."[24]

Browne survived Bastrop and proceeded to San Antonio, but not without further adventure. Between the two settlements he was set upon by a pack of fierce young dogs, used in the pursuit and treeing of runaway Negro slaves. When he finally reached San Antonio he stopped on the outskirts at a Mexican's cabin to see a man who had been scalped only a few days before on the trail to Eagle Pass—Browne's destination. The raw brutality of the mid-century West was brought home to Browne in that shanty in San Antone. The victim, Browne was told, was a well-known Texas horse thief who had always managed to avoid punishment by the law. But after stealing his last mount, an animal worth over $200, he had tried to escape to the Rio Grande and was seized by Comanches near the Agua Fria, scalped, left for dead, and his horse re-rustled.

The scene in the shack was to be engraved on Browne's memory:

> I went to see him in company with the physician who was attending him. The poor fellow was lying on a rough bed in the corner of the room. He suffered great pain, as I judged, for he seldom stopped groaning. He must have been a man of great muscular strength, but was now emaciated and presented a very cadaverous appearance; his dark beard and moustache contrasting fearfully with the deathlike pallor of his skin.
>
> His mind seemed quite unsettled. Sometimes in the midst of his groans, he would stop suddenly and utter the most horrid imprecations. When the doctor approached, he wept like a child and begged him, for God's sake, to put an end to his sufferings at once. A bandage was on his head. The doctor removed it and displayed a spectacle from which I could not but shrink, aghast—a round, raw spot about the size of the palm of the hand, puffed up and swollen at the edges where the scalp had been torn from the skull after the circular incision of the knife. The poor man shrieked with pain when the dressing commenced and it required all the power of

24 *Ibid.*, 369–70.

two stout Mexicans to hold him upright in the bed. This had to be done frequently so that it did not surprise me that he should beg to be put to death.

The doctor told Browne that the horse thief was the third such case he had had of a man surviving a scalping, but he added that men in such condition seldom survived very long.[25]

A somewhat shaken agent made his way into the city. Browne found San Antonio to be practically a metropolis in comparison to the other settlements he had visited. (The city, dating back to the Spanish Presidio de San Antonio de Béxar and the Villa de San Fernando de Béxar, jumped in population from 3,500 in 1850 to 10,000 by 1856.) He also found that the revenue officer for San Antonio was living twelve miles out of town and principally engaged in the buying and selling of live-stock, rather than in the tending of federal fiscal affairs in the area. Browne knew exactly what to do. He recommended strongly that the gentleman resign the San Antonio position, and he soon had his written resignation in hand. He then quickly appointed a temporary replace-ment until the Collector of the District of Saluria could get a permanent officeholder. To hold the fort, Browne chose former Mayor King of San Antonio, a man of great standing and character.[26]

Confidential Agent Browne reached Eagle Pass safely, without being scalped or even half-scalped. In that small town across the Rio Grande from Piedras Negras, Coahuila, he found a revenue officer who had never received any instructions from the Treasury Department and who had collected no duties, ever, on any articles brought into Texas from Mexico. Browne patiently briefed him on Customs rules and procedures, left him instructions to follow, and then moved on. Eagle Pass was not yet an important customs point. It was settled only in 1849 as a result of the Mexican War and the California Gold Rush, being set up as a temporary military post—Camp Eagle Pass—some four miles below a supply center (Camp California) for Texas Argonauts who were on their way to California via the Gila Trail. Fort Duncan was established in 1850 be-tween the two camps to create a strip settlement along the river; a

25 *Ibid.*, 370.   26 N. A. 177-1-84.

saloonkeeper soon followed, and El Paso del Aguila was born. By 1851, stages connected it to the other El Paso, El Paso del Norte.[27]

Browne's next stop was Laredo. This was then, as now, the chief port of entry to Texas from Mexico and was already an old settlement when he saw it for the first time. It was established in 1735 by the Spaniards, and a mission was set up there in 1762. By 1835 it was a settlement of 1,700 people. In 1846 the Texas Rangers seized the town from Mexico, the Republic of Texas having left it as a sort of no man's land, not trying to extend its government over the important port of entry. Mirabeau B. Lamar took command of Laredo during the Mexican War, and when Webb County was organized in 1848, Laredo was made its seat of government. Its population jumped during the California Gold Rush.[28]

The Customs officials of Laredo were much more businesslike than the sole officer in Eagle Pass. In fact, Browne found that their force of Mounted Inspectors, the forerunners of the modern Border Patrol, had caused revenue collections to double, even though the importation of livestock had been temporarily prohibited by the Mexican government. From Laredo he sent a report to Secretary of the Treasury James Guthrie on Valentine's Day, by military express via San Antonio and Corpus Christi, on conditions in the zone between Eagle Pass and Laredo. In this communication he strongly urged retention of the Mounted Inspectors, whose terms of employment were due to run out as of March 1, 1854.[29]

Browne felt that the Rio Grande frontier was important not only because of the duties collected there but also "because of the immense frauds in the way of returned debenture goods." In fact, he felt that the Rio Grande Valley stations were far more important than the relatively small amount of duties collected would suggest. Moreover, he was confident that he could prevent the evasion of customs by a more rigid system of protection and control. He flatly stated that the Mounted Inspectors force *must* be continued. To his mind, it was absolutely essential to the protection of the nation's frontier. Without the Mounted Inspectors, he advised Guthrie, the deputy collectors of customs would be helpless— so helpless, he added, that they themselves might as well be discontinued

[27] Webb, *Handbook of Texas*, I, 532.   [28] *Ibid.*, II, 28.   [29] N. A. 177-1-84.

as a worthless expense. In any case, thought Browne, the number of deputy collectors could be cut in half if Congress should decide to include stock, principally cattle, in the list of free articles of import. Browne favored this change. But he cautioned the Department of the Treasury against any greater reduction because, as he said:

> Texas is becoming now a populous state. The tide of emigration is gradually setting westward. The consumption of imported goods will be greater every year. Without a rigid guard along the frontier, the whole state might be supplied with foreign goods free of duty under the debenture system. Boxes and bales could be passed over into Mexico at the points designated by the law and smuggled back within a distance of a few miles on the same day.[30]

Perhaps Browne had the scalped horse thief on his mind when he wrote Guthrie from Laredo:

> The most difficult duty that now devolves upon me will be the inspection of the Rio Grande from this point to Brownsville. A detachment of soldiers sent down a few days since to Redmund's Ranch, to aid in the capture of a desperado who has been engaged in instigating the Mexicans on the American side to violate the revenue laws,[31] have just returned and represent a lawless state of things in that vicinity. Three murders took place a few days ago, supposed to be by Indians near that place and great difficulty is experienced by the Deputy Collector in performing his official duties and enforcing the law.[32]

[30] N. A. 177-1-82.

[31] This would appear to be Juan Nepomuceno Cortina, the so-called Rogue of the Rio Grande, either a bandit or a patriot (depending upon which side of the Rio Grande one dwells) who, though uneducated, and, indeed, illiterate, was a natural leader in the 1840's. He fought in General Mariano Arista's command versus Zachary Taylor at Resaca de la Palma and at Palo Alto in 1846, then settled on the family ranch, Santa Rita, just west of Brownsville. Murders were attributed to him, and between 1850 and 1859 he was the region's outstanding cattle rustler. Although indicted by the local grand jury, he was never convicted or even prosecuted. Cortina got into a scrape with the Brownsville City Marshal in 1859 and shot him in the shoulder. This finally made him *persona non grata* on the left bank, and he fled to Mexico. But he returned in a series of daring raids which came to be called the Cortina Wars. He captured the Brownsville jail and released the prisoners on one bold foray, routed both militia and Texas Ranger forces, but was finally whipped by Major S. P. Heintzleman and Rip Ford of the Rangers. Webb, *Handbook of Texas*, I, 416-17.

[32] N. A. 177-1-84.

Browne hoped to be able to straighten things out. He secured a six-man escort of troopers from Colonel Gustavus Loomis,[33] commanding officer at Laredo, to accompany him as far as Ringgold Barracks.[34] Browne found that the letters which the Secretary of War had kindly furnished him, addressed to commanders of various military stations in Texas, were worth their weight in gold. (He asked Guthrie, in one of his reports home, to pass on his gratitude to the Secretary of War.) He cited several examples of the courtesy and help extended to him by the army. He was given wagons by Major James Belger[35] at San Antonio, as well as transportation by Major George B. Crittenden[36] at Fort Inge,[37]

[33] Colonel Gustavus Loomis was a real "Regular." Born in Vermont, he graduated from the United States Military Academy (1811) in time for duty in the War of 1812, being taken prisoner at Fort Niagara. He served in the Black Hawk and Seminole Wars before being posted to the Indian Territory in the 1840's. During the 1850's he pulled duty at such Texas posts as Forts Belknap, McIntosh, and Ringgold Barracks, before returning to Florida for another crack at the Seminoles. He served in the Civil War and retired in 1863, after being carried for more than forty-five years on the Army Register. George W. Cullum, *Biographical Register of the Officers and Graduates of the U.S. Military Academy* (2 vols., New York, D. Van Nostrand, 1868), I, 118.

[34] Fort Ringgold, first called Ringgold Barracks, then Camp Ringgold, was a cavalry post on the Rio Grande adjacent to Rio Grande City in Starr County. It was set up on October 26, 1848, and named for a victim of the Battle of Palo Alto—Major David Ringgold. It was made a permanent camp, despite epidemics, in 1850 but abandoned in February, 1859. However, the outbreak of the Cortina Wars led to the return of the garrison in December of that year. Abandoned again from 1861–65, it became Fort Ringgold in 1878 and served as a military post until World War II. Webb, *Handbook of Texas*, I, 631.

[35] Brevet Major James Belger, brevetted for meritorious conduct "particularly in the performance of his duty in prosecution of the War with Mexico," enlisted in the Second United States Infantry at Fort Brooke, Florida, in 1837. He worked his way up as a quartermaster expert and served in San Antonio from 1851 to 1856. Guy V. Henry, *Military Record of Army and Civilian Appointments* (2 vols., New York, D. Van Nostrand, 1873), II, 44.

[36] A Kentuckian, George B. Crittenden graduated from the United States Military Academy in 1832 but resigned the following year to become a counselor at law. However, he was reappointed to the United States Army in 1846 and was brevetted for gallant and meritorious conduct in the Battles of Contreras and Churubusco during the Mexican War. After the war he stayed on in the Army, being assigned duty with the Mounted Rifles at Fort Leavenworth, Fort Kearny, Fort Vancouver, and in scouting assignments in Texas as well as duty at such posts as Fort Inge, Fort Clark, and San Antonio. He resigned his commission in 1861 to enter Confederate service. Cullum, *Officers and Graduates of the U.S. Military Academy*, I, 409–10.

[37] Fort Inge, in Uvalde County, on the east bank of the Leona River, was established on

J. Ross Browne often poked fun in text and picture at himself, as in this self-caricature, but he was serious in his investigative work in the West for the government. He once enunciated his credo thus: "It has always been my chief aim to promote to the best of my ability the development of our material resources and however I may have fallen short of the objects of my ambition, none will deny that I have labored long and faithfully in an honorable cause."

J. Ross Browne liked to escape "back to Nature" from pettifogging politicians and crooked civil servants in the Mint and Customs and Indian Services by joining Captain Jack Hays and his merry band of Coast Rangers on hunting and camping trips in the redwoods of the Mendocino Coast of California near Needle Rock and Bear Harbor.

Paisano Press

Disgusted by the pretensions of such nonports as Gardiner, Oregon, Browne satirically and facetiously suggested that the open and dangerous Redwood Coast of California be given a port of entry. He singled out the inaccessible cove euphemistically called "Bear Harbor," and reminded the Treasury Department, tongue in cheek, that "Wherever goats can travel, so can public funds."

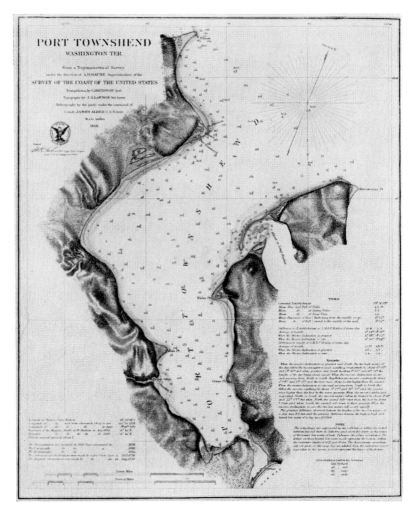

Port Townsend, Washington, which Browne investigated in 1854, has not even yet forgiven the Secret Agent for his scathing description of the "very benighted place." Debauched Indians and bad whisky made the greatest impression on Browne in the Puget Sound port. His sarcasm was uninhibited: "The principal luxuries afforded by the market of this delightful seaport are clams and the carcasses of dead whales that drift ashore, by reason of eating which the natives have clammy skins and are given to much spouting at public meetings."

Sutro Library

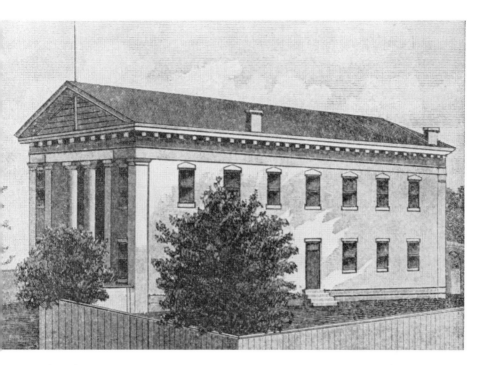

The Treasury Department's secret agent was bored with the pork-barreling and empire-building of tank towns in the Far West with delusions of grandeur. The former State Capitol at Benicia, for example, recently abandoned for one in Sacramento, loomed over a near ghost town in 1854. Half of the buildings in the drowsy town lay empty, and Browne reported to Washington on the somnolent port: "Benicia is now, like nearly all other towns in California, standing upon her own bottom."

California State Division of Beaches and Parks

The Secret Agent in the Southwest—as J. Ross Browne saw himself.

The commercial recession which began in late 1854 did little to discourage the looting of the public treasury, and when Browne reached Monterey (*above*) he ran into a scandal involving reckless charges of dishonesty, leveled by Judge Pacificus Ord against the Inspector of Customs, Thomas G. Richards. Browne took no side in the quarrel but collected data and forwarded it to Washington. The Inspector was replaced.

California State Division of Beaches and Parks

A half-dozen years after the Gold Rush, the port of Sacramento was so quiet that the Collector of Customs used two of the three rooms in the Customs House as sleeping quarters. Indeed, so quiet was Collector Charles C. Sackett's district that Browne recommended it be abolished. As far as the Agent could determine, Sackett was collecting $3,430 a year, in pay, for doing exactly nothing.

by Colonel Joseph Plympton[38] at Fort Duncan,[39] and by Colonel Loomis at Fort McIntosh.[40] The spoils-hating efficiency expert was pleased to find the military completely unlike the revenue service on the isolated and unsettled frontier. It was high in efficiency.

For geographical reasons, Special Agent Browne recommended that Eagle Pass be detached from its position in the District of Saluria[41] and included in the District of Brazos Santiago.[42] He felt that the latter

March 13, 1849, and named in honor of Lt. Zebulon M. P. Inge, killed at Resaca de la Palma. When Browne was there it was a compound of a dozen buildings around a parade ground shaded by elms and hackberries. Many of the buildings were crude and flimsy—some of the officers' quarters were of jacal—but it was a shipshape post till abandoned in 1869. Today, only ruins remain. Webb, *Handbook of Texas*, I, 627.

[38] Joseph Plympton of Massachusetts was appointed a second lieutenant in the Fourth Infantry in 1812. He served in the infantry for many years, winning the brevet rank of colonel for his conduct at Cerro Gordo. In 1854, when Browne met him, he was colonel of the First Infantry. He died in 1860. A. L. Morrison, *History of San Luis Obispo County* (Los Angeles, Historic Record Co., 1917), 633.

[39] Fort Duncan, a mile or so from Eagle Pass, was set up on March 27, 1849, by Capt. S. Burbank. It consisted of a storehouse, two magazines, a stone hospital, and officers' and enlisted men's quarters in 1854. Abandoned in 1859, it was regarrisoned for the Cortina Wars, then again abandoned with the outbreak of the Civil War in 1861. Webb, *Handbook of Texas*, I, 624.

[40] The original name of the post was Camp Crawford when it was established in 1849, but on January 7 ,1850, the name was changed to honor Col. J. S. McIntosh, killed in the storming of Molino del Rey in the Mexican War. It consisted of a star-shaped earthwork of an acre on a bluff above the Rio Grande, with a stone powder magazine. Abandoned in 1858, it was revived in the Civil War. *Ibid.*, I, 628.

[41] Great things were expected of Saluria in Browne's day, but it is a ghost town today on the northeastern tip of Matagorda Island, in Refugio County near McHenry Bayou. It was a development of promoter James Power in 1845. He had lots laid out in a townsite; he got settlers to come in and businesses established. The government did its part by erecting a lighthouse there, and two Texas Governors made their homes in Saluria, Henry Smith and Edmund J. Davis. But the thriving young port of J. Ross Browne's day was blockaded by the Union Navy during the Civil War, and when invasion appeared imminent, the Confederate defenders stationed at Fort Esperanza determined upon a scorched-earth policy. They burned the town, blew up the lighthouse, and drove most of the local cattle over to the mainland. The fort itself was defended until November 29, 1863, by Daniel Shea's artillery battalion, but finally the Confederates retreated to the mainland before the Federals commanded by Nathaniel P. Banks. The inhabitants returned to refound Saluria, but in 1875 the great Indianola Hurricane swept the town, washing it away and killing thirty of its forty-three tenacious residents. This spelled finis to Saluria. *Ibid.*, II, 537.

[42] Brazos Santiago Pass is the channel between the southern tip of Padre Island and the north end of Brazos Island. The waterway is the link between the Laguna Madre and the Gulf of Mexico and is northeast of Brownsville. *Ibid.*, I, 212.

could command the whole line of the river to its upper reaches. When, in due course of time, the Rio Grande Valley's commerce should greatly expand, Laredo could become a port of entry for a mid-district. He also suggested that Brownsville[43] be made port of entry for the District of Brazos Santiago rather than Point Isabel,[44] which lay several miles to the northwest of the mouth of the Rio Grande. Browne had the best of reasons to support his recommendation of the change. First and foremost, there was no commerce (as of 1854) at Point Isabel. Second, the lightering of cargoes to Point Isabel from vessels at Brazos Island, and their subsequent overland transfer to Brownsville, were both expensive and inconvenient to shippers. Brownsville was the major place of business in the lower Rio Grande Valley, and Browne was convinced that it would remain so. Some merchants of Brownsville urged the Confidential Agent to work for the shift of the port of entry; others were satisfied with it where it was. It appeared to Browne that, usually, the bigger merchants were of the former mind while the smaller retailers opposed the move. He gave the transfer a lot of thought and finally had to side with the merchant princes of southwest Texas because of the inconvenience and wastefulness of repeated transshipments of goods. He wanted to see direct delivery aboard ship on the river from Brazos Island to Brownsville. He thought that Point Isabel should be made a port of delivery for the mosquito fleet of small, coasting vessels running to Brazos Santiago.[45]

Browne also wanted Corpus Christi[46] separated from the District of

[43] Brownsville, twenty-two miles from the mouth of the Rio Grande, named for Major Jacob Brown, hero of Fort Taylor (renamed Fort Brown) in the Mexican War, became the seat of Cameron County in 1848; incorporated in 1850. It has been, since J. Ross Browne's day, *the* port for the Rio Grande Valley and for northeast Mexico as well. *Ibid.*, I, 229.

[44] Point Isabel, now Port Isabel, is on the tip of a peninsula in the Laguna Madre inside of Padre Island, three miles west of Brazos Santiago Pass. It was settled as early as 1770. Soldiers of Zachary Taylor occupied it in the Mexican War, and in 1849, Forty-niners used it as a port. In 1853 a lighthouse was erected but trade drifted steadily away, to Brownsville. *Ibid.*, II, 394.

[45] N. A. 177–1–82.

[46] Corpus Christi began life as a settlement when Henry Lawrence Kinney quartered his forty-man private army there and set up a trading post in 1840. Zack Taylor stopped there in 1845 en route to Mexico, and the site was continued as an Army depot until 1855. The

Saluria and made into a district itself, with Aransas[47] as its port of entry and Copano[48] and Corpus Christi proper designated as ports of delivery. This made good sense, for only Aransas could be reached by either steamers or sailing vessels of any substantial draft and, thus, of any real cargo. Aransas was the head of navigation of Corpus Christi Bay. The whole District of Saluria looked to Browne like a mystical, never-never land. He suggested that Powderhorn replace the existing port of entry, La Salle.[49] His reasoning was that Powderhorn,[50] insignificant as it was,

town became the seat of Nueces County in 1846, and, like so many Gulf towns of Texas (many of which, unlike Corpus, are ghost towns today) became a boom port with the migration to California after the discovery of gold in 1848. A post office was in existence by 1850, the town was incorporated in 1852, and by 1854 the United States government had recognized the town as a port. Vessels were unloaded outside a breakwater and goods lightered ashore. Blockaded and captured by Federal forces in the Civil War, Corpus Christi had a renaissance in the 1920's when it became a busy deepwater port. Webb, *Handbook of Texas*, I, 415.

[47] Aransas, now a ghost town, was a rival to Corpus Christi in Browne's day. It was founded about 1845 on the southwest end of St. Joseph Island, almost due east of Corpus Christi, and was first called St. Joseph. A stage and a ferry connected the town with mainland points. It became a port of call for the Morgan Line, the first Texan steamship line (1836), and a post office. When the Civil War broke it was a prosperous port. The Union blockade stopped shipping and ruined the town. Federal troops captured it twice, and the second time, in the summer of 1862, burned every building to the ground. *Ibid.*, I, 57.

[48] Copano was another of James Power's projects, in south Refugio County, overlooking Copano Bay, a westward extension of Aransas Bay. A port by 1845 and a post office by 1850, its wharves and shell-concrete warehouses starved to death when no railroad came near. Its decline continued until 1870 when the entire population—Power's widow and daughters —moved away. *Ibid.*, I, 410.

[49] La Salle, in Calhoun County on Matagorda Bay, now a vanished ghost town, was about six miles south of Indianola, and was founded in the 1840's. A prognosticated boom never materialized, chiefly because the La Salle and El Paso Railroad, though chartered, was to exist on paper only. Plans for making the village into a port were abandoned. When Federal troops landed at La Salle in the Civil War, the handful of inhabitants moved to Indianola. *Ibid.*, II, 31.

[50] Powderhorn, later Karlshaven and still later Indianola, was founded by Charles Morgan of the Morgan Line. When he found port charges too high at La Vaca, he built Indianola as a rival harbor, and made it the chief port of call of his steamships. Germans settled there in the 1840's. In 1850 the Federal Boundary Commission sat there. Between 1850 and 1861 it was an important military depot for everything from bully beef to (live) camels imported by Jeff Davis for an abortive United States Army camel corps. It was a pre–Civil War center for slaughtering cattle, for hides and tallow, for shipping livestock to Cuba and the East Coast of the United States. The Hurricane of September 15, 1875, was

loomed head and shoulders over the former in importance since La Salle did not even exist except as a speck on a map drawn by the proprietor of the undeveloped "development" of that name. Browne found that the gentleman did not see eye to eye with him on this, of course, since he was not only the owner of the site of La Salle but also the former collector of customs of the District.[51]

Another of Browne's recommendations for tightening up customs control of the Gulf Coast of Texas was the stationing of boarding officers at Saluria or Decrow's Point, because the entrance to Matagorda Bay was entirely unprotected and the haven itself a smuggler's paradise. He found Saluria, formerly the port of entry, to be inaccessible by land and of no commercial importance. Indianola, a mile or two from Powderhorn, and eventually merged with it to form a community, was the business and population center of the area. Since Powderhorn was considered the actual head of navigation and could accommodate steamers and sailing vessels drawing up to eight feet of water, Browne's vote went to Powderhorn. He did not forget that he was given the task of coming up with money-saving ideas for the government. He suggested that the Texas Coast revenue service be streamlined by dispensing with the services of two boatmen at Powderhorn, at a saving of fifty dollars a month, since the two had absolutely nothing to do. They would not be missed, Browne assured Guthrie. He suggested that the twenty-five-dollar monthly salary of each man be used to employ boarding officers at Decrow's Point.[52] His last report from Texas—at least, his last surviving *Tejano* report—was mailed from Rio Grande City and concluded with these words: "My stay in Texas has been greatly prolonged by

---

the beginning of the end for Indianola, the most important of Texas's ghost towns. For the first time, the Gulf broke over Matagorda Island and tidal waves scoured Indianola. The population drifted to La Vaca. *Ibid.*, II, 883.

[51] N. A. 177–1–82.

[52] Decrow's Point may have been named for Daniel Decrow, one of Stephen Austin's Old Three Hundred Families, or for his kin, Thomas Decrow. The settlement, on the lower end of Matagorda Island fronting the pass, founded in 1834, was swept away by the tidal waves of the Indianola Hurricane of 1875. Thomas Decrow, his wife, and all other inhabitants were lost. John Henry Brown, *History of Texas* (2 vols., St. Louis, L. E. Daniel, 1893), II, 536. Webb, *Handbook of Texas*, I, 480.

the inconvenience of getting from point to point but I trust the tour has been complete and thorough, and advantageous to the Government as well as to the Officers of the Revenue. I leave on Saturday for California."[53]

It is unfortunate that only a fragment of Browne's Texas reports are available. For, thorough and careful as always, he submitted statements on the situations in Galveston, Austin, San Antonio, Eagle Pass, Laredo, and Rio Grande City, as well as the (now ghost-town) Gulf ports. Notes made by Treasury Department officials on the backs of J. Ross Browne's letters to Secretary Guthrie indicate that many, if not all, of his recommendations were carried out. In the case of Texas, for example, it appears that an inspector at Galveston was dismissed in line with Browne's recommendation, that the boatmen at Powderhorn-Indianola were dropped, and that a boarding officer was appointed for Decrow's Point.[54]

Browne was able to work wonders, himself, on the hitherto unpoliced customs frontier. He threatened E. Jones and Company of San Antonio with criminal action for evasion of duties on imported Mexican livestock. He would not accept the excuse which the company offered for not having paid duty on the mules and brood mares. Their "out" was that the late Deputy Collector had declared the animals duty exempt. After explaining the Treasury Department's instructions and regulations patiently, but to no avail, Browne threatened the Company with prosecution. He soon had the two hundred dollars worth of duty in his hands. He deposited the money with the Assistant Quartermaster General in San Antonio. By June 13, 1854, his Texas business closed and his sense of duty reasonably satisfied, Browne was in Aspinwall,[55] writing to Secretary Guthrie that he hoped to be in San Francisco in two weeks.[56]

[53] N. A. 177-1-82.

[54] *Ibid.*

[55] Aspinwall, founded in 1850 in conjunction with the building of the Panama Railroad, and named in 1852 for the railway's chief promoter, *yanqui* William Aspinwall, is now the major Panamanian city on the Caribbean, Colón.

[56] N. A. 177-1-85.

CHAPTER FOUR

The City That Knew How

THE FIRST DAY OF JULY, 1854, saw J. Ross Browne back at the Golden Gate, to become reacquainted with San Francisco, "The City That Knows How," in the claims of its boosters. One thing was certain in the 1850's: it was a city that knew how to politic, to graft, and to featherbed. Browne would open there a Pandora's box of "irregularities." But, despite all the headaches which governmental graft and malingering caused him in San Francisco, he became fonder and fonder of the city. Not long after he had become settled, he wrote his wife: "I like the country much better than I did in '49. In fact, I have determined to come out here to live. The climate is splendid for children. All the California children are young giants." In the summer of 1855 he did bring his family to California, to stay. He built a frame house on a twelve-acre tract of the old Peralta Grant in Oakland along the Estuary. It would be his family home for fourteen years.[1]

But Browne, in the opening days of July, speedily got down to the business at hand. His very first report, sent on July 15, made it clear to Secretary Guthrie that the Collector of Customs did not see eye to eye with the newly arrived agent. But, at least, Collector Richard P. Ham-

[1] *Muleback*, viii.

mond[2] was willing to go along with him to the extent of adopting some of his suggestions toward reducing the staggering costs of the operation of the San Francisco Customs House. Browne sized Hammond up, on a quick first impression, as a man of great intelligence and integrity. In later communiqués he was forced to re-evaluate him somewhat, but he continued to vouch for Hammond's political bill of health, telling Guthrie that the Collector was "an ardent supporter of the Administration."[3]

Browne's first major recommendation was a bombshell. Small wonder that Hammond greeted it with something less than ardor; the Special Agent demanded that the expenses of operating the Customs House be reduced by $100,000 a year! He flatly guaranteed to Hammond and to Secretary Guthrie, too, not only that it could be done without detriment to public service, but that the economizing would actually redound to the public's great advantage. Twenty inspectors he found to be doing, literally, nothing. Or, at least, nothing save claiming and cashing their checks.

He did not make this claim (or any other) without substantiation. In order to support his sweeping recommendations for reform, he prepared a set of tables on the number of vessels arriving in port, the amount of

[2] Maj. Richard Pindell Hammond was born in Hagerstown, Maryland, in 1820. He secured an appointment to the United States Military Academy, thanks to Andrew Jackson's good offices, and graduated with honors on July 1, 1841. He served with distinction in Florida, in the Coast Survey, and in the Mexican War. In the latter conflict, he was brevetted twice for gallant and meritorious conduct. When Mexico City was captured, Hammond was selected to be the secretary of the city government and acting judge advocate. In January, 1848, he was sent to California as a special government agent. After his survey was completed he remained in California on leave and finally resigned his commission in 1850. The founder of the city of Stockton, Capt. C. W. Weber, invited him into a partnership, and he prospered in real estate there before being elected to the state assembly (1852) of which he became speaker. Upon the expiration of his term in 1854, he was named collector. After his "encouraged" resignation, he went into ranching in San Joaquin County at Cherokee Lane near Stockton, became a business and civic leader, regent of the University of California, and confidant of railroad magnate and Governor, Leland S. Stanford. He died on November 28, 1891. "His ideals were high and governed all his actions, and his motives were never questioned," said historian J. M. Guinn. But he was eased out of the collectorship by Browne's investigations. J. M. Guinn, *History of the State of California and Biographical Record of San Joaquin County* (2 vols., Los Angeles, Historic Record Co., 1909), II, 18–21.

[3] N. A. 177–1–88.

goods carried, and so forth. With this he was able to call to the attention of Hammond and Guthrie the consistency in the amount of business from month to month and year to year. With this weapon in hand he could denounce the "reserve force" of inspectors built up, supposedly, for cases of necessity. Of course, the emergencies never arose; the necessity was never there. This was the most absurd, wasteful, and obvious frill in the San Francisco operation, and it was the first to go. Browne's figures also supplied damning evidence of the slipshod administration of the establishment, and led to a coolness between Hammond and Browne and to the latter's losing his respect for the former. It was made clear that it took double the work force of 1853 to do but two-thirds of the work—weighing, measuring, gauging, etc.—in the following year. Browne singled out certain offices for particular attention and, almost, for scorn. He found that the tonnage measurer, for example, had worked on 130 vessels in the fiscal year 1853–54. According to Browne's estimates, these tasks should have taken, on the outside, three hundred hours. This was just fifty full working days at the Customs House during the entire year. Yet the man was paid eight dollars a day, for every workday of the year. Browne's strong suggestion was that the officer who inspected coasting licenses, and who was busy only half of the time, be allowed to absorb the light chores of tonnage measuring.

Browne found many absentees from the swollen (on-paper) work force. Some were on extended sick leave, others were away on "urgent political business."[4] Browne, like Abraham Lincoln, loathed the political hangers-on who impeded government. Lincoln would sadly say, "I am afraid this thing is going to ruin republican government—the incessant human wriggle and struggle for office." Browne, when only twenty-five years old, made his feelings on the subject so clear that the book reviewer of the *Edinburgh Review* quoted them to his British audience when he described Browne's distaste for "the hollowness of political distinction, the small trickery produced in the struggle for power; the overbearing aristocracy of station and the heartless and selfish intrigues by which public men maintain their influence. I became thoroughly disgusted with so much hypocrisy and bombast. It required no sage monitor to

[4] *Ibid.*

convince me that true patriotism does not prevail to a very astonishing extent in the hearts of those who make the most noise about it. The profession I had chosen enabled me to see behind the scenes and study well the great machinery of government. I cannot say that I saw a great deal to admire."[5] Nothing which Browne had seen between 1846 and 1854 had watered down these strong feelings of his.

Browne wanted the labor force markedly reduced in numbers. There were far too many laborers figuratively leaning on their shovels. He recommended that the excess of man power be disposed of at once. He also felt that the position of Assistant Naval Officer could be done away with entirely. Investigating the government's Union Street Warehouse, he was not so much struck by a lazy labor force as he was by the structure itself. He found it to be a white elephant, a dead loss to the government for the unexpired term of the lease. This document, too, he examined and described to Guthrie as illegal and unauthorized. Browne found that San Francisco's merchants were storing practically all of their goods in private warehouses, not in the expensive Union Street building.

When he turned his attention away from the harbor and to the United States Mint, he found it in bad shape, as well. It could not meet the coinage demands of the city. Browne heard many complaints of the Mint's inefficiency. His first investigation of these complaints demonstrated to him that the Mint's staff was cramped, short on silver (for refining purposes) to cover the deposits of gold, and all but out of such necessities as acids.

He was able to devote very little attention to the lighthouses of the Pacific Coast, but he did remind Secretary Guthrie that a Captain Graham had been sent out to inspect them. Graham, however, reported Browne, was ill and unable to make his survey. He urged Guthrie to give the navigational aids some attention. Contractors were impatiently waiting for their money for work done on some of the structures. There was little or nothing that Browne could do, except try to mollify the angry contractors. He had no authority to act in this area, especially since a duly appointed inspector had been sent to San Francisco.[6]

[5] "Ar(ticle) III, Etchings of a Whaling Cruise," *Edinburgh Review*, Vol. LXXXVI, No. 173 (July, 1847), 68.
[6] N. A. 177-1-88.

A much thornier problem was that of Edward Fitzgerald Beale, the late commissioner of Indian affairs for California. Browne met him but had no instructions to investigate his accounts, nor any desire to do so. He preferred to let the Secretary of the Interior handle that politically explosive matter. Many were of the opinion that Beale had been crucified politically. Bayard Taylor had dubbed him a "pioneer in the path of empire," and Beale, indeed, was something of a hero because of his cloak and dagger missions with government dispatches before and during the Mexican War. He had fought in the Battle of San Pascual, testified for Frémont in the latter's court-martial, and carried the news of the gold discovery in California to the East. President Millard Fillmore appointed him to the superintendency of Indian affairs in California on March 3, 1853, but his political enemies secured his replacement in that post by means of a whispering campaign. Undismayed, Beale went on to a variety of projects, including a camel corps for the army based at Fort Tejon in the Tehachapi Mountains, before his death in 1893. A friend of Frémont, U. S. Grant, James G. Blaine, and—especially—Kit Carson (each had saved the other's life), he was much liked in California and apparently well deserved of Charles Nordhoff's description of him: "A sparkling combination of scholar, gentleman and Indian fighter."[7]

Dodging the highly controversial Beale case, Browne went on to areas of his own responsibility. He found several areas of government work in San Francisco in which he was pleased. The Appraiser's Office, for example, appeared to be doing an admirable job. The Appraiser General was Samuel J. Bridge, of Massachussetts. When he left San Francisco for the East Coast on September 5, 1857, the newspapers bade him a fond farewell, reminding their readers of his ability and of the esteem held toward the faithful public official.[8] He returned to San Francisco later to settle for one of the lesser posts in the office and was one of the several appraisers until he sailed for the East Coast again on July 3, 1865, on a three-month leave granted him because of his ill health.[9] He finally had to resign because of his impaired health, in May,

[7] *Dictionary of American Biography*, I, 88–89.
[8] *San Francisco Daily Alta California*, September 5, 1857, p. 2, col. 1.
[9] *Ibid.*, July 3, 1865, p. 1, col. 3.

1870, after twenty-nine years in the San Francisco Customs House.[10] Browne also found that the United States Marine Hospital was not only well built but well run.[11]

The Confidential Agent had little to do with merchant seamen, for the most part. This was a pity since San Francisco was the world's capital of shanghaiing and could have used a dosage of Browne's brand of reform. But he did lend an ear to the complaints of agents of the Pacific Mail Steamship Company who told him that the United States Consul in the port of Acapulco, Mexico (Charles L. Denman, an Englishman appointed in California, according to the *Official Register* of 1855), was forcing Pacific Mail captains to take men aboard their ships for passage to San Francisco. The Consul's claim was that they were destitute American mariners and, therefore, rightly entitled by federal law to a trip home. But the Pacific Mail Company officers insisted that the traffic was a fraud. The men were not Americans, they said, but foreigners who paid the Consul something under the fifty-dollar fare to San Francisco. The latter would then frank them through as destitute seamen, at a cost of ten dollars to the government, that sum being paid to the steamship line. The Consul would pocket a nice profit; the men in question would get a cut-rate trip to booming San Francisco; and the steamer company would be out forty dollars per passenger.

Browne could hardly believe that a responsible consular officer would either stoop to such a fraud or be so negligent as to allow others than American seamen to take advantage of the law for their relief. But he looked into the matter, of course. To his disgust, he was able to secure affidavits from two of the transported seamen who were not American citizens.[12] Moreover, one of the complainants was a friend of Browne's, Captain Richard H. Pearson of the Pacific Mail line. He trusted him completely and knew there could be no collusion between a man like Pearson and the seamen to embarrass the Consul in the Mexican port.[13]

10 *Ibid.*, May 24, 1870, p. 1, col. 3.

11 N. A. 177–1–88. 12 N. A. 177–1–89.

13 Pearson brought the *Oregon* into San Francisco in April, 1849, and, though crews of other ships were deserting right and left, was able to sail for Panama on April 12, thanks to his seamanship and discipline. He was one of Pacific Mail's top captains. John Haskell Kemble, *The Panama Route* (Berkeley, University of California Press, 1943), 36.

Actually, Browne discovered that there was not much which he could do, except report his findings to Washington. The two sailors refused to admit paying the Consul any money, and Browne was anything but sure of the dependability of their sworn affidavits. He knew full well how lightly regarded was the testimony of merchant seamen—"As a general rule, the oaths of this class of men, and more especially of foreign sailors, are not worthy of implicit confidence."[14]

Browne's general appraisal of San Francisco was doubtless enlightening to Washington. His study of economic conditions showed prices decreasing and some unemployment resulting from a business slow-down. He suggested that the labor force be trimmed and that the inflated salaries of public officials be reduced. It was clear to Browne that the boom days of the Gold Rush, itself, were over. Since he found many temporary workers receiving a high rate of pay, the same as that given permanent workers, he recommended that their pay be cut, and first. But even more important, he felt, was a reduction in the pay of superior officers in federal employ, as opposed to menials.[15] However, some months later he did encounter some civil servants who were under-compensated, so his pay-cut recommendation was not to be an "across the board" affair. (On August 17, 1855, he would urge the Treasury Department to raise the pay of certain San Francisco Mint employees.)[16]

Some of the reforms which Browne suggested as being long overdue in San Francisco required the action of Congress. The actual abolition of offices in the proliferating, far-flung branch of Big Government was one. The two positions which he particularly wished to knock in the head were those of Deputy Naval Officer, held by David Hayden, and Deputy Surveyor, held by George W. Guthrie. All of the duties of the (chief) Naval Officer and of the (chief) Surveyor of the Port were being done by the two deputies or by clerks. The nominal heads of the two departments had nothing to do but sign their names to an occasional document. An exasperated Browne wrote to his superior on July 20: "I am prepared to prove, if necessary, that they are not actually employed upon

[14] N. A. 177–1–89.
[15] N. A. 177–1–90.
[16] N. A. 177–1–260.

their official duties one hour a day during the entire year." Yet each man received $15,000 from the public's pockets per annum. In addition, they profited from a shart of forfeitures, penalties, and so on. These ran the Surveyor's yearly take, for doing next-to-nothing, to $22,000 and the Naval Officer's to $23,000.[17]

Since the Deputy Naval Officer was doing practically all of the work of the Naval Officer (William B. Dameron), and to all extents and purposes *was* the Naval Officer other than in rank, name, and pay, Browne urged that the offices of deputies be abolished altogether and the shiftless chiefs required to perform their neglected duties. As Browne understood the policy of the Treasury Department, any jobs which turned up as useless sinecures were to be done away with. He informed the Secretary of the Treasury that the Collector of Customs and all other top officers of the Customs House staff readily admitted that the two men in question did no useful duty except for the routine signing of their names to documents executed by their staffs. Browne's examination of the books of the two offices reinforced his original appraisal of the two deputies. They were carrying on their work in able fashion. (Indeed, they were each carrying two men's work.) But his criticism of the system of sinecures created by politicking knew no bounds. "I beg leave to impress the opinion," he wrote, "derived from personal observation, that in all cases where public officers perform no actual duty, the result is injurious to the Government."[18]

Browne was not surprised to find the accounts of the two do-nothing officers themselves to be somewhat out of order. Surveyor William Van Voorhies[19] had accumulated $2,222.42 in fees which should have been

[17] N. A. 177-1-90.

[18] *Ibid.*

[19] A hotheaded, partisan (but sincere) professional Democrat, Van Voorhies held various state and federal posts in California. He was an assemblyman from San Francisco during his long career, secretary of state of California, and a member of the second State Constitutional Convention. The Tennessean, who belonged to the Southern or "Chivalry" faction of the Democratic party, began his career in the West as a postal agent for the Pacific Coast (1848). He was, actually, a special courier from President Polk to the people of California, urging them not to go it alone but to be patient and become citizens of a state in the United States. (Polk feared that Benton and Frémont were desirous of seeing a Pacific republic arise on the coast.) After helping to save California for the Union, he appointed C. L. Ross

used to pay—that is, to help pay—the salaries of Customs House employees. Former Surveyor Hart Fellows, he found, had a similar balance on the books of $3,825.94.[20] Browne swore that he would get this money back to where it belonged, in Uncle Sam's Treasury, by forcing the two men to pay it to the Assistant Treasurer of the United States (J. R. Snyder) in San Francisco. If they did not turn it over freely, he was ready to enter suit against them.

Another workless sinecure which the inspector general turned up was the post of Measurer of Tonnage. He urged that the office be completely abolished. Browne found the incumbent, Louis McLane, extensively engaged in private business at his private office, neither active in nor interested in the affairs of the Department except on payday. The gentleman also turned out to be one of the owners of the building which housed the Customs Office! An incredulous Browne barely managed to keep his astonishment in check when he wrote the Department on July 29, 1854. But he managed to content himself with wry understatement: "It is certainly an unusual thing, if not one of questionable propriety, for one of the owners of a customs house to occupy a subordinate situation in it, where all the operations of the Department may possibly be subject to his scrutiny." Browne then notified Guthrie that he had asked Collector Hammond to remove the landlord–Measurer of Tonnage at once.[21]

The following day Browne sent another report, which outlined his planned reductions in staff and the resultant savings in the cost of operating the Customs House. By dropping twenty-five inspectors, two assistant weighers and measurers, two gaugers, ten laborers, and three clerks (all with the agreement of Collector of Customs Richard P.

---

temporary postmaster for San Francisco and tried to establish routes and post offices, but with no more luck than Browne had in 1849. Van Voorhies soon gave up the mails and turned to law. In 1853, President Pierce named him surveyor. He was replaced when Pierce left office, and turned to journalism, soon earning the reputation of being the bitterest Democrat in California because of his writings. He died in 1884. "William Van Voorhies," *Quarterly of the Society of California Pioneers*, Vol. II, No. 1 (1925), 5–6. Van Voorhies once joked: "My occupations on the Pacific Coast have been multifarious, to wit: Law, merchandizing, mining, restaurant keeping and—least reputable of all—office holding." *First Steamship Pioneers* (San Francisco, H. S. Crocker, 1874), 270.

[20] *Sacramento Union*, December 27, 1878, p. 3, col. 2.

[21] N. A. 177–1–93.

Hammond), he would save the Department at least $90,150 per year. By throwing in the eminently disposable posts of deputy surveyor and deputy naval officer, the savings total would be $105,150 per annum. He urged the immediate reduction of the rent paid for the government warehouse on Union Street. The existing rent, of $2,000 per month, he considered to be "a gross fraud upon the Government." If all these measures were carried through, Browne pointed out, the government would save $136,350 a year. He reminded the Secretary that overstaffing was not only wasteful of public money but that it also encouraged idleness and general inefficiency. He then documented his charges with tables of proof which he appended to his official report.[22] (However, he would continue to whack away at the oversized Customs House staff until August 3, 1855, when, after removing a final half-dozen inspectors, he would report the work force trimmed as far as practicable.)[23]

Browne's methods were effective. They worked. By the end of Browne's first month in the city, Surveyor Van Voorhies had begun the liquidation of his balance by paying July Customs House salaries out of it. The problem of Hart Fellows was stickier. The latter stoutly denied any wrongdoing, claiming that the fees were legally his to keep. Although Browne quoted Departmental chapter and verse to him, he was adamantine. But finally Browne's persistance paid off. Fellows was worn down and acceded to the agent's demand for the money. Graciously, Browne wrote to the Treasury Department that he did not feel that former Collector Fellows was trying to defraud the government. It was just a misunderstanding of the law. While he was at it, however, Guthrie's confidential agent wondered aloud why the accounting officers of the Treasury Department had allowed the two balances to remain improperly in the hands of the two individuals in San Francisco for such a long time.[24]

After carefully studying the statistics on ship arrivals in port during the fiscal year 1853–54, Browne found that 735 ships had called at San Francisco from foreign or Atlantic Coast United States ports.[25] This made him feel secure in recommending the abolition of more superfluous

[22] N. A. 177–1–97.   [23] N. A. 177–1–263.
[24] N. A. 177–1–98.   [25] *Ibid.*

positions at the Customs House, starting with the Spirit Entry Clerk.[26] Still sizing up Collector Hammond, he ventured the opinion to Guthrie that Hammond was not too bad. Browne thought that it was a case of the Collectors having to wrestle with problems inherited from his careless predecessors in office. Browne became a little annoyed at Hammond, however, when the latter gave in to pressure after the walls of the government's bonded warehouse on Union Street collapsed and fell in. Frederick Macondray and other moneybags of San Francisco were soon hounding Hammond for damages. Even though Browne showed the merchant princes that the collapse was not caused by the government's overloading the leased warehouse but rather because of defects in materials used in the construction of the building, Hammond gave in and paid for the repairs. Browne was angry at him for doing this. He told him it was wrong to do it. The special agent was afraid that it would set a precedent. He worried aloud to Guthrie over the possibility of a future custom of private parties seeking "to build cheap houses and rent them to the Government, with the advantage of the use of Government funds for their repair or reconstruction."[27]

On August 1, Special Agent Browne called the Treasury Secretary's attention to a shameful situation on the Pacific Coast. This was the growing coolie trade and its relationship to the Customs House and the Treasury Department. Browne cited repeated violations of the Passenger Acts of February 22, 1847, and May 17, 1848.[28] The laws in question were being openly flouted in connection with the immigration of Chinese to San Francisco. The coolie trade was beginning to boom, and shipowners and masters were finding infinite ways to evade the law. The statutes which limited the number of passengers on ships specified the main, lower, and orlop decks, for example, but said nothing of the exposed outside or weather decks because the lawmakers never dreamed that greedy men would ship human cargo (coolies) in such space. Little did the solons know the mentality of bucko mates and avaricious shipowners. Vessels like the *Potomac, Australia,* and *Libertad* took advantage of these legal loopholes to transport Chinese to San Francisco like livestock. The *Libertad* case was particularly flagrant and tragic. Browne

[26] N. A. 177-1-113.   [27] *Ibid.*   [28] *Ibid.*

warned Guthrie that the coolie trade evil had "become so great as to cause serious alarm on the part of the Municipal and State authorities. . . . Vessels coming into port now carry from one to two passengers for every ton and the result is that large numbers of them die on the passage or in port. The case of the *Libertad* can hardly be surpassed in all its inhuman and disgusting details by that of any slaver in the African trade."[29]

Yet, sadly reported Browne, Judge Ogden Hoffman[30] contended that the brutal traffic was strictly legal. The jurist insisted that the statues on the books applied only to the decks specifically identified in the legislation. Browne countered that the 1847 law limited the number of passengers who might be taken "on board" a vessel, and to Browne this was clear enough. If a man was on *any* deck—or dangling from the rigging, for that matter—he was aboard the ship. But Hoffman was adamant, as only a judge can be. This decision of Ogden Hoffman led to a stepping up of the coolie trade. Notices were posted in China of the great opportunities in the Big City of the Golden Mountains (San Francisco, California), and ship after ship pointed its prow toward the Golden Gate with up to one thousand Chinese aboard. Guthrie's secret agent predicted that an "epidemic which will force the people of California to rise up in self-defense against these violations of law and humanity must be the consequence unless active measures are taken to prevent further abuse of this kind." (The people *did* rise up in a rash of anti-coolie disturbances which were a factor in the shocking tong wars which afflicted Chinatown for decades.)[31] Browne's solution of the problem was to

[29] N. A. 177-1-117.

[30] Although he was angered and disgusted by the justice's decision, Browne and Hoffman became fast friends and the latter joined Browne's jolly crew of Coast Rangers. The Judge was an outstanding figure of California's bench, a New York–born Columbia and Dane Law School (Harvard) graduate who was appointed United States District Court judge in March, 1851, when he was twenty-eight, by President Millard Fillmore. A fine linguist and a constant reader, he brought intelligence and stability to law enforcement in the West, even though he did not see eye to eye with Browne on the overcrowded coolie clippers. Oscar T. Schuck, *Representative and Leading Men of the Pacific* (San Francisco, Bacon and Co., 1870), 535–37.

[31] See Richard H. Dillon, *The Hatchet Men* (New York, Coward-McCann, 1962).

change the law to a clear-cut limitation of the number of passengers on a ship, based on the tonnage of the vessel in question.[32]

Guthrie sent a circular on the government's passenger laws to Browne, in hopes it would be of help to him. After thanking him, Browne ruefully complained that the judges of San Francisco preferred to stipulate a rigid construction of the laws when they wanted to protect shipowners—so rigid, in fact, that human rights became mere results of technical forms.[33]

Special Agent Browne did his best to tighten up on the harbor where such evils as smuggling, shanghaiing, and buckoism were rampant. To see to it that the laws were enforced on the Embarcadero he had Lyman Ackley[34] appointed supervising inspector and captain of the night watch on the Bay. Ackley was also given command of the Revenue Barge which had formerly been in the hands of Captain John E. Grymes. The new Supervising Inspector was ordered to use the craft to visit all ships in the stream and to see that inspectors were both aboard them and doing their duty. Surveyor of the Port William Van Voorhies drew up a new set of orders. These he signed and sent to Collector Hammond for countersigning. They were then published and copies were used by Ackley to guide his actions.[35]

[32] N. A. 177–1–117.

[33] N. A. 177–1–153.

[34] Inspector Lyman Ackley, a Jacksonian Democrat from New Jersey, had come to California as a miner. He was appointed an inspector by President Pierce. Ackley prospered in the Golden State, and fifteen years after J. Ross Browne's orders had him clamping down on the lawless conditions of San Francisco harbor, he was able to describe his occupation, when asked to do so by the Marysville Pioneers Society, as "capitalist." Alonzo Phelps, *Contemporary Biography of California's Representative Men* (2 vols., San Francisco, A. L. Bancroft and Co., 1881), II, 50.

[35] N. A. 177–1–117.

CHAPTER FIVE

The Northwest Corner

ARLY IN AUGUST, 1854, J. Ross Browne left San Francisco for the Redwood Coast of California. He surveyed the situation at Humboldt Bay, at Trinidad and, lastly, at Crescent City where the Zurich-born S. H. Grubler was inspector. He then moved on via the Umpqua River and the Willamette River to Salem, Oregon Territory. In the latter capital he visited the office of the Surveyor General, for he was acting under the orders of the General Land Office as well as the Treasury Department in this area.[1]

Brown's visit to Humboldt Bay was primarily for the purpose of deciding whether or not a customs district should be set up there, separate from that of San Francisco and complete with ports of entry and delivery. He found the entrance to the Bay blocked by a bar on which an angry surf crashed. The channel was impracticable but not impassable. He also found a bustling triumvirate of communities on the Bay— Eureka, Bucksport, and Union or Union City. The latter was designated the point of entry, with Henry Wattson serving as inspector of customs. The three towns mustered, all together, about one thousand souls. The people carried on a small trade with the mines from Union, did some

---

[1] N. A. 177–1–123.

lumbering out of Eureka, and from Bucksport engaged in a tiny trade with the farmers of the Eel River Valley which lay to the south of Humboldt Bay. There were three very bad mule trails to the Trinity mines seventy to one hundred miles back in the wild interior. The chief business of the Humboldt Bay region was lumbering, of course, since the harbor was literally surrounded with forests of the mighty redwoods —*Sequoia sempervirens*. The industry, however, was in an economic decline in 1854. Finished lumber was bringing a low price on the market. Of three steam sawmills on the Bay, Guthrie's agent found only one to be operating. The inhabitants of the area needed no foreign imports, and the only possible justification which Browne could see for the establishment of a customs collection district at Humboldt Bay was so that lumber mills could ship their product directly to foreign ports when they found the price of lumber too low in San Francisco. They would receive from abroad various foreign products in exchange. Browne felt that there was little likelihood of such a trade popping up. Nor did he feel that this possible future foreign trade was the real reason for the pressure on Washington to establish a new customs district in California's northwest corner.

"If I may be permitted to state the facts plainly," began Browne, "they are simply these: The necessity for creating the proposed district arises solely from a very bad policy adopted by members of Congress of creating profitable offices for political favorites at the expense of Government. There is no more commercial necessity for a new district at Humboldt than there is for one at the headwaters of the Sacramento. If such a bill has been passed, it is a fraud upon the people." Browne offered to prove his case to Guthrie by the use of official San Francisco Customs House records. He pointed out, too, that Union, which had been designated the port of entry, was five miles from the mouth of Humboldt Bay and was inaccessible to vessels. All goods had to be lightered from Eureka in order to reach Union. Eureka, not Union or Union City, was the head of navigation of the broad bay. If any town deserved to be designated as a port of entry, advised the agent, it was certainly not Union but either Bucksport, just around the Point, or Eureka, three miles from the bay entrance.

64

Browne did not know who was introducing the bill to create a new customs district in the Eureka area, and he did not care. But he frankly, openly, and loudly opposed the erection of such a new district. In fact, he was in favor of reducing the already-established districts by three! "To appoint a collector, at $3,000 per annum, at Humboldt Bay, whose office would be a mere sinecure, would be simply to pay that sum into the pockets of some aspirant for popular favor in California for the purpose of securing his election, so far as it could be done, by the voters of the District of Humboldt Bay, at the expense of the people."[2]

After leaving Humboldt Bay, Browne swung through coastal Oregon in order to make a very careful survey of the District of Umpqua or Cape Perpetua. He went from the California line to Astoria at the mouth of the Columbia River before he was through. He found the port of entry for the District of Umpqua to be Gardiner, a "town" consisting of two houses, only one of which was occupied by humankind. This latter building was the residence and office—and entire world—of the Collector of the Port, Addison C. Gibbs.[3] The adjacent structure was a small warehouse containing a large iron safe for the deposit of public funds, and little else. Even the funds were lacking since there were no direct imports, never had been, and (probably) never would be. It was a difficult harbor to reach since a sandbar had first to be conquered. The passage of the river's mouth was always dangerous, although steamers could enter in good weather. Near the entrance was another, unnamed "town" of three houses, two of them empty. Opposite Gardiner were two more farmhouses, and perhaps a log hut or two hid in the vicinity. This handful of hovels constituted the entire settlement of the Port of Umpqua Bay in the year of our Lord 1854. Otherwise, it was a wilderness of mountains and forests from Gardiner to Scottsburg, twenty-five miles away.[4]

Undoubtedly, the farcical District of Umpqua suggested Browne's satire on the port of Bear Harbor, California, in his *Coast Rangers*.

[2] N. A. 177–1–124.

[3] Gibbs, who came to the Umpqua from California in 1850 and laid out Gardiner, was elected to the Oregon legislature in 1852, and in 1862 became Oregon's wartime governor. *Oregon Historical Quarterly*, Vol. II (1901), 329.

[4] N. A. 177–1–125.

(Bear Harbor was even less populous and less an effective haven than Gardiner.) Browne found government offices in Oregon to be political playthings, just as in San Francisco. Reverend H. K. Hines described the situation very well: "Oregon, like all other territories under the vicious system of territorial government adopted by our national legislature, for all the time of her existence as a Territory was made the prey of party spoilsmen. Politically, nothing could settle down into a nominal and healthy state. With every change of national administration, the executive and judicial officers were changed. The people of the Territory had no voice in the selection of these officers."[5]

Browne found Umpqua Bay to be an inlet only one-half mile wide, formed by the Umpqua River with some nineteen feet of water said to overlay the bar and the narrow, tortuous channel. The agent doubted that there was that much depth of water. There were a few Umpqua Indian families besides the three or four white families in the area. Gardiner, five miles from the river's mouth, was technically a port since two steamers had, indeed, reached it. The first had come during 1853. The second was the *America*, with J. Ross Browne aboard, arriving in 1854. Some twenty-five miles upriver was Scottsburg, which could be reached once or twice a month during flood tides by two small steamboats of about thirty tons each. There was no navigation of the stream in times of low water, and there was no road to Scottsburg, or into the interior. The little hamlets were faced with a dense, forbidding wall of forest. The only breaks in the curtain of hemlock, cedar, alder, vine maple, spruce, and fir were the small valleys of Smith's River and Scofield's River which emptied into the Umpqua above Gardiner. The former tributary was navigable for about thirty-five miles, but the latter for only fourteen.

The agent thought that some trade might possibly develop in time for the tiny "port" between the angry sea and the brooding, impassable mountains. But he was sure that Umpqua would never be important as a commercial point. Whatever imports would be made by Oregon, he felt sure, would come via the Columbia River.

Addison C. Gibbs, the collector of the port, was paying fifty dollars a

[5] *An Illustrated History of Oregon* (Chicago, Lewis Publishing Co., 1893), 161.

month for the rent of his office, which was actually his living quarters. Browne looked over the building and decided it was worth no more than thirty dollars per month. He told the Collector that the Treasury Department would no longer allow such a sum as was being paid. In fact, no more than twenty dollars should be paid as rent in Gardiner. But Browne could not bring himself to be as ruthless with the lonely Gibbs as he had been with the time-on-their-hands boys of the San Francisco Customs House. The Collector's only companion much of the time was the government's boatman, Madison Scobey. Guthrie received a communiqué from his roving agent on August 8: "Inasmuch as the compensation of the Collector is small and he has no other means of subsistence, at a place where there is neither trade nor population, it would hardly be practicable for him to live without his trifling perquisite. The hire of a boatman stands upon the same footing. This boatman is required perhaps once or twice a month, but it would be difficult to obtain temporary assistance where there are no people and scarcely reasonable to compel the Collector to run the boat used for boarding vessels. The best remedy from these expenditures would be to add the District to that of Astoria and to place an inspector at Umpqua who could perform the duties now performed by the Collector."[6] Regardless of the post's small compensation ($1,503.90), Gibbs found a rival for the position in the person of a man named Snelling—or so went the Oregon Coast rumors. But on September 25, 1854, he was able to write Browne that the rumor was apparently false. He also took the opportunity to inform the Treasury agent that D. W. Tracy, owner of the government's building at Gardiner, desired more rent. Even though Gibbs attempted to soft-soap Browne by ending his letter thus, "I have just finished reading *Yusef* and was much pleased with the work," Browne shot back a reply which advised him that if any more rent was paid than he had specified, it would have to come out of Gibb's salary.[7]

The agent discovered Port Orford to be a small mining and lumbering settlement about eighty miles south of the mouth of the Umpqua River and, he guessed, some fifty miles from the California border. In

[6] N. A. 177-1-125.
[7] N. A. 177-1-164.

spite of its name, it had no harbor, only an open roadstead. But it did have an inspector of customs—Robert W. Dunbar. Dunbar was appointed in Oregon to the $2,000 post. He was a former Virginian. There were no roads leading inland from the port by courtesy, or at least no tracks large enough to take a wheeled vehicle.

Thirty miles north of Port Orford, Browne found the unnavigable Coquille River. It had no real settlement, but he found a few settlers squatting near its mouth. (Upriver Coquille would have 4,730 inhabitants by the Census of 1960.) Sixty miles or so further lay Coos Bay and the Coos River. This stream was navigable for a few miles, and Empire City, at its mouth, boasted a population of about 100 people, making it something of a metropolis for that desolate stretch of coast. Coal mines had just been discovered, but Browne was afraid that they would turn out to be low-grade, unprofitable lignite.

Another thirty miles brought him to Randolph,[8] a town of perhaps 75 miners near the beach. There were no inspectors of customs at these "ports" except for Coos Bay. There the Collector had appointed an aide to board any coasting steamers foolish enough to call. The official was Rollin S. Belknap, and he not only boarded ships and examined papers, but he was the port's pilot, too, and somehow managed to eke out a precarious living thanks to the fees allowed him by law for various kinds of extra work.[9]

With his work on the Oregon Coast finished, Browne struck up the Umpqua Valley, thence over the Calapooya Mountains to the valley of the Williamette River. He then carefully and diligently made an examination of interior Oregon, visiting such still-thriving communities as Corvallis, Albany, Salem, Eugene (then called Eugene City), Oregon

[8] Randolph has vanished entirely since J. Ross Browne's day, but Port Orford and Empire City (now simply Empire) are still with us. The former, long a village, from which cedar logs were slung out to anchored lumber schooners via a cable from the bluff, was finally incorporated in 1935. In its day, some fairly important people resided there, including Sherman and Seward, Jack London and Joaquin Miller. Empire City is just a few miles out of North Bend. It was settled by Jacksonville gold miners turned coal miners, who also dabbled in lumber-milling and shipping. As Browne predicted, the coal was low grade and not very profitable; as North Bend grew, Empire City shrank. *Oregon: End of the Trail* (Portland, Binfords and Mort, 1940), 380, 384.

[9] N. A. 177–1–125.

City, Milwaukee, Portland, St. Helens, Rainier, and Astoria. He even explored the Columbia River for some distance by boat.[10]

From Astoria, Browne next wrote his headquarters on August 21 that he had put an end to the travesty of service performed by Peter G. Stuart, surveyor and inspector at Pacific City. This minute port (or, better, nonport) lay south of Shoalwater Bay on the northern Oregon Coast, southwest of present-day Tillamook, and just inside Cape Kiwanda on Nestucca Bay. But Stuart lived in Oregon City, 130 miles or so from his ostensible post—and it was a hard, almost impassable, 130 miles of mountain and forest. Surveyor Stuart had never even been in his "port"—actually no more than a hamlet of three or four houses—since his appointment.[11] He carried on his private business in Oregon City, where he lived. He had discharged but one vessel since his appointment, and he had carried out this task not at Pacific City but at Vancouver. Browne found that the ostensible Surveyor and Inspector of Milwaukie was Robert W. Dunbar, who was also supposed to cover Port Orford. He could not very well be in two places at once, but it turned out that he was actually in a third! Like Stuart, he preferred interior, sunny Oregon to coastal, foggy, Oregon. Dunbar lived in Oregon City. He flatly declined to live in Milwaukie, which lay just south of Portland. The absence of the two men from their duty, all of the time, was not noticeably missed. There was simply no need for a revenue officer in the two, or three, "ports" which they were supposed to administer, because there was no revenue. "I have deemed it my duty to stop at once such a fraud upon the Treasury," noted Browne. Seriously he continued: "I trust that the offices will be abolished and that Congress may deem it expedient before creating any others of a similar kind to establish them at cities where there are inhabitants and ports where there is some prospect of commerce."[12]

Stuart's statement that he found it "impracticable" to live in Pacific City at the federal compensation allowed by law was, to Browne, tantamount to a resignation. He told the Collector of Customs in Astoria,

---

[10] N. A. 177-1-126.

[11] N. A. 177-1-127.

[12] N. A. 177-1-126.

John Adair, not to pay Stuart any more salary. The same thing went for Dunbar, Browne advised Adair. The Surveyor-Inspector of Milwaukie had never discharged a ship. Indeed, he had never performed a single day's service of any kind in his official capacity (except to draw his pay), to the best of Browne's knowledge. With one stroke, Browne was, thus, able to save Uncle Sam and the American taxpayers the sum of $2,000 per year in the wilds of Oregon. The appointment of surveyors and inspectors was not up to the Collector at Astoria, but Browne strongly advised Collector Adair to refuse to pay the appointees as public officers because they had refused to take up residence at their proper stations. Since the Inspector and Surveyor of Portland (William M. King and his assistant) had little to do, they could perform any revenue business required on the Columbia and Williamette rivers. Browne bluntly told Adair that he expected him to direct the Portland office to handle such work in the future.[13]

While he was in the area, Browne paid a business call on Peter Skene Ogden, the chief factor of the Hudson's Bay Company.[14] The proceeds of the sale of the ship *Albion*, $2,255.09, had been paid to him as chief factor of the British company. Browne was not sure why the money had been paid over to Ogden, but he intended to find out. He asked him to turn the money over to Collector Adair, but the Canadian refused. The sum, reported Browne, had been wrongfully given to the Hudson's Bay Company by the Clerk of the United States District Court, James C. Strong. Browne observed to his superior that "there has been some peculation upon the Treasury in this matter and of the most flagrant character, and if the parties can be brought to justice, it shall be done."

It was on July 27 that Browne had promised to look into matters in Washington Territory, which had ben carved out of Oregon Territory on March 3, 1853. It was August 22 when he started for Puget Sound from Astoria, planning to spend a fortnight in Washington Territory

[13] N. A. 177-1-127.

[14] Ogden was a daring explorer, fur trader, and businessman who was made the head of the Columbia River District of the Hudson's Bay Company's operations, at Fort Vancouver. He was a good peacemaker between Yankees and Britons before he died in 1854, shortly after Browne visited him, in Oregon City. He was sixty years old. *Dictionary of American Biography*, VII, 640-41.

before returning to California for an inspection of that state's southern districts.[15] Washington turned out to be as sorry a situation as Oregon or California, with incompetency and bickering quite *de rigueur*. Back and forth he zigzagged over the American Northwest. Finally, he crossed the Cowlitz River to Cowlitz Landing at the head of canoe navigation and made his way to civilization, of sorts, again at Olympia. From the latter town, he wrote Guthrie on September 2 about the complicated and ramified *Albion* affair. He had suspended the charge made against the Treasury Department for expenses incurred in the seizure of the British bark. He insisted that any expenses be paid out of the proceeds of the sale of the *Albion* and her cargo. After legal expenses had been paid, $2,571.91 was left in the hands of Clerk of the Court James C. Strong, but he had turned it over to Ogden. Browne had notified J. S. Clendennin, the United States attorney for the Territory of Washington, that the money had been paid over to the Hudson's Bay Company, representing the consignees or owners, in error. It was a misunderstanding. It should have gone to the United States government by a deposit to the office of the Assistant Treasurer of the United States, Jacob Rink Snyder, in San Francisco, in charge of the Sub-Treasury for the Pacific Coast. After ascertaining all the facts, the Secretary of the Treasury could then dispose of the balance as the law required.

Browne was never loathe to carry a big stick when he felt that his government was in danger of being fleeced. He wrote a letter to Clendennin which he concluded with these words:

> I shall lay all the facts of this case before the Secretary of the Treasury and I deem it my duty to state that should there be any further delay in procuring this money, or in having it placed to the credit of the Treasurer of the United States, I shall endeavor on my return to Washington to have such measures taken as will prevent the recurrence of such neglect of duty on the part of public officers on this Coast in future.[16]

But the problem continued to swell like a poisoned donkey. When he again demanded the money from Ogden, the latter refused to deliver it

[15] N. A. 177–1–126.
[16] N. A. 177–1–128.

71

without an order from the Clerk of the Court. The Clerk, for his part, refused to turn the receipt over to District Attorney Clendennin. "It is rumored that he has lost it or retains it for improper purposes," groaned Browne. He was stymied. Court would not sit until the first Monday in October, and he was due back in California in September. There was also a rumor that Judge O. B. McFadden would decline the appointment to the bench of new Washington Territory. This would complicate matters still more. Clendennin quickly denied this tale, telling Browne that McFadden had definitely decided to accept the appointment.[17]

Browne was not so sure. He clipped a letter to the editor from the *Democratic Standard* of Portland and sent it on to Washington, D.C. The letter-writer had protested McFadden's appointment as Chief Justice of the Supreme Court of Washington Territory and had reminded the press and his fellow readers that the jurist was finding it very slow and difficult to make his way to the Territory. To the writer, who signed himself "A Citizen of Clark County," McFadden seemed most clearly not to want the job after having so actively sought the appointment. The *Standard* ran an editorial which supported the views of the letter-writer of Jacksonville. Browne also clipped this and forwarded it to Guthrie.[18]

As for the other member of the new bench, Browne described him candidly: "Judge Monroe has been intoxicated for some months past and I think the money would be quite as safe in the hands of Governor Ogden as it would be in those of the Court." Browne regretted that he did not have the extraordinary powers which would have allowed him to clean up the entire *Albion* affair. He would have demanded the money, himself. He would have deposited it, himself, in the San Francisco Sub-Treasury.[19]

In a postscript, he mentioned another thorny Washington Territory case. It was his opinion that United States versus Moses was one of the most flagrant cases of fraud on the part of a public official. He felt that A. B. Moses, appointed collector of Olympia, first port of entry for Puget

[17] N. A. 177–1–129.
[18] N. A. 177–1–128.
[19] N. A. 177–1–129.

Sound, in February, 1851, should not be let off easily but should suffer the full penalty of the law.[20]

From Olympia, Browne's trail led to Steilacoom, Nisqually, Port Townsend, and Bellingham Bay. He reported from Steilacoom on September 4, 1854, complaining first about the irregularity of the mail in Oregon and Washington Territories. This circumstance led him to repeat himself in his reports, several times over, to make sure that at least one copy of his communiqués would reach the Department within a reasonable time. He was surprised to find no port of entry in Olympia, where it had been located in 1851. But the Collector had moved it to Port Townsend. He had simply packed up his books and papers and moved himself and his office to the Olympic Peninsula town where the trade was. Browne thought that Collector Isaac N. Ebey's transfer was both sensible and correct. Said Browne, "Port Townsend is the proper place for a port of entry, and the change will be beneficial."[21]

Browne took passage in the revenue cutter commanded by A. Benton Moses, surveyor of Nisqually, who was under fire (like so many of his federal colleagues in the West) for suspected fraud. Moses took him to visit Steilacoom, Alki, Seattle, Port Townsend, Bellingham Bay, and San Juan Island. Browne hoped to be able to get to Victoria, British Columbia, if he could get Captain James Alden to take him there in the spry Coast Survey steamer *Active.*[22]

The pace was beginning to wear down the inspector. He complained:

> It is very difficult and tedious traveling in this country owing to the absence of the usual means of conveyance. There is not a stage or steamboat in the Territory, and scarcely a road that amounts to more than a trail, and all the water travel is done in [small] boats and canoes.

Perhaps travel weary, Browne allowed himself to confess to a profound disillusionment with the Pacific Northwest:

> I have been very much disappointed in my expectations as to the progress of this country and I cannot but think that Governor Stevens is oversanguine as to its future importance. Having no pecuniary or political interests on this coast, I am prepared to say that it is a good country for

20 *Ibid.*
21 N. A. 177–1–130.
22 *Ibid.*

coarse lumber and nothing more. Its agricultural prospects are far below those of Oregon or California and, as to its coal mines, I have not yet seen them but the people of the Territory are not very sanguine about them.

Browne tabulated the centers of population for the Treasury Department. He found Olympia to be a town of 400 people, mostly lumbermen. Steilacoom, some 30 miles to the northeast, boasted about 150 persons and Nisqually, about 5 miles or so from Steilacoom, added to the sum total civilization but "one warehouse and a blind man, the only white inhabitant." Alki, adjacent to Seattle, had a population of between 30 and 40, while the erstwhile metropolis, Seattle, itself, could count but 125 heads of citizenry. "There are no other towns," Browne commented, "and but a few scattering settlers on the east side of the Sound up to Bellingham's Bay, where there is a sawmill, a coal mine, and some fifty or sixty inhabitants."[23]

On the west side of Puget Sound he found only a few squatters and even fewer hamlets than on the eastern shore. Teekalet or Port Gamble was the metropolis of the area. There some 40 people lived and worked, principally in a large sawmill. In Port Madison a sawmill employed 15 or 20 men, and in Port Ludlow a mill had about 20 more. Port Townsend was a "city" of 20 citizens. "There is no trade of any importance," he observed of Port Townsend, "there being but two stores, but it is the proper place for the port of entry."

Browne was impressed with Port Townsend, after a fashion, and turned to it (or perhaps, turned *on* it) when he was composing satire on the follies and frauds of the West. In his volume, *Crusoe's Island*, written fifteen years after his visit, as well as in his official reports to Washington on the Indian wars of Oregon and Washington, he dwelt on the little port. He poked fun at the town in a little essay titled "The Great Port Townsend Controversy, Showing How Whiskey Built a City." Port Townsend was not amused. Although Port Townsend never became the great haven predicted by its early boosters, its citizens became touchy about criticism as their dreams of glory and avarice ran on. Full of local pride, they found the very name J. Ross Browne to be an anathema.

But Browne did not poke fun at people and places just for the sport of

[23] *Ibid.*

74

it. He was disgusted by the conditions in Port Townsend, its squalor, and, particularly, the degradation of its Indians, such as the chief whom he called the Duke of York. He wrote:

Few persons who have visited the Pacific Coast of late years are ignorant of the fact that the city of Port Townsend is eligibly situated on Puget's Sound, near the Straits of [Juan de] Fuca; and none who have seen that remarkable city can hesitate a moment to admit that it is a commercial metropolis without parallel.

Port Townsend is indeed a remarkable place. I am not acquainted with quite such another place in the whole world. It certainly possesses natural and artificial advantages over most of the cities in the Atlantic States or Europe. In front there is an extensive water privilege, embracing the various ramifications of Puget's Sound. Admiralty Inlet forms an outlet for the exports of the country and Hood's Canal is an excellent place for hoodwinking the revenue officers. On the rear, extending to Dungeness Point, is a jungle of pine and matted brush through which neither man nor beast can penetrate without considerable effort. This will always be a secure place of retreat in case of an invasion from a war canoe manned by Northern Indians. With regard to the town itself, it is singularly picturesque and diversified. The prevailing style of architecture is a mixed order of the Gothic, Doric, Ionic, and Corinthian. The houses, of which there must be at least twenty in the city and suburbs, are built chiefly of pine boards, thatched with shingles, canvas, and wooden slabs. The palace and out buildings of the Duke of York are built of driftwood from the saw mills of Port Ludlow, and are eligibly located near the wharf so as to be convenient to the clams and oysters and afford his maids of honor an opportunity of indulging in frequent ablutions. There is somewhat of an ancient and fish-like odor about the premises of his highness, and it must be admitted that his chimneys smoke horribly, but still the artistic effect is very fine at a distance. The streets of Port Townsend are paved with sand and the public squares are curiously ornamented with dead horses and the bones of many dead cows, upon the beef of which the inhabitants have partially subsisted since the foundation of the city. This, of course, gives a very original appearance to the public pleasure grounds and enables strangers to know when they arrive in the city, by reason of the peculiar odor, so that even admitting the absence of lamps no person can fail to recognize Port Townsend in the darkest night. When it was a port of entry under the laws of the United States, there was a collector of customs stationed in a small shanty on the principal wharf, whose business it was to look out for smugglers and pay the salary of an inspector who owns some sheep on San Juan Island, and holds joint possession of that disputed territory with the British government. The collector of customs, being unable to attend to the many important duties that devolved upon him without assistance, was allowed two boatmen, whose duty it was to put him on board of suspicious vessels in the offing, and one of whom, by virtue of a special commission, was ex-officio deputy collector and made up the accounts of the district.

The principal luxuries afforded by the market of this delightful seaport are clams and the carcasses of dead whales that drift ashore, by reason of eating which the natives have clammy skins and are given to much spouting at public meetings. The prevailing languages spoken are the Clallam, Chenook, and Skookum-Chuck or Strong Water, with a mixture of broken English; and all the public notices are written on shingles with burnt sticks and nailed up over the door of the town hall. A newspaper, issued here once every six months, is printed by means of wooden types whittled out of pine knots by the Indians and rubbed against the bottom of the editor's potato pot. The castoff shirts of the inhabitants answer for paper. For the preservation of public morals a jail has been constructed out of logs that drifted ashore in times past, in which noted criminals are put for safe-keeping. The first and last prisoners ever incarcerated in that institution were eleven Northern Indians who were suspected of the murder of Colonel Ebey at Whidby's Island. As the logs are laid upon sand to make the foundation secure, the Indians, while rooting for clams one night, happened to come up at the outside of the jail and, finding the watchman who had been placed there by the citizens fast asleep with an empty whiskey bottle in the distance, they stole his blanket, hat, boots, and pipe, and bade an affectionate farewell to Port Townsend.

The municipal affairs of the city are managed by a mayor and six councilmen who are elected to office in a very peculiar manner. On the day of election, notice having been previously given on the town shingles, all the candidates for corporate honors go up on the top of the hill back of the waterfront and play at pitch penny and quoits till a certain number are declared eligible; after which all the eligible candidates are required to climb a greased pole in the centre of the main public square. The two best then become eligible for the mayoralty and the twelve next best for the common council. These fourteen candidates then get on the roof of the town hall and begin to yell like Indians. Whoever can yell the loudest is declared mayor and the six next loudest become the members of the common council for the ensuing year.

While I had the misfortune to be in public employ (and for no disreputable act that I can now remember), it became my duty to inquire into the condition of the Indians on Puget's Sound. In the course of my tour I visited this unique city for the purpose of having a '*wa-wa*' with the Duke of York, chief of the Clallam tribe.

The principal articles of commerce, I soon discovered, were whisky, cotton handkerchiefs, tobacco, and cigars, and the principal shops were devoted to billiards and the sale of grog. I was introduced by the Indian Agent to the Duke, who inhabited that region and still disputed the possession of the place with the white settlers. If the settlers paid him anything for the land upon which they built their shanties it must have been in whisky, for the Duke was lying drunk in his wigwam at the time of my visit. For the sake of morals, I regret to say that he had two wives, ambitiously named Queen Victoria and Jenny Lind, and for the good repute of Indian ladies of rank it grieves me to add that the Queen and Jenny were also very tipsy, if not quite drunk, when I called to pay my respects.

The Duke was lying on a rough wooden bedstead, with a bullock's hide stretched over it, enjoying his ease with the ladies of his household. When the agent informed him that a *Hyas Tyee,* or Big Chief, had called to see him with a message from the Great Chief of all the Indians, the Duke grunted significantly, as much as to say "that's all right." The Queen, who sat near him in the bed, gave him a few whacks to rouse him up and by the aid of Jenny Lind succeeded, after a while, in getting him in an upright position. His costume consisted of a red shirt and nothing else but neither of the royal ladies seemed at all put out by the scantiness of his wardrobe. There was something very amiable and jolly in the face of the old Duke, even stupified as he was by whisky. He took me by the hand in a friendly manner and, patting his stomach, remarked, "Duke York, belly good man!"

Of course I complimented him upon his general reputation as a good man, and proceeded to make the usual speech, derived from the official formula, about the Great Chief in Washington, whose children were as numerous as the leaves on the trees and the grass on the plains.

"Oh, damn!" said the Duke, impatiently, "him send any whisky?"

No, on the contrary, the Great Chief had heard with profound regret that the Indians of Puget's Sound were addicted to the evil practice of drinking whisky, and it made his heart bleed to learn that it was killing them off rapidly and was the principal cause of all their misery. It was very cruel and very wicked for white men to sell whisky to the Indians, and it was his earnest wish that the law against this illicit traffic might be enforced and the offenders punished.

"Oh, damn!" said the Duke, turning over on his bed and contemptuously waving his hand in termination of the interview, "dis *Tyee* no 'count.' "

While this *wa-wa,* or grand talk, was going on, the Queen put her arms affectionately around the Duke's neck and giggled with admiration at his eloquence. Jenny sat a little at one side, and seemed to be under the combined influence of whisky, jealousy, and a black eye. I was subsequently informed that the Duke was in the habit of beating both the Queen and Jenny for their repeated quarrels, and when unusually drunk was not particular about either the force or direction of his blows. This accounted for Jenny's black eye and bruised features, and for the alleged absence of two of the Queen's front teeth, which it was said were knocked out in a recent brawl.

Some months after my visit to Port Townsend, in writing a report on the Indians of Puget's Sound, I took occasion to refer to the salient points of the above interview with the Duke of York, and to make a few remarks touching the degraded condition of himself and tribe, attributing it to the illegal practice on the part of the citizens of selling whisky to the Indians. I stated that his wigwam was situated between two whiskey shops and that the Clallams would soon be reduced to the level of bad white men in Port Townsend, "which, to say the least of it, was a very benighted place." The report was printed by order of Congress though I was not aware of that fact till one day, sitting in my office in San Francisco, I received a copy of the *Olympia Democrat* (if I remember correctly), containing a series of grave charges against me, signed by the principal citizens of Port Townsend. I have lost the original documents but shall endeavor to supply the deficiency as well as my memory serves. The letter was addressed to the "United States Special Agent," and was substantially as follows:

"Sir,—The undersigned have read your official report relative to the Indians of Puget's Sound and regret that you have deemed it necessary to step so far aside from the line of your duty as to traduce our fair name and reputation as citizens of Port Townsend. You will pardon us for expressing the opinion that you might have spent your time with more credit to yourself and benefit to the government.

"Sir, it may be that on the occasion of your visit here the Duke of York and his wives were drunk; but the undersigned are satisfied, upon a personal examination, that neither Queen Victoria nor Jenny Lind suffered the loss of two front teeth, as you state in your report; and they are not aware that Jenny Lind's eyes were ever blacked by the Duke of York, nor do they believe it, although you have thought proper to make that statement in your report.

"The undersigned do not pretend to say that there is no whisky sold in Port Townsend; but they do deny, sir, that you ever saw any of them drunk, or that the citizens of Port Townsend, as a class, are at all intemperate. On the contrary, they claim to be as orderly, industrious, and law-abiding as the citizens of any other town on the Pacific Coast or elsewhere.

"Sir, it is scarcely possible that you can have forgotten so soon the marked kindness and hospitality with which you were treated by the citizens of this place during your sojourn here; and now the return you make is to blacken the reputation of our thriving little town, and endeavor to destroy our future prospects. You are, of course, at liberty to choose your own line of travel but if ever you visit Port Townsend again, we can assure you, sir, you will enjoy a very different reception. Had you confined your misstatements to the Indians, we might have excused it on the ground that it is not customary for public officers to adhere strictly to facts in their reports; but when you go entirely out of your way and commit such an unprovoked attack upon our character, we feel bound to set ourselves right before the world.

"In charity, we can only suppose that you have been grossly deceived in your sources of information; yet when you profess to have witnessed personally the evil effects of whisky in Port Townsend, and go so far as to pronounce it a benighted place, we cannot evade the conclusion that you must have had some experience in which you say you witnessed; either that, or you deliberately committed a base slander upon the citizens of this place. Although the undersigned consider themselves included in your sweeping assertion, it cannot have escaped your memory, sir, that on the occasion of your visit to Port Townsend you found them engaged in peace-

ful avocations as useful and respected members of society; and they positively deny that any of them have ever sold whisky to the Indians or committed the crime of murder.

"Sir, the undersigned have made inquiry into the portion of your report
in which you state that no less than six murders were committed here
during the past year, and can only find that two were committed, and
neither of them by citizens of this place. The conclusion, therefore, to
which the undersigned are forced, is, that you were at a loss for something
to say and invented at least four murders for the purpose of contributing to
the interest of your report.

"Sir, when a respectable community are engaged in trying to make an
honest living, we think it hardly fair that you, as a government agent,
should come among them and, without cause or provocation, slander their
character and injure their reputation. We therefore enter our solemn protest against the unfounded charges made in your report, and respectfully
recommend that in future you confine yourself to your official duties.

"(Signed) J. Hodges, B. Punch, T. Thatcher, B. Fletcher, Warren
Hastings, Wm. Pitt, J. Fox, E. Burke, and eleven others."

Here was a serious business. I can assure the reader that the sensations
experienced in the perusal of such a document, when addressed to one's
self through a public newspaper and signed by fifteen or twenty responsible
persons are peculiar and by no means agreeable. For a moment I really
began to think I was a very bad man, and that there must be something
uncommonly reprehensible in my conduct.

Upon the whole, I felt that I was a little in fault and had better apologize.
There was no particular necessity for introducing Queen Victoria's front
teeth and Jenny Lind's black eye to Congress; and, to confess the truth, it
was really going a little beyond the usual limits of official etiquette to
"ring in" a public town possessing valuable political influence.

I therefore prepared and published in the newspapers an Apology which,
it seemed to me, ought to be satisfactory. The following is as close a copy
of the original as I can now write from memory:

SAN FRANCISCO, CAL., April 1st, 1858

"To MESSRS. J. HODGES, B. PUNCH, T. THATCHER, B. FLETCHER, WARREN
HASTINGS, WM. PITT, J. FOX, E. BURKE, AND ELEVEN OTHERS, CITIZENS,
PORT TOWNSEND, W. T.:

"Gentlemen—I have read with surprise and regret your letter of the 10th ult. in which you make several very serious charges against me in reference to certain statements contained in my report on the Indians of Puget's Sound. Not the least important of these charges is that I stepped aside from the line of my duty to traduce your fair name and reputation as citizens of Port Townsend. You entertain the opinion that I might have been better employed—an opinion in which I would cheerfully concur if it were not based upon erroneous premises. I have not the slightest recollection of having traduced your fair name and reputation or made any reference to you whatever in my report. When I alluded to the beachcombers, rowdies, and other bad characters in Port Townsend, I had no idea that respectable gentlemen like yourselves would take it as personal. Of course, as none of you ever sold whisky to the Indians or committed murder, you do great injustice to your own reputation in supposing that the public at large would attribute these crimes to you because I mentioned them in my report.

"You deny positively that either Queen Victoria or Jenny Lind had her front teeth knocked out by the Duke of York. Well, I take that back, for I certainly did not examine their mouths as closely as you seem to have done. But when you deny that Jenny Lind's eye was black, you do me great injustice. I shall insist upon it to the latest hour of my existence that it was black—deeply, darkly, beautifully black, with a prismatic circle of pink, blue, and yellow in the immediate vicinity. I cheerfully retract the tooth, but gentlemen, I hold on to the eye. Depend upon it, I shall stand by that eye as long as the flag of freedom waves over this glorious republic! You will admit, at all events, the Jenny had a drop in her eye.

"While you do not pretend to say that there is no whisky sold in Port Townsend, you do insist upon it that I never saw any of you drunk. Of course not, gentlemen. There are several of you that I do not recollect having ever seen, drunk or sober. If I did see any of you under the influence of intoxicating spirits, the disguise was certainly effectual, for I am now entirely unable to say which of you it was. Besides, I never said I saw any of you drunk. It requires a great deal of whisky to intoxicate some people and I should be sorry to hazard a conjecture as to the gauge of any citizen of Port Townsend. I do not believe you habitually drink whisky as a beverage—certainly not Port Townsend whisky, for that would kill the strongest man that ever lived in less than six months, if he drank nothing else. Many of you, no doubt, use tea or coffee at breakfast, and it is quite possible that some of you occasionally venture upon water.

"Gentlemen, you were pleased to call my attention to certain customs houses, Indian claims, and pre-emption claims when I was at Port Townsend; but when you claim to be as orderly, industrious, and law-abiding as the citizens of any other town on the Pacific Coast, or elsewhere, you go altogether beyond my official jurisdiction. I think you had better send that claim to Congress.

"That it is not customary for public officers to adhere strictly to facts for their reports is a melancholy truth. You have me there, gentlemen. Truth is very scarce in official documents. It is not expected by the public, and it would be utterly thrown away upon Congress. Besides, the truth is the last thing that would serve your purpose as claimants for public money.

"You are charitable enough to suppose that I may have been grossly deceived in my sources of information. Well, you ought to know all about that, for I got most of that information from yourselves. As to my remark that Port Townsend is a benighted place, I am astonished that you did not see the true meaning of that expression. It was merely a jocular allusion to the absence of lamps in the public streets at night.

"You do not think it can possibly have escaped my memory that I found you engaged in your peaceful avocations as useful and respectable members of society on the occasion of my visit to Port Townsend. Now, upon my honor, I cannot remember who it was, particularly, that I saw engaged in peaceful avocations, but I certainly saw a good many white men lying about in sunny places fast asleep, and a good many more sitting on logs of wood whittling small sticks and apparently waiting for somebody to invite them into the nearest saloon; others I saw playing billiards and some few standing about the corners of the streets, waiting for the houses to grow—all of which were unquestionably peaceful, if not strictly useful, avocations. I have no recollection of having seen any person engaged in the performance of any labor calculated to strain his vertebrae.

"The result of your inquiries on the subject of murder appears to be that only two murders were committed in Port Townsend during the past year, instead of six as stated in my report. Well, gentlemen, I was not present and did not participate in any of these alleged murders and cheerfully admit that your sheriff, who gave me the information and whose name is appended to your letter, may not have counted them accurately. At all events, I take four of them back and place them to the credit of Port Townsend for the ensuing year. I utterly disclaim having invented them, though I would at any time much rather invent four murders than commit one. Nor can I admit that I was at a loss for something to say. There was abundance of fictitious material presented in the course of my official investigations, without rendering it at all necessary for me to resort to imaginary murders. And I further insist upon it that, if I did not personally witness the violent death of six men in Port Townsend, I heard the King's English most cruelly murdered there on at least six different occasions. Gentlemen, you need not take any farther trouble about setting yourselves right before the world. I trust you will admit that you are all right now, since I have duly made the *amende honorable*.

"Wishing you success in your 'peaceful avocations,' and exemption from all future anxiety relative to the price of lots in Port Townsend, I remain, very respectfully, your obedient servant, etc."

Strange to say, so far from being satisfied with this apology the citizens of Port Townsend were enraged to a degree bordering on insanity. The mayor, upon the reception of the mail containing the fatal document, called the Town Council together, and the schoolmaster read it to the Town Council, and the Town Council deliberated over it for three days and then unanimously resolved that the author was a "Vile Kalumater, unworthy of further Atension, and had beter stere cleer of Port Townsend for the Future!" For two years they did nothing else, in an official point of view, but write letters to the San Francisco papers denouncing the author of this Vile Kalumy and assuring the public that his description of Port Townsend was wholly unworthy of credit; that Port Townsend was the neatest, cleanest, most orderly and most flourishing little town on the Pacific coast. By the time the Fraser River excitement broke out, the people of California were well acquainted through the newspapers with at least one town on Puget's Sound. If they knew nothing of Whatcomb (*sic*), Squill-Chuck, and other rival places that aspired to popular favor, they were no strangers to the reputation of Port Townsend. Thousands who had no particular business there went to take a look at this wonderful town, which had given rise to so much controversy. The citizens were soon forced to build a fine hotel. Many visitors liked the society and concluded to remain. Others thought it would soon be the great centre of commerce for all the shipping that would be drawn thither by the mineral wealth of Fraser River, and bought city lots on speculation. Traders came there and set up stores; new whisky saloons were built; customers crowded in from all parts; in short, it became a gay and dashing sort of place and very soon had the appearance of a city. When the Fraser River bubble burst, nobody was killed at Port Townsend because it had a strong reputation, and could still persuade people that it was bound to be a great city at some future period.

During the following year I made bold to pay my old friends a visit. A delegation of the Common Council met me on the wharf. There were no hacks yet introduced, but any number of horses were placed at my disposal. The greeting was cordial and impressive. A most complimentary address was read to me by the mayor of the city in which it was fully and frankly acknowledged that I was the means of building up the fortunes of Port Townsend. After the address the citizens with one accord rushed to me and, grasping me warmly by the hand, at once retracted their injurious imputations. These gratifying public demonstrations over, we adjourned to the nearest saloon and buried the hatchet forever in an ocean of the best Port Townsend whisky. It is due to the citizens to say that not one of them went beyond reasonable bounds on this joyous occasion, by which I do not mean to intimate that they were accustomed to the beverage referred to. At all events, I think it has been clearly demonstrated by these authentic documents that "whisky built a great city."[24]

Browne's tongue-in-cheek apologia not withstanding, Port Townsendites have always preferred another California writer to the Irishborn iconoclast. John Muir, in his *Steep Trails*, spoke well of the Quimper Peninsula town in the eighties:

All vessels stop here and they make a lively show about the wharves and in the bay. The winds stir the flags of every civilized nation while the Indians, in their long-beaked canoes, glide about from ship to ship, satisfying their curiosity or trading with the crews.[25]

Browne, in terms of belligerency, was no T. R., but he was ready to jump into another Nootka Sound incident in 1854, if need be, or at least have another go at "Fifty-four forty or fight." He was quick to meddle into the conflict between Uncle Sam and John Bull over the San Juan Islands. Friction would continue in this archipelago until Kaiser Wilhelm I, chosen to arbitrate the dispute, awarded the islands to the United

[24] *Crusoe's Island*, 270–83.
[25] (Boston, Houghton Mifflin, 1918), 219.

States in 1872. But first, the so-called Pig War of 1859 would be fought between John Bull and Brother Jonathan, and George Pickett would demonstrate his firmness in an action almost absurd when compared to his gallant, and tragic, charge at Gettysburg.

The Treasury Agent was sensible enough to wish to avoid trouble for the United States if he could. This was particularly true in 1854 since Browne had little regard for Uncle Sam's defensive posture, considering the country ill prepared for war. He investigated the uneasy truce which reigned over Orcas, Lopez, and San Juan Islands, and their satellites, and made an on-the-spot report to Secretary Guthrie:

> The difficulty regarding the importation of sheep to the Island of San Juan remains as last reported. The British authorities are, *de facto,* in possession although the Inspector (Henry Webber) placed there by Col. Ebey is suffered to remain. Americans are prohibited from trading there and several fishing vessels have been warned off. The British authorities come and go with their supplies as they please. That they have not the shadow of a claim to the Island is apparent from the spirit and wording of the Treaty [of June 5, 1846, which gave Vancouver Island to Great Britain but located the international boundary on the 49th parallel] and I think that, pending negotiations on the subject, our Naval forces on this coast should be directed to drive them from the Island or protect our people in the same privileges enjoyed by them.
>
> I shall see Col. Ebey and Captain Alden on this subject and report the result of their proceedings since the origin of the difficulty. Any hasty measures which would involve our people in a collision with the British authorities should be avoided.
>
> The difficulty can be settled in Washington [D.C.] but not here, and if it becomes necessary to maintain our rights by force, we should take care to have force enough on the spot before we undertake to do it. Otherwise we only render ourselves ridiculous and invite further encroachment.[26]

In another letter Browne expanded on his San Juan Island observations:

> Mr. Ebey still retains his inspectors on the Island of San Juan. The British authorities are virtually in possession of the Island. It is not for a

[26] N. A. 177–1–130.

Collector of Customs to raise an army of citizens and declare war against a foreign power; and if our Government, with a knowledge of the facts, deems it expedient to permit the British authorities to declare boundary lines where they please, I am much afraid the Collectors of Customs must acquiesce, however repugnant it may be to their sense of justice. Mr. Ebey, with his army of two inspectors and four boatmen, will never be able to regain nor hold possession of San Juan. Acting Governor Mason will not help him because he thinks the matter should be decided in Washington [D.C.]. Lest Mr. Ebey should deem it expedient, in the absence of further instructions from the Department, to commence hostilities with the small force at his command, I beg that immediate attention be given to the subject in Washington and venture to hope that bloodshed may be avoided.[27]

In this same letter, posted in San Francisco on September 23, 1854, Browne sent Guthrie a map of his route of inspection of the Oregon and Puget Sound country. He mentioned the hardship of traveling in America's northwest corner, saying: "The journey was attended with great inconvenience and some personal risk from the Indians, but I am happy to say that I succeeded in accomplishing the object of my visit."[28]

In general, Browne found the revenue affairs of the Northern Districts (Washington and Oregon) to be loosely managed and suffering from a lack of commerce. Indeed, he found even the inducements to smuggling to be trifling. But if there was little shipping, there was plenty of sipping. John Barleycorn was as present a threat to the government in the Northern Districts as John Bull himself. Browne reminded Guthrie of this:

> I took occasion in a letter from Olympia to refer incidentally to the fact that Judge Monroe has not been in a proper condition since the date of his appointment to perform his duties as a public officer. It is greatly to be regretted that so talented and popular a gentleman should reduce himself to such a condition by habitual intemperance, but I do not think that the public interests should suffer from the confirmed errors of consequent incapacity of any individual. With great reluctance, I recommend his removal from the office of District Judge.[29]

[27] N. A. 177–1–131.
[28] *Ibid.*
[29] *Ibid.*

"Judge" Clendennin was widely criticized, too, not only for intemperance but for inaction. But Browne thought that he could be salvaged. The application of large dollops of good counsel to Clendennin, he felt, would bring him around. He did not, therefore, suggest his removal as district attorney along with that of Judge Monroe. While he was at it, Browne looked into the charges of misconduct leveled against Collector of Customs Isaac N. Ebey by Surveyor A. Benton Moses of Nisqually. The agent decided that they were founded on jealousy and personal hostility and little, if anything, else.[30]

[30] *Ibid.*

CHAPTER SIX

San Francisco and
the Hinterland

BACK ON THE EMBARCADERO on September 23, Browne
found that vessels were clearing from port for Australia and the Sandwich Islands via Teekalet or Port Gamble. He examined the manifest of
one ship carrying 25 tons of hay and 250,000 board feet of lumber—
supposedly. But only the hay was aboard the ship upon its departure
from San Francisco Bay. The hay was landed at Teekalet, and the
lumber was sworn to as being aboard. This was perjury. Guthrie's agent
vowed to put a stop to the rampant skulduggery of coastal commerce.
He particularly promised to secure a tight control of entering and clearing vessels at all Pacific Coast ports.[1]

A second letter of the twenty-third was concerned with the internal
affairs of the troublesome San Francisco Customs House. Browne found
that the workday there ran from only 10:00 A.M. to 3:00 P.M. And few
employees, he discovered, put in a good day's work even in terms of that
sort of truncated workday. There was not an ion of doubt in his mind of
the necessity of reducing the number of "desks" (i.e, positions) under
the Customs House roof. He preferred to leave it up to the Collector and
the Deputy Collector, for the most part, to decide who would stay and

[1] N. A. 177-1-131.

who would have to leave. But he thought it better to reduce the number of employees than to cut salaries in general.

Business in San Francisco had decreased in the year preceding Browne's visit to such an extent that the onetime boomtown now resembled cities of other states. Business activity no longer skyrocketed; it was regular, though with fluctuations. Browne felt that the years immediately ahead would see a gradual increase. He was positive that the decrease in business activity which he saw would continue for a time, however, unless new gold mines should be discovered or some other, similar, excitement should artificially stimulate commercial activity. All California needed was a new bonanza to create new population and new imports.

To his dismay, Browne found that the Collector had not carried out all of his earlier recommendations. But Hammond agreed to proceed with them as of October 1. Hammond had fired thirteen inspectors but then had rehired or reinstated three of them. (And just why, Browne could not determine.) It was the Confidential Agent's opinion that fifteen more men could easily be dispensed with. He so recommended to the Department of the Treasury. He also suggested that one of the two revenue boats, together with its crew, be discontinued at the end of September, 1854.

One matter which continued to perturb the businesslike Browne was the fact that the Customs House was a hangout for politicians and job-seekers, full of business but not revenue business. In San Francisco the Customs House appeared to have taken the place of the London coffee-house or the Paris sidewalk café. Certain of the Customs House staff actually lived in the building, as though it were a lodginghouse. This irregular housekeeping arrangement led to bull sessions and impromptu political conclaves as well as card games at all hours. The San Francisco Customs House was in danger of turning into a social club at best, a Tammany Hall at worst. A disgusted Browne wrote Guthrie: "The Customs House is little better than a place of meeting for the discussion of pending elections."[2]

[2] N. A. 177-1-133.

The gaggle of political hacks hanging about the Customs House was, of course, a symptom of the bad government which had grown out of the spoils system in the West. Browne made no bones about his distaste for the corrupt and improper system of purchasing friends at the expense of the United States Treasury. He wished that his "feeble powers" were greater so that he could do something to eradicate the shabby evil. But he was sure that complaints against his labors, and his "feeble powers," were already being made to Washington by the politicos whose nests he was bothering. He knew that his efforts would be maligned as "inimical to the Administration." But he made his position clear on this matter:

> It will make no difference with me what the result may be in the pending elections so long as I hold an appointment from the Treasury Department. I believe the system to be wrong in itself and injurious in its tendency, and shall act upon that belief while in office and at all other times. Should this course be prejudicial to the Administration, I shall regret such a result extremely but am prepared, nevertheless, to adhere to the principle and shall always carry it out to the best of my ability.[3]

To document and substantiate his suggestions and charges, Browne submitted to Washington dozens of tables at this time, including lists of Customs House clerks, by name, with those to be dismissed checked on the list.

Regardless of the elections looming up ahead, Browne went right on with his unpleasant duty. Some of the men whom he was busily removing from their sinecures had powerful connections "outside," as they termed it, and in Washington itself. But the bullheaded Browne would not let these considerations, completely irrelevant, to his way of thinking, dissuade him from his duty for a moment. And his duty, as he saw it, was to herd the useless hangers-on away from the public trough. He absolutely refused to keep worthless and workless men on the government payroll just because they were suspected of being good, or at least friendly, politicians. Soon Browne was openly warned that he was striking at friends of the Secretary of the Treasury and of the Presi-

[3] *Ibid.*

dent himself. These warnings led him to address the Secretary in regard to his feelings toward a situation in which he might have to attack a personal friend of Guthrie: "Permit me to say, with due respect, that such a consideration would weigh as little with me as any other."[4]

Browne was indeed a *rara avis*. He suggested that his own pay be cut! He received six dollars a day in subsistence. This sum was paid him for the hiring of guides, for clerical assistance, and for miscellaneous expenses. But in his tour of the Puget Sound country he had used the revenue cutter and, elsewhere, had traveled in steamboats, on muleback, or on foot. In no case had he needed or hired guides, he reported. Nor had he engaged any clerks. Therefore, he thought that the Department should discontinue the allowance.[5]

Sickened by the politicking grafters who ran amuck on the Coast, he wrote home to his wife: "Thank God, I have no ambition in that way [politics] and I can safely say that it is not in the power of mortal man, however shrewd, to make me believe wrong is right. . . . I mean to cut down the expenses of the Customs House at least a hundred thousand dollars a year." He steadfastly refused all "presents" thrust upon him by worried thimbleriggers, and he wrote Lucy: "There shall at least be one agent here against whom nothing can be said."[6]

To reinforce his opinion that no district should be created at Humboldt Bay, Browne had asked the inspector there, A. J. Heustis,[7] to prepare and send him a report on Humboldt Bay commerce. When he received this document in September he forwarded it to Secretary Guthrie (on the twenty-fourth), mentioning that although Heustis was a natural aspirant for the position of collector, should the new Humboldt Bay District be created, he was trustworthy, nevertheless, and his statistics were reliable. Heustis' tables showed Browne that 183 vessels entered Humboldt Bay in the fiscal year 1853–54, with an average tonnage of 165

---

[4] N. A. 177–1–135.

[5] N. A. 177–1–138.

[6] *Muleback*, viii.

[7] A. J. Heustis was a pillar of the Methodist church and a local preacher of the Eureka area as late as 1883. Local historians termed him "a man of considerable ability" (and Browne felt he could trust him.) C. V. Anthony, *Fifty Years of Methodism* (San Francisco, Methodist Book Concern, 1901), 226.

tons. These ships ranged from a 91-tonner to a 922-ton vessel. Across the bar had sailed 90 schooners, along with 65 brigs, 22 barks, and 6 steamers. They had brought in mostly merchandise, dry goods, and groceries—3,236 tons in all. They took out lumber, and lots of it—20,567,000 feet. Heustis also gave Browne figures on the typical run from San Francisco to Humboldt Bay, which averaged twelve and one-half days. But Inspector Heustis also informed him that fast ships could make the passage in as little as seven days.

To supply these ships with redwood lumber there were nine steam sawmills on the Bay, built at an aggregate cost of $325,000. About $125,000 more was invested in the area in teams, logging railways, and other ramifications of mill operations. According to Heustis, it took 125 men to run the mills by day only. On the basis of a day-and-night operation, 200 men were required.

Union had a population of 400 persons; Eureka, the same; Bucksport, about 300. According to Lieutenant James Alden's survey and chart, there were three and one-half fathoms of water over the bar, and the channel was from one-half to three-quarters of a mile wide. (These statistics were the only ones presented by Heustis which Browne accepted with decided reservations.) Finally, the Inspector reported that most routes inland were satisfactory for pack animals but not for wagons. Browne was already familiar with most of what Heustis said and, indeed, had already forwarded much similar information East. But he sent the entire document on to Guthrie for his perusal.[8]

On the twenty-fifth, Browne was in Benicia,[9] headquarters of the Customs District of Sonoma. Here he found very little business. He immediately ordered a reduction from $300 to $100 in the monthly rent paid for the Customs House there. He called the former sum "unwar-

[8] N. A. 177–1–139.

[9] Benicia, on Carquinez Straits east of San Francisco, might be considered to be the Port Townsend of California. For many years it has lived with its dreams of grandeur—dreams which have never quite come true. It is today a comfortable but hardly busy town which remembers its historic past. In 1849 it was a thriving port of entrepôt for the gold mines. In 1853–54 it was the state capitol. But even an army post and arsenal could not prevent Benicia from dwindling in size and importance as the nineteenth century wore on and such towns as Fairfield and Vallejo grew. *California, A Guide to the Golden State* (New York, Hastings House, 1939), 574.

ranted" and "extravagant." For this amount the government was getting all of two small three-room frame buildings. (At the very same time he was trying to reduce the rent of the San Francisco Customs House from $2,000 to $1,500 a month. There, he had pointed out to the owners that there had been a general decrease in San Francisco rents of 33⅓ per cent since the boom days of 1849 and 1850. The owners finally agreed to submit his suggestion to a committee of prominent merchants for a sort of arbitration.) In sleepy Benicia he did not have to bother with such complicated dickering. He simply told the Collector of the Port, Lansing B. Mizner[10] (whose name the *Official Register* of 1855 charmingly corrupted into "Lansing Bettizner), to see to it.[11]

Visiting Sacramento next, he got the rent of the Customs House there reduced from $75 to $25 per month. This office was a three-room building, but two of the rooms were bedrooms. Browne patiently pointed out to the Collector that the government was not obliged to furnish its Customs men with sleeping quarters, but only with offices for the performance of their duties. He would allow no further rent to be paid for sleeping accommodations. There was no business of any real importance in Collector Charles C. Sackett's district, and Browne recommended that the district be abolished. Ironically, his recommendation followed hard on the heels of empire-builder Sackett's appointment of a deputy collector to aid in what he apparently considered to be his strenuous duties.[12]

Sackett, a New Yorker, was a good collector. He was collecting $3,430 a year for doing nothing. However, he was widely respected in the Sacramento Valley in at least two fields, law and journalism. He was a

10 The Mizners were one of the most interesting and eccentric families in California, if not in the nation. Papa of the brood which came to include architect Addison and artist Wilson was Lansing Bond Mizner, a politician, lawyer, railroad promoter, land speculator, and presiding officer, for years, in the state senate. He had bet on Benicia as *the* up-and-coming city of the Pacific Coast and was stuck with his bet—and the large holdings of real estate which he had bought up. A great Benjamin Harrison man, he was named minister plenipotentiary to the five Central-American republics by President Harrison. He died in 1893. Alva Johnston, *The Legendary Mizners* (New York, Farrar, Straus and Young, 1953), 3–6.

11 N. A. 177–1–142.

12 N. A. 177–1–144.

successful attorney and justice of the peace in Sacramento during his lifetime and was, as well, a correspondent on Red Bluff and San Francisco newspapers. He died of consumption on October 29, 1863, when he was still less than fifty years of age.[13]

Browne left Sackett and moved south. On September 28 he was in Stockton, headquarters of the Customs District of San Joaquin. Here he found he had to tackle a problem far different from ships and ghost ports, or the staffing of a large customs house. He had to deal with a situation reminiscent of those he had found on the Rio Grande in Texas. "Large numbers of stock," he wrote Guthrie, "are brought into this District from Mexico upon which there are reasonable grounds to suppose no duties are paid. Without a thorough knowledge of the Southern passes, it will not be possible for me to put a stop to this system of fraud. I have determined, therefore, in visiting the Southern Districts, to go and return by the way of Tejon Pass and make a general reconnaissance of the San Joaquin Valley. Tomorrow I leave Stockton to join Colonel [Jack] Hays,[14] who is on a surveying tour of part of my proposed route."[15]

The meeting of Hays and Browne was the start of a long and strong friendship. Jack Hays was the founder of the informal group of hunters (which Browne joined) which came to be known as "The Coast Rangers," thanks to J. Ross Browne's articles in *Harper's*. On this fall 1854 tour of inspection of Hays's, Browne apparently had his son along, for he wrote his wife on the twenty-sixth that "Buck [his boy] and I are now on our way to Stockton . . . to meet Jack Hays, the great Texan Ranger, who is to carry us on a tour of exploration connected with his affairs as Surveyor General." Browne also mentioned that Buck planned

[13] *San Francisco Daily Alta California*, October 30, 1863, p. 1, col. 2.

[14] Colonel John Coffee (Jack) Hays was one of the most remarkable men to leave his imprint on the West. He was a soldier and an officer in the Mexican War, a great hero of the Texas Rangers, an Indian fighter, an explorer. He helped the Republic of Texas survive to become a state of the Union. He left Texas to go to Arizona's Gila River as an Indian agent but turned up in California, eventually, as sheriff of San Francisco, United States surveyor general, land speculator and town developer, rancher and "capitalist." James Kimmins Greer, *Colonel Jack Hays* (New York, E. P. Dutton and Company, 1952), 9.

[15] N. A. 177-1-146.

to study surveying in Colonel Hays's office during the winter months. Eventually, it was from Hays that J. Ross Browne bought the lots for his famed home of Pagoda Hill.[16]

At this juncture Browne warned the Treasury Department against heeding the frequently made claims that an unusual state of affairs existed in California. This unusual state was the excuse made for the justification of exorbitant rents, for one thing. Except for somewhat higher land values, rents, and labor costs than elsewhere, Browne found California to be shaking down to a resemblance of most other states in the union. J. M. Scofield,[17] collector of Customs in Stockton, had written Browne a letter in which he insisted that rents of "decent" property were sky high in Stockton. Browne, with commendable restraint, did not ask him the price of "indecent" property but contented himself with ordering him to reduce the Customs House rent from $200 a month to $45 immediately. If he could not do so, he was to find new quarters at the latter rental fee.[18]

California's vaunted rainy season caught Browne in the field, and he had to return to San Francisco after bogging down. On October 11 he wrote from the Golden Gate city about his San Joaquin Valley trip. The rains and flooding had made it impossible for him to get to Tejon Pass[19] via Tulare Lake,[20] but not before he had learned of large numbers of

---

[16] Greer, *Colonel Jack Hays*, 293.

[17] Scofield was a Virginian, born in Prince Edward County, who had become a Texan by 1836. When his father died in the town of Buck Snort, on the Brazos, he was taken in tow by a famous *Tejano* gambler and horse racer, Robert Porter. By the time he was nine years old he had been on his first big drunk—and with Sam Houston!—circa 1844. After many narrow squeaks on the Texas frontier, from Comanches, he left his surveying profession and came to California. He mined in Amador County, taught school in Coulterville and in Oregon, and by 1881 was the proprietor of Idlewild Vineyards in Stanislaus County's thermal belt. *History of Stanislaus County* (San Francisco, W. W. Elliott, 1881), 179.

[18] N. A. 177–1–147.

[19] Tejon Pass, like Fort Tejon, which was set up by Lt. Col. Edward Fitzgerald Beale in August of the year, was named for a dead badger (*tejon*, in Spanish) found in one of the canyons of the area by a party of Mexican soldiers exploring the Tehachapi Mountains. The pass and the fort were the link between southern California and northern California.

[20] Tulare Lake once filled much of the San Joaquin Valley west of Visalia, making it an impassable swamp. Today it is much shrunken—a result of damming of rivers, land reclamation, and drainage.

cattle being imported to California from Sonora, Mexico, in the prior two or three years. However, by 1854 these cattle were scattered all over the state's mining regions and were quite beyond any possibility of having duty levied upon them. Browne thought he could control the smuggling of cattle into California by stationing a deputy collector at Fort Yuma, to receive duties on imported Mexican stock. This was his number-one recommendation to his chief.[21]

He wrote:

> Fort Yuma is the point at which they must pass, and once beyond that it is nearly if not quite impossible to get at them. The Inspectors stationed at Tejon Pass and other points, Pacheco's and Livermore's Passes,[22] are of little use, though it appears to be necessary to have some guard at those places. In a few days I shall make a tour through the South when I hope to be able to establish such a system of guards there, subject, of course, to your approval, as will effectively put an end to further abuse.[23]

The San Joaquin District appeared to Browne to be of very little use to the government as it stood. Stock-owning in Stockton was in small lots, and the cattle were in the hands of second or even third purchasers, who had acted in good faith in buying the animals and who knew nothing of the payment or nonpayment of duties on them at the point of entry into California. He found Collector Scofield fairly busy, but solely with his own affairs, not the government's. He ran a private commission and forwarding firm, and was very busy on the wharves. It was Messrs. Sullivan and Company, of Mariposa, who, unaware that Browne was a confidential agent of the federal government, told him that Scofield was a busy auctioneer and that he also handled all of their goods for them.

[21] N. A. 177–1–150.

[22] Andrew Lester was inspector at Livermore Pass and Pacheco Pass, as they are commonly rendered. He made news in 1860 when, according to the papers, he was the only federal official holding a valuable office in the state who refused to abandon the Democratic party when ordered to do so by newly elected President Abraham Lincoln. *San Francisco Daily Evening Bulletin*, August 17, 1860, p. 2, col. 3. E. Edwards Hewett was inspector at Pacheco Pass and Zion Pass. Twenty years later he was Col. Hewett, prominent in Southern Pacific Railroad affairs, and he was also tax collector of Los Angeles before his death in 1895. *San Francisco Call*, June 9, 1895, p. 2, col. 2.

[23] N. A. 177–1–150.

Browne reported to Guthrie on this without emphasis or comment other than to wryly add: "I do not state this in the way of complaint against the Collector. Every public officer in California does as little for the Government and as much for himself as possible, and Mr. Scofield is as honest as others." Browne indicated that the Sacramento Collector had hired a deputy because he was too busy with his own auction house to be bothered by Customs affairs. The agent bluntly told Sackett that the salary paid him by the United States government was justification enough for his attending to business in his office. The agent candidly admitted to Secretary Guthrie that neither the Sacramento nor the Stockton office was "neglected" by the greatly distracted Collectors, but that what little revenue business there was to be found in either city could be disposed of in a few hours each week.

The situation was similar in Benicia. There, the lease for the Customs House had been renewed at the original $300-per-month rental when it should have been no more than $50. Half of the buildings in the drowsy town were empty. In fact, Benicia was beginning to resemble Gardiner, Oregon, or even Bear Harbor, California, the ghost ports. In the Carquinez Strait town, the government's unwitting largesse was being promoted and exploited to the hilt. "Benicia is now, like nearly all other towns in California," reported Browne, "standing upon her own bottom and if she changes her position it must be by some unforeseen circumstance."[24]

The lessor of the Customs House property, a Mr. Argenti,[25] was not about to give the government a break. His contract was all correct and legal, and he intended to soak Uncle Sam for the full $300 per month, even though he openly admitted to Browne that he would find it difficult to rent the building for $10 a month should the government move

24 *Ibid.*

25 This was probably Felix Argenti, an Italian banker who died in 1861 with—so said the papers—a claim against the government for millions of dollars still unsettled. Before he died of apoplexy, he became famous in California as a romantic figure. He was said to be a nobleman's son who had fought several duels in Italy as a result of his journalistic efforts and who had spent nine months in a dungeon for insulting the King's mistress in print. Released, he had gone to New York to settle but rushed to California in '49. *San Francisco Daily Alta California*, May 20, 1861, p. 1, col. 1.

97

its office. J. Ross Browne sought some kind of loophole to free the Treasury from this unabashed blackmail. He thought that, perhaps, the lease was binding only on the Collector and not upon the government. Or that, perhaps, the rent could be cut to $100 for the office portion of the property, while Mizner and his men could be made responsible for the rent on the remainder, which they occupied as lodgings.[26] In October, Argenti was ready to come down to $150 to $250 a month, but Browne firmly refused all compromises and told him, flatly, that the government would pay him $100 and not one cent more, as of November 1.[27]

Browne was unable to lick the Benicia holdup. He was pained to learn that Collector Mizner had not followed his orders and asked Argenti to reduce the rent but that he had ignored his instructions entirely and told the Italian to continue the rent at the same $300 per month.[28] However, Browne had his revenge. He saw to it that Lansing B. Mizner was removed from office a year later. The *Alta California* realized that something was in the wind, and when the story broke the editors noted, "The removal of Lansing B. Mizner was unexpected, though we doubt not there are men in town who are looking for it."[29]

The agent was more successful on the Colorado River than on the Carquinez Strait. Secretary James Guthrie scrawled an order to a subordinate in his heavy hand on the back of Browne's letter to him concerning the smuggled cattle from Sonora. It read: "Please look at the law of September 1850 creating the Districts in California and see to what District Fort Yuma belongs. It is situated on the Colorado River and, I think, it is in the Dt. of San Diego. If so, authorize the Coll. of that Dt. to appt. a Depy. at Fort Yuma with instructions to collect duties on livestock."[30]

Back in San Francisco, Browne complied with the Secretary's instructions and abolished the office of Deputy Surveyor, even though the gentleman holding the post was named Guthrie, like Browne's chief,

[26] N. A. 177–1–150.
[27] N. A. 177–1–154.
[28] N. A. 177–1–257.
[29] *San Francisco Daily Alta California*, September 15, 1855, p. 2, col. 2.
[30] N. A. 177–1–150.

and, moreover, was a loyal, faithful, and efficient officer who was never absent from duty during office hours.

Since Guthrie[31] was almost indispensable (he had had long experience in the Philadelphia Customs House before migrating to California), Surveyor Van Voorhies quietly hired him as miscellaneous clerk and "forgot" to advise Browne of his action. J. Ross Browne had preferred not to interfere with the persons actually holding an office, feeling that personnel matters as such were the legitimate province of the heads of the offices which he was examining. Browne's feeling was that his job was to study duties, work-load, and so forth, not the characters or personalities or even work capacities of the particular job-holders of the moment. So, he was not irritated by Van Voorhies' maneuver. The latter lumped together the duties of the old Miscellaneous Clerk position with those of the Spirit Entry Clerk and the Deputy Surveyor and gave them all to Guthrie. The only fly in the unguent was the drop in pay— from $4,000 to $3,333 per annum. Van Voorhies petitioned the Secretary for a higher rate of pay for the man who was probably his most valued employee. Browne took a hand, too, advising the Secretary of the Treasury that he concurred fully with Van Voorhies in the matter.[32]

Apparently the Tammany-like pressure in San Francisco was beginning to wear on Browne as the fall of 1854 faded. On October 13, Guthrie's trouble shooter wrote him a frank and personal letter which explained his feelings about politics and politicking versus government service:

> Will you permit me once more to trouble you with a private letter? I fear I have already trespassed upon your time but I am very anxious to present you with an unvarnished account of men and things in California. There is not a sensible businessman or disinterested Democrat in San Francisco who does not approve of your reductions in the Customs House. Nevertheless, there is some talk about the office of ruin to the Party, alienation of friends, &c. Now, I conscientiously believe that any aspirant for

[31] George Whitney Guthrie was a New Yorker who was a member of the Customs House staff from 1854 to 1861. He then branched out into newspaper publishing, the *City Directory* indicating his interest in the *Mirror, Daily Republic, National,* and the well-known *Herald.* (See various city directories of the period.)

[32] N. A. 177–1–151.

political favor in California who predicts these things is attached to the Administration just to the extent of his own prospects of success, and no more. The Administration can never lose a friend in the honest performance of its duty to the people and the country. Much is said about the victory "we" have just achieved. Now, the plain truth is, the Broderick[33] faction killed itself by its own corrupt course and the Administration Party was successful because the measures of the Administration were popular and the Party was strong.

I hope to see the Customs House a different sort of establishment from what it has been here in times past, and it affords me pleasure to state that it is now so, to a great extent. The Collector is a gentleman of talent and integrity and in every respect qualified to render this a model Customs House. But he and myself have the misfortune to differ in regard to questions of political expediency which, unfortunately, enter into all the operations of the Customs House. It is probably not much worse here than in New York but it is bad enough there, and I think a careful examination would do that establishment no harm. At all events, I hope to see the San Francisco Customs House not merely better conducted than it has been before, which I truly believe to be the case now, but conducted upon strictly business principles. . . . Until that Utopian period arrives, the Department can never feel secure from fraud on this remote frontier where it is excluded from all knowledge of the motives which govern men in their political struggles.[34]

To Browne's surprise, the government was able to secure property for the site of the new Customs House at a very fair price. He feared that abuses would crop up during construction, however. (He was proved right, as usual.) He warned:

It will be necessary to keep a vigilant eye upon the expenditures. I have but little confidence in men in California—less now than in '49. The city

[33] Opinion seems to be that the martyrdom of David C. Broderick, killed in a duel with Chief Justice David Terry of California, was undeserved, if his death was not. A disreputable public figure, he was a Forty-niner who built up a Tammany machine in San Francisco and, as a state senator close to Governor Bigler, was able to control patronage. After years of corrupt effort he was elected United States Senator and served two years before his death. His henchmen were "shoulder-strikers" (toughs), and editor James King of William called him "David *Catline* Broderick." L. E. Feldman, "Broderick, a Reassessment," *Pacific Historical Review*, Vol. XXX, No. 1 (February, 1961), 39–46.

[34] N. A. 177–1–152.

of San Francisco is the very hotbed of all sorts of corruption, political, moral, and financial.

It is hard to tell in whom to put faith. As a principle, therefore, I would say, no man in this country should be trusted in the expenditure of public money further than absolutely necessary and any man, however high his reputation, should be deemed open to temptation and to corrupt influences where honesty goes by degrees of comparison. To be "moderately correct," as the highest degree is here, appears to me tantamount to Cobbett's definition of the Moderate Reformer in England, whose virtue he compared to "moderate virtue" in woman.[35]

As work progressed on the new Customs House building, Browne examined it and reported that it appeared to be well done. However, he warned Guthrie not to be surprised to find a million-dollar-price-tagged building on his hands before it was through. He discovered that the foundation alone, for example, cost the government $145,000.[36]

Still bruised from his violent contacts with politicos, Browne next took on San Francisco's big businessmen. He attempted to get the only-nominal duty on ice imported from Sitka, Russian Alaska, upped to a more reasonable figure. This did not please the American-Russian Company, of course. Beverly Sanders, it appeared, when he was collector, had worked out a monopoly with the Empress of Russia. The Russian-American Company and the American-Russian Company had practically become one, at least in terms of the Alaskan ice business. They secured it at Sitka at a low price and entered it in San Francisco, to be sold at a high price—$30 to $50 a ton. They were successful in excluding all rivals from competition. Traders going to Sitka offered as high as $25 a ton there, but could pry none loose from the tentacles of the monopolists.[37]

By the fall of 1854 it was obvious that a serious decrease in business was taking place on the West Coast, from San Diego to Puget Sound. There was simply not enough population in the state as yet to continue the frenetic commercial activity which the Gold Rush had engendered. On October 15 there were but four foreign vessels in all of San Francisco

[35] N. A. 177–1–153.
[36] *Ibid.*
[37] N. A. 177–1–153.

Bay, excepting beached and mud-bound hulks. Browne was optimistic, however. He thought that the extreme depression would not last much longer. It had not come as a bombshell to Browne, as it had to many others. He had been aware of the steady, month-after-month decrease in foreign trade.[38]

Everywhere he looked, Browne found profiteering and swindling. He sent to Washington on October 18 a clipping on the Meiggs[39] Swindle. This, he pointed out, was the commonest kind of copy to be found in the newspapers. He reminded Guthrie that such stories substantiated his dire warnings in earlier reports concerning the financial and political immorality of the Golden State. He had been told that army and navy officers, too, had misused public funds. But he could get no names of the guilty from his informants. Still, he advised the Secretary of the Treasury to compare carefully the weekly returns of the Assistant Treasurer of the United States with the returns of army and navy officers who deposited monies in the San Francisco Sub-Treasury. He urged him also to look carefully for large sums drawn one week but not matched by a corresponding disbursement in the subsequent week or two. The inference was that the party concerned, if he did not make a disbursement, was either pocketing the funds or lending it or banking it. Of the latter possibility, Browne observed, "Some party must enjoy the advantage of three or five percent per month during the interval of delay." The only way which J. Ross Browne could figure out for the Sub-Treasury to check on this kind of financial finagling was to require officers making drafts to state on the back of them the object for which the money was intended. These could then be compared with returns to see if the money was actually disbursed as promised. Once more he warned Washington of the moral bankruptcy of the West Coast and its metropolis: "Public officers are a long distance from the seat of government here and can

[38] N. A. 177-1-158.

[39] Henry ("Harry") Meiggs, the absconding alderman of San Francisco, was a pioneer in the Pacific Coast lumber industry for whom San Francisco's historic Meiggs Wharf was named. When he overextended himself financially he tried to cover up by using forged city warrants. Discovered, he fled to Chile, where he became a great railway builder in the Andes. It is said he eventually paid most of his San Francisco bad debts—$800,000. *Dictionary of American Biography* VI, 501–502.

enjoy almost entire immunity from punishment by losing their vouchers in a fire, suffering the loss of books and accounts, or some other convenient disaster."[40]

When Browne found himself linked by the newspapers with Colonel Thomas J. Henley[41] as being responsible for the removal of Edward F. Beale as Indian agent, he protested that it was not only untrue but absurd, to boot. He thought it was an attempt by a portion of the press to smear him and to discredit the administration in Washington at the same time. "I am determined not to write or procure one line to be written in any newspaper in California during my visit here," he stated. (This must have been a difficult decision for a natural, facile, and prolific writer.) Beale himself publicly regretted the story and told Browne so. He knew of no reason for it unless some indiscreet and misguided editorial writer was a little overzealous in defending him. Browne advised Guthrie that he had never heard Beale utter a single hostile word toward the administration.[42]

In addition to finding the federal service in the West veined throughout with dishonesty, Browne found it to be flabby with personal rivalries and jealousies. B. F. Shaw complained to him about Collector Isaac N. Ebey at Puget Sound in almost the same terms and charges as those made by Surveyor A. Benton Moses of Nisqually. According to Shaw, men were carried on the government rolls as boathands when they were actually in Ebey's service as cooks or other menials. Browne was no Diogenes and he did not know the men personally, but he was convinced that it was all a private quarrel. "There is a great jealousy existing between Federal officers and disappointed politicians in Washington Ter-

[40] N. A. 177-1-159.

[41] If there is indeed, truth in the old cliché about smoke betraying fire, then there was something wrong with Col. Henley. When he was postmaster of San Francisco the *Sacramento Union* accused him of throwing undelivered letters into trash and wastepaper bins. Draymen would then, it was said, dump the mail into a hole in a wharf. This hole eventually blossomed with signs—"Letters Sent Via This Line Must Bear U. S. Postage Stamps," "Mail Expected Every Tide," and "Get in Line, Damn Your Soul, Only One at a Time Goes down the Hole." *Sacramento Daily Union*, October 27, 1856, p. 3, col. 1. The *Alta* accused him of Indian Agency frauds, too, in 1858. *Sacramento Daily Union*, December 20, 1858, p. 2, col. 1.

[42] N. A. 177-1-160.

ritory and between men in different pursuits whose interests frequently clash where the community is so small; and I think that where absolute fraud cannot be detected, the better plan is to let them settle their own difficulties."[43]

[43] N. A. 177–1–166.

CHAPTER SEVEN

Southern California

November 3 found Browne at Tejon Pass, high in the Tehachapi Mountains. He reported that his inquiries had elicited the information that no herds of Mexican stock had been driven over Walker Pass (the southernmost of the Sierra Passes, east of modern Bakersfield) or over Tejon Pass for two years. The routes had been entirely discontinued by the drovers, and there were few immigrants using the passes, either. Therefore, Browne instructed the Collector at Stockton to discontinue the inspector's posts at the passes, since neither officer was performing a day's work for the District. Both were public land surveyors, in any case, busy with their work for the Surveyor General, Hays.[1]

Browne worked his way south and wrote from San Diego on November 7 that the War Department wanted back the building which it had turned over to the Treasury Department for customs use in that port city. They planned to raze it for its lumber. Browne opposed the idea, of course, unsure that another building could be found there at a reasonable rent.[2]

Two days later he was in San Pedro, reporting that John T. Jones,

[1] N. A. 177–1–169.
[2] N. A. 177–1–170.

assemblyman-elect of that area was asking for compensation for his services as inspector of customs for the port of San Pedro. The Collector at San Diego, William Caswell Ferrell,[3] had appointed Jones upon the resignation of Inspector Stevens on June 30, 1852. Jones served from July 1, 1852, until January 3, 1853, when a gentleman named Toler showed up with the appointment of surveyor and inspector of customs for San Pedro—and to succeed Stevens. Here was the usual confusion, of which Browne found so much, but, at least, there was no chicanery, so he urged that Jones be compensated for the time he served the port in good faith in the hiatus between Stevens and Toler.[4]

In his next stop, Monterey, Browne on November 14 ran into reckless charges of dishonesty in office. These were being launched against Thomas G. Richards, inspector of customs at the old capital of Spanish and Mexican California. The charges were preferred by Judge Pacificus Ord.[5] Browne investigated but could come to no conclusion from the facts at hand as to just who was in the right. He did collect some old letters of recommendation in behalf of Richards, some dating back to 1847. With these he sent to Washington letters defending Richards by such men as Delos R. Ashley, Robert F. Peckham, Jonathan H. Watson, and Lt. Simon Blunt, U.S.N. (for whom Blunt's Reef is named), all well-known and respected gentlemen of the Pacific Coast. (Nevertheless, Richards was replaced, and Isaac B. Wall was named collector at Monterey.)

Small wonder that Browne, once he was back in San Francisco, was as disgusted with the satellite ports as he was with the metropolis. He sourly described his beloved California as a "country settled chiefly by speculators and political adventurers." Because of the great distance be-

[3] William Ferrell was a Tarheel who came to San Diego in 1850 and was chosen district attorney in the first election. He was an able lawyer and a founder of "New" San Diego, adjacent to the old Spanish town, with William Heath Davis. He was a school commissioner, assessor, and city trustee as well as a collector of customs, but in 1859 went to Baja California, to live like a hermit. William E. Smythe, *History of San Diego* (San Diego, The History Company, 1907), 273.

[4] N. A. 177-1-171.

[5] Judge Ord was General Ord's brother and Monterey's representative to the California Constitutional Convention. *First Steamship Pioneers*, 237-40.

tween San Francisco and Washington and the uncertain-to-poor communications between the two cities, not to mention the superfluity of scoundrels in California, Browne urged that a special agent be permanently stationed in California. This officer should have complete authority to protect the government's interests and should be responsible to the heads of various departments of the government. He would, thus, be a general officer, not a special agent of any one department as J. Ross Browne was of the Treasury Department.

After four months of constant, hard, labor on the Pacific Coast, Browne was tired. He confessed that he could not possibly accomplish everything confided in him in anything less than two years. Although he had written 150 reports and letters, and traveled from San Diego to Canada, he found that he had only made a bare beginning. His experience had convinced him that a permanent agent on the Coast would save the federal government at least half a million dollars a year. He suggested that the office of appraiser general might be converted to a position in which that officer could perform such duties. (The office was a nominal one when Browne wrote.) However, he could not recommend the incumbent, Samuel J. Bridge, even though he had praised the Appraiser General's office when he had first arrived as being of that rare condition in San Francisco, well run. After a second or third look at Bridge, Browne came away with a low opinion of him. He felt that he was not only incompetent but could not say "no" to influential people and, finally, was a usurer whose "sole and absorbing passion" was avarice.[6]

Nor would Browne allow himself to be considered for the new position. "I desire to return to my family and to engage in some pursuit more congenial to my taste."[7]

He urged that a new man be chosen also for his own post of Special Agent of the Treasury. He was tired and depressed. He wrote:

Although I have never had a single unpleasant word with any person, here or elsewhere, while I have held the appointment, I am satisfied that no man can act honestly towards the Government in such a capacity with-

[6] N. A. 177–1–187.
[7] *Ibid.*

out devoting his whole energy to it, discarding all hope of making a competency for his family, and doing many acts toward his fellow men that cannot be but repugnant to the feelings of a gentleman.[8]

Luckily, J. Ross Browne was not one to stay in a depressed state of mind for long. Rested up, his brain-fag gone, he would be his old self again in a day or so. He once wrote his wife on this subject:

> Do not be at all troubled about me, my dear child, I am well and hearty, having got rid of the gout, rheumatism, liver-complaint, yellow jaundice, dyspepsia, and heart disease on the same day that my sick-headache left me. As to mental trouble, mine is seldom deep enough to do any damage. Nothing can keep me down-hearted (save family afflictions) more than six hours. All the ills of life to which I am subject vanish in conversation or letter-writing. Always bear in mind when I write to you in a doleful strain that I am that minute rid of the evil.[9]

Browne's philosophical attitude toward life always came galloping to his rescue when he was plunged into these blue funks. He was soon able to view California with more detachment. As he once wrote Lucy: "The world is such a pleasant joke. The more serious people are in their pursuits the more absurd they seem to me."[10]

On November 14 he reported on the Tejon Indian Reservation and Beale. He and Colonel Henley, Beale's successor as superintendent of the Department of the Interior's Indian Office California Superintendency, had looked over the Reservation and found it quiet and prosperous. The Indians were, at the moment, apparently as satisfied with Henley's measures for their comfort and protection as they had been with Beale's. Browne prayed that Congress would not, as rumored, reduce the size of the Tejon Reservation from 25,000 acres to 10,000 acres. Such a reduction would be ruinous. (It was.) He added: "If any portion of the land is left open to white settlers, there must inevitably be an end to all hope of reclaiming the Indians."[11]

[8] N. A. 177–1–188.
[9] *Muleback*, x.
[10] *Ibid.*, 22.
[11] N. A. 177–1–189.

In 1856, Browne suggested that Assayer Agoston Haraszthy of the San Francisco Mint be fired, pointing out: "He is a very efficient officer but of late has been engaged a great deal in his private affairs. When he came here it was supposed that he was very poor. It is now generally believed that he is worth some thirty or forty thousand dollars, owns a large ranch [*above*], etc. . . . I consider him an unsafe man and would recommend his removal."

Wine Institute, San Francisco

Although Secret Agent Browne asked Washington to sack the "Father of California Viticulture," Agoston Haraszthy, when the latter was Assayer of the United States Mint in San Francisco, the investigator believed it would be almost impossible to replace the talented Hungarian with a competent man. He reported to Secretary of the Treasury Guthrie: "Having my confidence in public officers so often shaken of late, I scarcely know what to do about suggesting the name of a suitable person to fill his job."

Wine Institute, San Francisco

At Eagle Pass and Laredo, Texas—and, later, in California—J. Ross Browne checked on the importation of Mexican cattle into the United States. He recommended that the efficient Mounted Inspectors be retained and that cattle be included in the United States Customs list of free articles of import. "It would certainly be a beneficial measure to Texas and California."

To his surprise, Browne found a cattle problem in Stockton, headquarters of the Customs District of San Joaquin. Far to the south, but
under Stockton's jurisdiction, Mexican cattle were being driven into the
Central Valley via Tejon Pass. Eventually Browne controlled this trade—
"upon which there are reasonable grounds to suppose no duties are paid"
—by stationing a deputy collector of Customs at Fort Yuma to receive
duty on the Mexican steers.

Sutro Library

Doubtless the most historic institution which J. Ross Browne examined in his California tour of inspection was the old Spanish Customs House at Monterey, founded in 1814 and the site of the capture of Monterey, by mistake, by Thomas ap Catesby Jones in 1842 and of the "legitimate" recapture in 1846 by Commodore John D. Sloat.

California State Division of Beaches and Parks

The government's confidential agent sympathized with the plight of the reservation Indians of Oregon and Washington, commenting: "They cannot be made to understand why Government should take their country away from them and then compel them to work for a living. They say Government deprived them of their national heritage; now let it support them."

Sutro Library

J. Ross Browne led a double life; he was a humorist but he was also a "muckraker" before the term was invented. Uncovering corruption in the federal service proved to be a distasteful job, but Browne's strong sense of duty and honor led him to expose "the hollowness of political distinction, the small trickery practiced in the struggle for power, the overbearing aristocracy of station, and the heartless and selfish intrigues by which public men maintain their influence."

Just at the time Browne was losing favor in Washington, because he was so painfully honest as a public servant, the streets of San Francisco boomed again as the result of the Washoe silver bonanza. Before returning East, the government agent visited Nevada (1860), and his writings about Washoe remain among the best on the Silver State.

Sutro Library

Browne's repeated contacts with the erstwhile noble red man in California, Oregon, and Washington would bear fruit when he wrote with fine irony of their shabby treatment by the government—supposedly their protector. At Tejon he saw a fine reservation built by Beale which, in a few short years, would decay under Henley and then die of starvation, from lack of funds. Browne later wrote:

> In 1853 laws were passed for the establishment of a reservation system in California, and large appropriations were made to carry it into effect. Tracts of land of twenty-five thousand acres were ordered to be set apart for the use of the Indians; officers were appointed to supervise the affairs of the service; clothing, cattle, seeds, and agricultural implements were purchased; and a general invitation was extended to the various tribes to come in and learn how to work like white men. The first reservation was established at the Tejon, a beautiful and fertile valley in the southern part of the state. Headquarters for the employees and large granaries for the crops were erected. The Indians were feasted on cattle and everything promised favorably. True, it cost a great deal to get started, about $250,000, but a considerable crop was raised, and there was every reason to hope that the experiment would prove successful. . . .[12]
>
> In order that the appropriations might be devoted to their legitimate purpose and the greatest possible amount of instruction furnished at the least expense, the Executive Department adopted the policy of selecting officers experienced in the art of public speaking and thoroughly acquainted with the prevailing systems of primary elections. A similar policy had been found to operate beneficially in the case of Collectors of Customs, and there was no reason why it should not in other branches of the public service. Gentlemen skilled in the tactics of state legislatures and capable of influencing these refractory bodies by the exercise of moral suasion could be relied upon to deal with the Indians, who are not so far advanced in the arts of civilization and whose necessities, in a pecuniary point of view, are not usually so urgent.[13]

Browne undoubtedly had Henley in mind. In July, 1855, the *Alta California* quoted a newspaper, the *Southern Californian*, on the decay of the Tejon Reservation after Henley took over. Totally incompetent,

[12] Browne, "The Indians of California," *Crusoe's Island*, 289.
[13] *Ibid.*, 290.

he cared little for his red-skinned wards. But the *Alta California* doubted that even as incompetent a superintendent of Indian affairs as Henley could be turned out of office, because his political ties and services were so important.[14]

J. Ross Browne's exposé of the condition of the Indians of California continued:

> They [the Indians] could not make out why men should drink so much whisky and swear so hard unless they were gambling and if any farther proof was necessary, it was plain to see that the game was one of hazard, because the players were constantly whispering to each other and passing money from hand to hand and pocket to pocket. . . . For men who possessed an extraordinary capacity for drinking ardent spirits, who could number among their select friends the most notorious vagrants and idlers in the state, who spent their days in idleness and their nights in brawling grogshops, whose habits, in short, were in every way disreputable, the authorities in Washington entertained a very profound antipathy. I know this to be the case, because the most stringent regulations were established prohibiting persons in the service from getting drunk, and official orders written warning them that they would be promptly removed in case of misconduct. Circular letters were also issued and posted up at the different reservations forbidding the employees to adopt the wives of the Indians, which it was supposed they might attempt to do from too zealous a disposition to cultivate friendly relations with both sexes. . . .[15]

> In one respect, I think the policy of the Government was unfortunate— that is in the disfavor with which persons of intemperate and disreputable habits were regarded. Men of this kind—and they are not difficult to find in California—could do a great deal toward meliorating the moral condition of the Indians by drinking up all the whisky that might be smuggled on the reservations, and behaving so disreputably in general that no Indian, however degraded in his propensities, could fail to become ashamed of such low vices. . . .[16]

> In accordance with the views of the Department, it was deemed to be consistent with decency that these untutored savages should be clothed in a more becoming costume than Nature had bestowed upon them. Most of

[14] *San Francisco Daily Alta California*, July 6, 1855, p. 2, col. 1.
[15] Browne, *Crusoe's Island*, 290–91.
[16] *Ibid.*, 292.

them were as ignorant of covering as they were of the Lecompton Constitution. . . . The blankets, to be sure, were very thin and cost a great deal of
money in proportion to their value. But, then, peculiar advantages were
to be derived from the transparency of the fabric. In some respects, the
worst material might be considered the most economical. By holding his
blanket to the light, an Indian could enjoy the contemplation of both sides
of it at the same time, and it would require only a little instruction in
architecture to enable him to use it occasionally as a window to his wigwam. . . . Nor was it the least important consideration that when he
gambled it away or sold it for whisky he would not be subject to any inconvenience from a change of temperature. The shirts and pantaloons
were, in general, equally transparent and possessed this additional advantage that they very soon cracked open in the seams and thereby enabled
the squaws to learn how to sew. . . .[17]

The Indians were also taught the advantages to be derived from the
cultivation of the earth. Large supplies of potatoes were purchased in San
Francisco at about double what they were worth in the vicinity of the
reservations. There were only twenty-five thousand acres of public land
available at each place for the growth of potatoes or other esculents for
which the hungry natives might have a preference; but it was much easier
to purchase potatoes than to make farmers of the white men employed to
teach them how to cultivate the earth. Sixteen or seventeen men on each
reservation had about as much as they could do to attend to their own
private claims and keep the natives from eating their private crops. . . .
Not that they were all absolutely worthless. On the contrary, some spent
their time in hunting, others in riding about the country, and a considerable number in laying out and supervising private claims, aided by Indian
labor and Government provisions. . . . The official reports transmitted to
Congress from time to time gave flattering accounts of the progress of the
system. The extent and variety of the crops were fabulously grand. Immense
numbers of Indians were fed and clothed—on paper. . . .[18]

It may seem strange that the appropriations demanded of Congress did
not decrease in a ratio commensurate with these flattering reports. The
self-sustaining period had not yet come. On the contrary, as the Indians
were advancing into the higher branches of education—music, dancing,
and the fine arts, moral philosophy and ethics, political economy, etc.—it

[17] *Ibid.*, 292–93.   [18] *Ibid.*, 295.

required more money to teach them. The number had been considerably diminished by death and desertion but then their appetites had improved and they were getting a great deal smarter. . . .[19]

But the most extraordinary feature in the history of this [Indian] service in California was the interpretation given by the Federal authorities in Washington as to the Independent Treasury Act of 1846. That stringent provision, prohibiting any public officer from using for private purposes, loaning, or depositing in any bank or banking institution any public funds committed to his charge, transmitting for settlement any voucher for a greater amount than that actually paid, or appropriating such funds to any other purpose than that prescribed by law, was so amended in the construction of the [Interior] Department as to mean "except in cases where such officer has rendered peculiar services to the Party and possesses strong influences in Congress." When any infraction of the law was reported, it was subjected to the test of this amended reading and if the conditions were found satisfactory, the matter was disposed of in a pigeonhole. An adroit system of accountability was established by which no property return, abstract of issues, account current or voucher was understood to mean what it expressed upon its face, so that no accounting officer possessing a clue to the policy adopted could be deceived by the figures. Thus it was perfectly well understood that five hundred or a thousand cattle did not necessarily mean real cattle with horns, legs, and tails, actually born in the usual course of nature, purchased for money, and delivered on the reservations, but prospective cattle that might come into existence and be wanted at some future period. For all the good the Indians got of them, it might as well be five hundred or a thousand head of voters. . . .[20]

The results of the policy pursued were precisely such as might have been expected. A large amount of money was annually expended in feeding white men and starving Indians. Such of the latter as were physically able took advantage of the tickets of leave granted them so freely, and left. Very few ever remained at these benevolent institutions when there was a possibility of getting anything to eat in the woods. Every year numbers of them perished from neglect and disease and some from absolute starvation. . . .

It invariably happened, when a visitor appeared on the reservations, that the Indians were "out in the mountains gathering nuts and berries." This was the case in spring, summer, autumn and winter. They certainly pos-

[19] *Ibid.*, 296.　　　　　　　[20] *Ibid.*, 297.

sessed a remarkable predilection for staying out a long time. Very few of them, indeed, have yet come back. . . . In the brief period of six years, they have been nearly destroyed by the generosity of government. What neglect, starvation and disease have not done, has been achieved by the cooperation of the white settlers in the great work of extermination. . . .[21]

A more inoffensive and harmless race of beings does not exist on the face of the earth but wherever they attempted to procure a subsistence they were hunted down, driven from the reservations by the instinct of self-preservation, shot down by settlers upon the most frivolous pretexts, and abandoned to their fate by the only power that could have afforded them protection.[22]

From the Indians of Tejon, Browne turned his attention to the Customs House at Santa Barbara. This was a minor southern California port, and he ordered the Collector of Customs at San Diego not to pay any more rent for a surveyor's office at its satellite, Santa Barbara. The only business of the port was the shipping of a few boxes of wine grapes to San Francisco each year from a local vineyard. Occasionally, too, coasting steamers put in there on their San Francisco to San Diego run. There were only three or four stores run by gringos, little interior trade, and no Mexican cattle passing through the town. Although there was little business—"The population is almost exclusively composed of native Californians, whose only business so far as I have been able to discover, is gambling and horse racing"—Browne was not ready to dispense with a revenue officer in the area. He recommended that the office be continued but that no rent be allowed. (In San Pedro he had to allow a continuation of $30 rent because there were no dwellings there.) Surveyors José María Covarrubias[23] and (his successor) Pedro Carrillo[24]

21 *Ibid.*, 300–302.

22 *Ibid.*, 307.

23 Among the offices held by Covarrubias, besides surveyor and assemblyman, was that of sheriff of Santa Barbara County, but he was removed and fined $100 in 1877 for taking kickbacks from his jailer. *San Francisco Daily Alta California*, October 30, 1877, p. 1, col. 5.

24 Movie star Leo Carrillo's Honolulu- and Boston-educated grandfather held many offices in southern California, including that of alcalde of Santa Barbara in 1848, town surveyor as well as customs surveyor, justice of the peace in Los Angeles, and state assemblyman. Hubert H. Bancroft, *California Pioneer Register and Index, 1542–1848* (Baltimore, Regional Publishing Company, 1964), 110.

worked out of their homes, customarily, and this suited the cost-cutting agent to a *t*.[25]

On his trips to central and southern California and elsewhere, Browne kept detailed personal expense accounts. These occasionally came in handy in reporting, such as when he wished to summarize the cost of travel in the Far West. He had only to refer to his own expense accounts to determine that the steamer fare (1854) between San Francisco and Portland was $60.00, while the San Francisco–San Diego charge was $50.00, including meals and staterooms in each case. To go from San Francisco to Benicia required an outlay of $4.00, to Stockton or Sacramento, $11.00. San Jose could be reached by stage from San Francisco for $4.00, but by steamer for only $2.00 and sometimes for as little as $1.00. Browne found that the journey from his San Francisco headquarters to Monterey by stage was $8.00, by steamer $10.00. Hotels made an average charge of $2.50 to $3.00 for a room and a per diem of $4.00 was ample for meals, on land. On shipboard, meals were thrown in for the fare quoted. Browne also observed that the cost of travel was declining and, while he felt that $.10 a mile was not enough to budget for constant travel on the Coast, a $.10 mileage allowance and a $4.00 per diem was ample.[26]

On November 18, writing from San Francisco, Browne turned his thoughts again to the cattle being trail-herded from Mexico into California. In this recapitulation of his thinking on the matter of dutiable cattle, he reminded the Secretary of the difficulty at both the Rio Grande and the Canadian–United States Lakes border of collecting duty and added that it was quite impossible to do so in California, with its enormous ranches, some of which extended even beyond the state's boundaries. To try to place an inspector on each ranch would be impossibly expensive. "Yet, said Browne, "I doubt if one fourth of the stock imported into California from Mexico pays duty. Yet this is the principal trade of the Southern districts." His final recommendation was that the most inexpensive and practicable solution was to abolish the duty on livestock and to do away with two southern California districts, one-half of the inspectors in the Lakes border area, and the entire corps of efficient mounted ranger-inspectors of the Rio Grande.[27]

[25] N. A. 177–1–192.   [26] *Ibid.*   [27] N. A. 177–1–199.

His argument was this: "The people in Texas and California are universally in favor of free trade in stock. Constant difficulty arises between the importers and the officers of the Revenue in consequence of the general unpopularity of this duty upon stock." Then he added a telling point: "In no instance does the revenue pay the expense of collection." Browne realized that Guthrie had already called Congress' attention to the subject of alien cattle entering the United States, and it was true that the trade was a great importance to the thinly settled border states. But he had valid reasons for urging a reversal of policy in the handling of imported cattle. He reminded Guthrie:

> The sooner these states are settled by a stock raising and agricultural population, the greater will be the amount of revenue collected upon foreign importations. Every facility therefore, should be granted by the general government to bring about that result, and none would tend more to accomplish it than the removal of all restrictions upon the trade which gives value to their claims. In California it is especially important that immigration should be encouraged. The extensive tracts of public lands in the Sacramento, San Joaquin, Tejon Lake, Los Angeles, San Bernardino and other Valleys, that may be made available for settlement, are capable of supporting a dense agricultural population. These valleys are peculiarly adapted in climate and soil to grazing purposes. Let their resources be fully developed and the commercial importance of the state will no longer be dependent upon the products of the mines. Stock raising must be the primary means of settlement. I trust that, in view of these facts, you will deem it expedient again to impress upon Congress the importance of including stock in the list of free articles. It would certainly be a beneficial measure to Texas and California.[28]

[28] *Ibid.*

CHAPTER EIGHT

A Would-Be Croesus Or Two

B ROWNE'S ATTENTION WAS DIVERTED from longhorns to bullion when the trouble-plagued United States Branch Mint in San Francisco was forced to his attention even though he considered its Superintendent, Lewis A. Birdsall, and the Assistant United States Treasurer there, Jacob R. Snyder, to be sufficiently zealous and faithful officers. The two were embarrassed by a lack of material for refining purposes and by deficiencies of funds even though the Collector of Customs had advanced the Mint $23,000 to pay such pressing expenses as freight charges, and for such purchases as coal and nitrate of soda, the latter used in the refining process. The Mint's sorry image disturbed Browne. He commented in a letter to Washington of November 22, 1854: "People here are losing all confidence in this concern. They cannot get their gold coined and are forced to transport it to Philadelphia."[1]

Browne took steps to get the Mint operating again. When the vessel with a hastily ordered load of nitrate of soda failed to arrive on schedule from Iquique, Chile, to make the acid needed for refining, he ordered that supplies, in the future, should be built up for at least a year's work.[2] To see to it that a reliable supply was always at hand, he arranged with

[1] N. A. 177-1-205.
[2] N. A. 177-1-157.

a local acid supplier, the San Francisco Chemical Works, in August, 1855, to handle the Mint's needs. The contract proved to be one which effected savings for the government, too, as an added bonus.[3]

Toward the end of 1854, the Russians returned to plague him. But this time it was not over ice. The Russian Consul attempted to procure illegally the seizure of the ship *Sitka* by the United States government. The *Sitka* was a prize, taken by the Allied fleet and brought into San Francisco. This was a most unusual case, of course. (San Francisco had never had a Crimean War on its hands before.) Prize ships were new to the Embarcadero. It was an important case, too; the nations involved in the question were Great Britain, Russia, France, and the United States. Browne was afraid that other prize cases might follow that of the *Sitka*. Since the precedent established in this case might be of great moment, he did not want to proceed with only his own limited knowledge of international and revenue law. Accordingly, he wrote Guthrie for instructions—something he was most unaccustomed to doing. The normally resourceful and independent Browne, for the time being, only suggested that all prizes be entered at the Customs House and that an inspector placed on board each captured vessel.[4]

While Browne awaited instructions, the Russians continued their campaign to regain the *Sitka* by first getting the United States to seize it from France and Britain. But J. Ross Browne had no information concerning any violation of the United States revenue laws by the Allies and did not want to be a tool for the Russians.[5]

Russian Consul Kostromitinoff managed to irritate Browne further by taking a quantity of champagne out to the American ship *Zenobia*, lying in the harbor, for the celebration in honor of the Russian success at Petropavlovsk and the failure of the British and French to capture Sevastopol, whose fall after a long siege they had several times (prematurely) announced. Browne did not so much mind the Consul passing the bubbly around, but when he fired a noon salute from the *Zenobia* in honor of the Russian war effort, this was coming close to the last

[3] N. A. 177-1-251.
[4] N. A. 177-1-214.
[5] N. A. 177-1-217.

straw. Since Uncle Sam was neutral in the Crimean War, Browne did not like the idea of the Russians using an American ship in San Francisco Bay for such patriotic displays. In fact, he was convinced that the Consul was up to no good. "I think further evidence is not necessary to establish the fact that the Russian Consul and the Russian and American Ice Company are doing all in their power to produce difficulty between the United States and the Allied Powers."[6]

The agent also learned of the supposed violation of American revenue laws for which the Russians blamed the French and British captors of the *Sitka*. They claimed that butter and beef had been landed from her in San Francisco, without payment of duty. But Collector Richard P. Hammond, with Browne's backing, refused Kostromitinoff's demand that the vessel be seized. There was no evidence to take to court (the beefsteaks and butter had been consumed); Julien Jacob Conradi, captain of the *Sitka,* was a prisoner of war and could not even be called as a witness. Still the Russian Consul continued his pressure, demanding that a local court obtain the release of his countrymen from custody because they were in a neutral port. Browne finally tired completely of the Consul's machinations and exploded: "If this is not a direct cessation of neutrality by the local authorities of the United States, I think it would be difficult to determine the belligerent extent to which neutrality may be carried without a violation of peace. The secret of the whole movement is simply this—The Russian and American Ice Companies are using every exertion to produce, upon some pretext or other, a difficulty between the authorities here and the Allied Powers. By means of wealth, intrigue, and fraud, they are getting up a public sympathy in behalf of Russia which the people have no cause to feel. . . . The annexation of Sitka is held out as an additional inducement for an alliance with Russia and a war against England and France." (And here Browne allowed his anger to cloud his normal good sense, dismissing what more short-sighted people would later call "Seward's Folly," too.) "The annexation of Sitka is a proposition too absurd for serious comment. It is a place without commerce, without resources of any kind except the ice with which the country is covered for three-fourths of the year and in all

[6] N. A. 177–1–215.

respects is wholly unworthy of note." He went on to compare Alaska unfavorably with Hawaii. "With regard to the Sandwich Islands, the case is different. We have substantial commercial interests there and it is hoped that the result of the negotiations now pending will be satisfactory."[7]

Because of the rumors of possible annexation of the Kingdom of Hawaii by the United States, Browne prepared a brief dossier on the Islands for his chief on December 1, 1854. He took great pains to show the extent of Hawaiian-American trade, and noted that "very great interest is felt by the people of California in the question of annexation." Some forty ships from the Islands had called at San Francisco in 1853 and 1854, and forty-six had cleared at the Customs House for the Sandwich Islands. These ships—forty of which were American and three of which were Hawaiian—totaled 14,588.25 tons. With long, detailed, and carefully composed tables, Browne broke down the imports from Hawaii to California. They ran to such products as sugar, potatoes, specie, garden seeds, molasses, coffee, whale oil, syrup, and dried fruit. He also made a breakdown of San Francisco's exports to the Hawaiian Islands.[8]

In January, 1855, Browne turned his attention again to the operation of the Mint. He submitted a long and detailed study to Washington. He found a deficiency in the supply of acids for refining but, as yet, could find no neglect. He did suggest that Superintendent Lewis Aiken Birdsall might maintain better control over the money kept at the Mint. The half-million dollars in cash in the building's vault was "guarded" only by a not-very-responsible clerk who slept in an adjoining room. Browne suggested that a proper system of guards be set up.[9] (While he was at it, he looked into the security measures practiced at the Customs House and found them nil, too. By the fall, when the new collector, Milton S. Latham, took office, Browne's recommendations had led to the appointment of a chief watchman to oversee the guards, keep them on their toes and, in general, see to a high level of security in the new Customs House.)[10]

Returning to the East for a visit, Browne was soon on his way back to

[7] N. A. 177-1-217.   [8] N. A. 177-1-208.
[9] N. A. 177-1-222.   [10] N. A. 177-1-304.

California. He left New York on May 5 and was in Aspinwall, Panama (Nueva Granada), on May 15. While on the Isthmus he consulted with the Department's Special Inspector for Panama, Ran Runnels, as well as with the American Consul, Thomas W. Ward.[11]

Browne arrived in San Francisco with his family on May 30 and the very next day reported to Washington that he was back on the job. He soon busied himself with planning a further reduction of the staff of the Customs House. In June alone he removed ten inspectors at San Francisco as well as the inspectors at Monterey and Oakland, neither of whom had done a lick of work for their pay. He revisited Benicia, where he was pleasantly surprised to find a little business, mainly coal arriving from Cardiff, Wales.[12]

Rumors began to reach him at this time of improper disbursements made by Collector Hammond, whom he had trusted. The word was that Hammond had made advances which he had failed to report to Washington. The money had gone to contractors building the new Customs House. J. Ross Browne quickly submitted a statement of what he had learned but left it to the Secretary to decide on the propriety or lack of it in Hammond's actions.[13]

In July, Browne made a swing around the North Bay area, in the counties of Sonoma and Napa. He visited Petaluma, Napa, Lakeville (now a hamlet outside of Petaluma), Bodega, and Fort Ross to determine if any revenue officers were necessary or desirable at these points. His decision was negative. He found only local trade and farming going on in the group of historic but small and quiet settlements north of San Francisco Bay. In the Bodega, Fort Ross, and Russian River area of Sonoma County he found few settlers at all. (Yet one of them was a man after his own heart—the witty and observant British writer, Frank Marryat, who squatted on a farm in the area for a time before going home to Blighty to write his famous *Mountains and Molehills*, in late 1854 and 1855, before his untimely death six months after publication.) The wild, mountainous country was settled mainly by large ranch

[11] N. A. 177-1-235.
[12] N. A. 177-1-236.
[13] *Ibid.*

owners and cattle drovers, or cowboys. Browne was always on the lookout for smuggling, but he had few worries in this area. Although the lonely, rugged Redwood Coast might have seemed ideal for the smuggler, Browne set the record straight for Washington: "There would be no object in smuggling in such a country, as it would cost more than the amount of duties to transport smuggled goods by pack mules to any place of sale."[14]

On August 12, Browne sent word to Washington that he was preparing for another field trip to both the north and the south of the state. He listed the outfit which he would need to hit the areas he had missed on earlier trips—a wagon, two mules, one horse, saddle, bridle, harness, and camping equipment. His estimate of the cost of everything was about $1,000. While he was citing these figures he could not resist mentioning that for the services he had performed in the field for the Departments of the Treasury and Interior, he had, so far, ended up $500 in debt to the government. (However, this was because he figured in the cost of transporting his family to the Pacific Coast.) On this planned trip of 1855, he advised Guthrie, he would not be doing any work for the Interior Department as he had done in 1854. But he could not overlook the fact that the Register and Receiver representing the General Land Office in Benicia were doing absolutely no business at all. There were no land sales in their area. He hoped that Guthrie would inform the Commissioner of the General Land Office so that he could act on the matter. Browne also noted that he had found rents for Interior Department offices to be excessive, just as was the case with Revenue Service buildings.[15]

On August 17, 1855, Browne informed Secretary Guthrie that Colonel Benjamin Franklin Washington, former storekeeper of the Customs House and former editor of the *Times and Transcript*, was on his way East. He was, according to Browne, the best political writer in California and the best friend of the administration to be found in the Golden State. He had been persuaded to run for governor but then dumped at the convention in favor of another candidate, who was eventually nominated. Browne hoped that Guthrie could help him. (One wonders if Browne

[14] N. A. 177-1-248. [15] N. A. 177-1-255.

saw the irony of his own politicking in this instance.) He had great confidence in Washington and his capabilities, describing him as an able and devoted government servant who deserved to be retained in public service.[16]

In September, J. Ross Browne had the pleasure of handing J. B. Storer his commission as Collector of Customs at Benicia, for the District of Sonoma, replacing the thorn in his side named Lansing B. Mizner. But Browne promised Storer a dismissal by return mail if there were any truth to the rumor that he was a member of a certain political organization. He did not name it, but, presumably, it was an anti-administration group. Storer vehemently denied the rumors, saying that they were canards started because he had served under Mizner who was, indeed, opposed to those currently in office in Washington. To satisfy Browne, Storer gave the agent a letter of recommendation from John McDougall, governor of California in 1851 and 1852. McDougall lauded Storer for his "fealty to the Party."[17] (The Independent Democratic, Democratic, or Lecompton Democratic party; just which one is not clear.) Browne was not above party politics, although he did not befoul himself in low politicking.

The seventeenth day of September saw Browne back at his office in San Francisco after a tour of inspection of San Pedro, Los Angeles, Elizabeth Lake,[18] Santa Barbara, San Bernardino, and the entire coast line from Santa Barbara to San Francisco. The major concern of the Department's inspector general, as far as southern California was concerned, was the Collector of Customs for the District of Los Angeles, who resided some seventeen miles from the port of entry. Moreover, he gave no personal attention to the duties of his office and, in fact, let his deputy do all the work. Browne asked that he be required to move to San Pedro or to yield his office.[19]

[16] N. A. 177–1–262.

[17] N. A. 177–1–264.

[18] Little-known Elizabeth Lake was once said to be the hangout not only of bandit Tiburcio Vasquez but also of a "sea monster" and spirits whose screams and curses gave the Antelope Valley *laguna* a bad name. So thick was it with waterfowl in pioneer times that E. F. Beale once brought down three ducks with a single shot from his rifle—not his shotgun.

[19] N. A. 177–1–266.

Another federal scandal broke in mid-September, and it was a humdinger. Browne had to report that he had just investigated what appeared to be collusion between Mint Superintendent Lewis S. Birdsall and Assayer Agoston Haraszthy and a newly formed private gold-refining firm in San Francisco in which James King of William[20] and the powerful and well-known banking, staging, and express concern, Adams and Company, played important roles.[21]

Patient digging unearthed these facts. Birdsall, Haraszthy, and King of William were partners in the new firm, each with one-fifth interest, except that Haraszthy, the key man, had a two-fifths slice of the pie. It was the Hungarian who was to supply the knowledge of assaying and refining. He would also contribute a hush-hush invention of his to the company. He also agreed to send a competent chemist in his place when he found Mint affairs too pressing to attend to the business of the new company. Birdsall was to be the promoter. It was his job to do all in his power to secure business for the new firm—all, that is, short of efforts inconsistent with his duties at the Mint. James King of William was to keep the accounts, and Adams and Company was to put up the money. Browne found that the company was being formed for the specific

---

[20] These three men were destined to be among the most prominent men of the age, especially Haraszthy and King of William. Lewis Aiken Birdsall was a medical doctor whose daughter, Sophia, married Milton S. Latham who would become governor of California (1859–60) and United States Senator from California from 1860 until 1863. Birdsall had been thought to be a good and efficient officer until Browne's investigation, and when he finally resigned, as a result of Browne's discoveries, it was not under a cloud. Indeed, the *Alta* editorialized (November 15, 1855, p. 2, col. 2): "Dr. Birdsall, we presume, resigns because he is abundantly able to live without making a slave of himself and because he desires a little time to call his own." Agoston Haraszthy was the brilliant Hungarian pioneer of California who abandoned smelting and minting to become the dominant figure in viticulture and enology. He is considered today to be the father of the California wine industry. He died in Nicaragua when he fell into a stream and was eaten by alligators. James King of William, like Haraszthy, was one of the most colorful men to tread the streets of San Francisco. He adopted his strange name when he was in Washington, D.C., and there were so many other James Kings that he was often confused with them. He simply added his father's first name to create a unique "handle." As a crusading editor (the *San Francisco Evening Bulletin*), he resembled Browne somewhat in that he cried out against graft and corruption. Unlike Browne, he was sometimes accused of skimming off some of the creamier graft, himself. In any case, his penchant for name-calling led to his assassination and to the formation of the Committee of Vigilance of 1856, which lynched his murderer.

[21] N. A. 177–1–267.

purpose of taking advantage of the new and secret refining process discovered by the talented Magyar, Haraszthy. In their contract, all partners swore never to divulge the secret of the process.[22]

The very day following his first exposé of the plan, Browne sent a follow-up letter. This November 19 report stated that the assaying and refining establishment had aborted. It had not gone into operation. Adams and Company probably gave it a second look and backed out of the deal as unprofitable. J. Ross Browne was not certain of the degree of impropriety of the two federal employees since the arrangement was all off. But he did point out that Birdsall had sworn several times during Browne's investigation (but prior to the latter's obtaining a copy of the contract) that he had absolutely no connection with a private establishment—which was simply not true.

Again, Browne left it up to the Department to decide whether to sack the men or not. The problem was complicated by the fact that they were almost indispensable to the operation of the Mint. It would be nearly impossible to replace them with competent men. In a postscript to his letter, Browne went so far as to say:

> I may add that Mr. Haraszthy is a very capable and efficient officer and if he has erred at all in the matter it has been with the full knowledge of the Superintendent. It would be very difficult to fill his place and I feel assured that a letter of warning from the Department would prevent a recurrence of the impropriety so far as Mr. Haraszthy is concerned.[23]

On September 20, Browne actually forwarded to Washington a copy of the Hungarian's argument in defense of his actions in the matter. Haraszthy explained that he had asked permission to conduct private work with his gold-refining discovery and that Superintendent Birdsall had granted it.[24]

Browne was seemingly inclined to help Haraszthy, but he was ominously silent on Birdsall and his conflict of interest, lack of judgment, or whatever, in the affair.

22 N. A. 177–1–268.
23 N. A. 177–1–269.
24 N. A. 177–1–270.

The September 19, 1855, report of Secret Agent Browne stated that Guthrie's removal of Hammond as collector in San Francisco had created a lot of excitement and had stimulated the press to the printing of many unjust statements in regard to the Secretary's position and actions. Browne explained, without apology, that he had not tried to defend the Treasury Department's action, nor to explain the facts to the public or to engage in any way in the newspaper controversies.[25] (He believed it did no good, and perhaps did the government's image harm, to engage in wrangles of this kind.)

But he had other news, which was good news, in his communiqué. No further legal action appeared to be necessary in the case of former Collector Beverly C. Sanders. The latter was going to pay back to the government all the money in question.[26] (Actually, the trials of Sanders and Hammond, both, for improper use of Customs House funds would creak on and on until 1860 when, after postponements and disagreeing juries, the government gave up and entered a nolle prosequi, dropping the whole legal action.)

More good news from Browne was the information that the highly respected Milton S. Latham, of Sacramento, had accepted the appointment of collector of customs for San Francisco. Browne was sure that he would reform the Customs House and put a stop to the abuses there.[27]

As early as the twenty-seventh of the month, Browne could report that the new Collector was tightening up. J. Ross Browne continued his reforms with renewed vigor, and when two inspectors at the Customs House were put on report, he saw to it that one was immediately removed. (The other resigned.) He stressed the importance of Latham's mission in cleaning up the mess of the Customs House: "This is a very important branch of the revenue system. I venture to assert that there has been heretofore more smuggling resulting from the inefficiency of inspectors than from any other cause on this Coast, and especially in this District."[28]

[25] N. A. 177–1–271.
[26] *Ibid.*
[27] N. A. 177–1–272.
[28] N. A. 177–1–280.

When Hammond left office, he took $24,137.86 with him. He claimed the sum was his commission, made on disbursements. But Browne saw no reason why Hammond should have a right to such funds since in the case of Beverly C. Sanders, Judge Ogden Hoffman had ruled that the Collector had no right to the money in question. The government had brought suit in that case in the Circuit Court of Maryland for the full amount. Browne quoted Chief Justice Taney's opinion: "The defendant is not entitled to any salary as depositary, nor any fees or commissions over and above the maximum compensation of $10,000 as Collector of San Francisco." Browne felt that this should hold for Hammond, too.[29] (But it would not prove to be that simple, and both Hammond and Sanders survived long and drawn-out court battles.)

During that month of September, Secretary Guthrie recommended to Collector Latham that he appoint J. Ross Browne to the post of deputy collector of customs for San Francisco. Latham was only too happy to proffer the appointment to the roving agent, but Browne did not think his acceptance of the post would be proper. He wrote Guthrie:

> While grateful to you for the complimentary manner in which the offer was made, I cannot consent to hold any office upon which it has been my duty to report as Special Agent of the Treasury. Nevertheless, I shall be most happy to confer with Mr. Latham and, should he desire it, afford him all the aid in my power in the performance of his official duties.[30]

In October, Milton S. Latham was actually sworn in as the new collector in San Francisco. As was the custom, all officers had then to be reappointed and sworn in anew. Browne took advantage of the "new broom" atmosphere to set up what modern management would call a position-and-pay plan. He established grades of work with uniform compensation at each level for all the various jobs he found in the Customs House.[31]

He continued his probing all the while and found more examples of the "Let's gouge Uncle Sam" school of thinking. The United States was

[29] N. A. 177-1-282.
[30] N. A. 177-1-286.
[31] N. A. 177-1-287.

paying far more for drayage than anyone else in San Francisco and more for beef for the United States Marine Hospital than was necessary. The bully beef was costing the taxpayers just double the market price of meat.[32]

During this trying month of October, Browne referred to his "impaired health" for the first time, after four months of constant work at his desk.[33] Perhaps for this reason he looked forward to another trip to Washington and Oregon, by land. It may be that he hoped that travel would cure his woes while he obtained additional knowledge of the northern coasts. However, the Secretary turned down his request.[34] Lewis Birdsall lifted no loads off Browne's back when he demanded that the agent conduct a thoroughgoing investigation of his transactions, in order to squelch attacks and rumors which were mounting against him. Browne wearily promised to comply with what he politely called the angry Superintendent's "request."[35] One bright note of the month, at least, was the occupation of the new Customs House.[36]

The provisions of the Passenger Act were still being evaded on the Pacific Coast in the mid-fifties, and there was little that Browne could do about such vessels as the *Sierra Nevada*, which came into port with an excess of two hundred passengers. About the only action which he could take was to try to seek the conviction of the captain on a misdemeanor charge—something very hard to obtain in a local court at that time. There was little sympathy with either health or safety measures among the profit-minded leaders of San Francisco's water front. He did the best he could, sending the cutter to the Golden Gate's heads. As he explained the situation:

> The revenue cutter has been ordered to the entrance to count the passengers on board previous to the arrival of the vessel at the wharf. It is not contemplated, of course, to keep up this system of obstruction but it is absolutely necessary that some example should be made in order to prevent

32 N. A. 177–1–290.
33 N. A. 177–1–291.
34 *Ibid.*
35 N. A. 177–1–293.
36 N. A. 177–1–294.

a recurrence of the late enormous sacrifice of life on board these steamers and also to satisfy the public that the charges of partiality to the Panama Line and hostility to the Nicaragua Line, made by the owners of the latter against the officers of the Customs, are wholly unfounded.[37]

The sacrifices of life to which Browne referred were the cases of the overcrowded Nicaragua Line steam packets *Cortez* and *Sierra Nevada,* which had been converted into charnel ships by cholera.[38]

Browne made a quick trip up the Sacramento Valley on combined Land Office–Treasury Department business at the end of October. He found the Marysville situation resembling that of so many other cities he had examined. The Register of the Land Office was renting an office for $250 a month, when he could have contracted one for $40–$50. When Browne reported this to Washington, the Commissioner of the General Land Office disallowed the oversized rent. Browne found little business in Sacramento and, consequently, little to report from there. He felt that the Sacramento District definitely should be merged with the San Francisco District, with only an inspector left at Sacramento.[39]

After an examination of the Birdsall affairs—invited by Birdsall himself—Browne wrote Guthrie on November 4 that the best interests of the government would be served by accepting the Superintendent's resignation. However, he cautioned, a conciliatory action rather than a peremptory one was advisable, to avoid trouble. Browne feared a public uproar—with much embarrassment to Collector Latham—over the ousting, since Latham was Birdsall's son-in-law. The leading applicant for the post, if it should be vacated, he noted, was Major Richard Roman.[40] Public opinion of Roman's integrity was high, but Browne nosed about a bit and came up with some objections. For one thing, he felt that the

[37] N. A. 177–1–303.

[38] N. A. 177–1–314.

[39] N. A. 177–1–308.

[40] Peter F. Lott actually replaced Birdsall. Roman, not to be confused with the pioneer bookseller-publisher Anton Roman, who died in a tragic Redwood Coast train wreck, had to be content in terms of position with the post of treasurer of the state of California. When he died in 1875 he was eulogized by the Sacramento *Union* (December 24, 1875, p. 1, col. 6) as "a man of many sterling qualities of head and heart." He was also United States consul in Guaymas and appraiser of San Francisco.

banking house of Palmer, Cook and Company was a little too interested in the Major's securing the post. It looked as if they would exert pressure on Roman. Moreover, Browne—who did not know Roman personally—learned that he was a man of convivial rather than business habits.[41]

The Confidential Agent felt that his friend, Colonel B. F. Washington, would give far better general satisfaction than any other person. If this selection were not feasible, Browne suggested that a person of proven ability be sent to San Francisco from the East. For his part, he could recommend no one save Washington on the Pacific Coast. But Browne once again urged the Secretary of the Treasury that Superintendent Lewis Birdsall be removed gently, adding "If I have erred in the conciliatory course which I have taken, it is proper that the error should be attributed to the true cause—sympathy for an old man whose life would be embittered by the stigma attached to his name, and whose family would share in the same reproach."[42]

Besides his ties with Palmer, Cook and Company, Browne found that Birdsall was very close to the proprietor of a chemical factory and was in on the contract of Haraszthy and Adams and Company to establish a private assay office. Even if he were innocent as a lambkin, the Department had lost confidence in him, and in Browne's judgment he deserved to be removed (via resignation).[43]

In December, Browne found himself defending Judge Ogden Hoffman, whom he did not yet know personally, and with whom he had sharply differed over the coolie ships, from unwarranted attacks.[44] This was also the month when Browne lowered the boom on Cyril V. Grey, corresponding clerk of the Customs House. He accused Grey of perpetrating frauds during the administrations of T. Butler King, Beverly C. Sanders, and Richard P. Hammond. According to his investigations, Grey was wont to obtain money under false pretenses. "During the few years of his official career, he amassed a considerable fortune which it is not reasonable to suppose he derived from his salary of $3,600 per year." Then the agent added tartly: "Since his removal from office he has established himself in this city as Proctor in Admiralty [Law] and I can

[41] N. A. 177–1–311.
[42] N. A. 177–1–311.
[43] N. A. 177–1–312.
[44] N. A. 177–1–323.

safely say that he is more successful in procuring acquittals and evasions of law than gentlemen of the bar generally who have not had the same personal experience in frauds upon the Treasury. I consider Mr. Grey a dishonest and designing man and I hope to procure his conviction upon the charge."[45]

As the new year of 1856 opened, Browne threw his support behind the government and the city of San Francisco in the Limantour Case. This was the most bald-faced attempted fraud in the history of the West, with the possible exception of the Great Diamond Hoax of the 1870's. José Yves Limantour, of Mexico, with forged documents of Governor Micheltorena of Alta California and others, tried to reclaim as his own property the land on which San Francisco sat. (Before he was through, he had produced documents which might have given him almost the entire coast from San Diego to Mendocino County.) On November 19, 1858, Judge Ogden Hoffman gave his opinion in the case. He found all the documentary evidence submitted by Limantour to be fraudulent and the majority of his witnesses to be perjurers.[46]

One of the counsels for the defense, an attorney named Gale, asked for J. Ross Browne's aid in getting the federal government to help. Browne hoped that the government would take a hand in opposing Limantour's crooked game. Moral support, more than money, was needed to thwart his project. As Browne put it: "If the Limantour claimants knew that they had to contend against a higher power than that now arraigned against them, it would materially affect their chances of success." It was his notion that the United States government could make some kind of confidential agreement with the parties trying to defeat the claimants, to protect public property which was threatened by Limantour and his followers.[47] The federal government did become interested—very interested—and men like Volney E. Howard and J. H. McKune, law agents of the Board of Land Commissioners, took an active role in the long (1853-58) case.[48]

[45] N. A. 177-1-324.

[46] Kenneth M. Johnson, *José Yves Limantour v. The United States* (Los Angeles, Dawson's Book Shop, 1961), 68.

[47] N. A. 177-1-328.

[48] Johnson, *José Yves Limantour v. The United States*, 36.

Another visit to Stockton and the District of the San Joaquin refreshed Browne on the subject of cattle drives. This was in February, 1856. He discovered that the importation of stock from Mexico had dwindled away to a negligible trade by that time. The guards at the passes were now useless, and Browne approved of the Department's discontinuing them. By 1856 all livestock, except for a minute fraction, was being driven in via Fort Yuma. Very little, if any, was being herded over Walker Pass or Tejon Pass. The San Bernardino Valley, however, had become a major artery for cattle drovers by the mid-fifties. "I do not think from the examination which I made of these districts that the trade in stock from Sonora or other parts of Mexico amounts to sufficient to bear the expense of a more rigid system of inspection," counseled Browne. He again reiterated his belief that the best course was the removal, entirely, of any duty on cattle. He reminded Guthrie how important the encouragement of livestock importation was to the settling of public lands in California.[49]

While he was in Stockton, Browne looked into the books of the Customs House. He found no foreign trade being carried on. Browne ordered the Collector, in future, to keep records on the coastwise trade. "The trade is small," he admitted to Guthrie, "but as the business of the District is now conducted, these coasting vessels might be laden with foreign goods taken on board outside the Bay of San Francisco and brought up to the interior during the night without the knowledge of a single Customs House officer." After this Sacramento tour, Browne finally recommended that the Customs Districts of Sonoma, Sacramento, and San Joaquin be abolished, with only inspectors stationed at Benicia, Stockton, and Sacramento.[50]

In an April 5, 1856, letter to the Department, Browne was quite alarmed by the trend of the Limantour swindle cases. He felt that the decision was going in favor of the claimants by default. He called attention to the fact that no attempt had been made to call witnesses from Mexico and that no satisfactory evidence of fraud could be produced without them. It looked to him as if the claims would be confirmed, and

[49] N. A. 177-1-336.
[50] *Ibid.*

"the same will probably be the result before the superior tribunals unless a more energetic policy is pursued by the Government or its agents." He predicted great costs to the United States in securing titles to lands held by the government for civil and military purposes. These lands included the United States Marine Hospital atop Rincon Hill, the buildings on Fort Point except for Fort Winfield Scott itself, Goat Island or Yerba Buena Island, Alcatraz Island, the Farallones, and the Folsom estate east of California Street.[51]

That the claims of Limantour are fraudulent is now the general impression. The testimony of Auguste Jouan[52] before the U.S. Commissioner (Johnston) indicates clearly the character of the fraud and the means taken to obtain the confirmation of the grants. Unfortunately, Jouan is represented to be a person of disreputable character and his testimony does not carry with it the weight which would attach to a more reliable source. Nevertheless, it indicates that confirmatory evidence can be had if the proper means are taken.[53]

Guthrie thought that an agent like Browne could be hired and sent to Mexico to root out evidence in behalf of the government for a nominal fee, perhaps $1,500. Browne begged to differ. He felt that the government should concentrate on one point of attack—the lighthouse sites threatened by Limantour's land claim—and battle from that position. As for the cloak-and-dagger man in Mexico, he urged that for such an all-or-nothing case, the agent should be sent to Mexico to secure proofs at all costs and with all the means to defray the expenses of witnesses to California. Browne had a man in mind. He was former United States

---

[51] N. A. 177-1-342.

[52] Auguste, or Augustus, Jouan was sent to San Francisco in 1852 by Limantour to act as his agent. A slippery fellow, Jouan apparently felt that he could make more by working against the erstwhile French Navy captain than with him, and it was he who leaked out hints that Limantour's claim was a fraud. To shut him up, Limantour gave him a note for $20,000, payable in Mexico, but then in a superb double cross, preferred charges against him so that he was arrested in Mexico. A letter of Jouan's to Victor Prudon was found which proved of interest. It read in part: "Try to humbug Wilson and Chittenden, Dillon & Co., telling them that to do good business the documents are very precious." Johnson, *José Yves Limantour v. The United States*, 37–38.

[53] N. A. 177-1-342.

Attorney Inge. "There is no doubt that he could defeat the fraud," said Browne.[54]

Browne's worries were largely unnecessary. He did not know it, but the proper means were being taken to fight the case to the death. The case was in capable hands, and on November 19, 1858, Judge Ogden Hoffman gave his decision in District Court, concluding with:

> Whether we consider the enormous extent or the extraordinary character of the alleged concessions to Limantour; the official positions and the distinguished antecedents of the principal witnesses who have testified in support of them, or the conclusive and unanswerable proofs by which their falsehood has been exposed; whether we consider the unscrupulous and pertinacious obstinacy with which the claims now before the Court have been persisted in—although six others presented to the Board have long since been abandoned—or the large sums extorted from the property owners in this city as the price of the relinquishment of these fraudulent pretensions; or, finally, the conclusive and irresistible proofs by which the perjuries by which they have been attempted to be maintained have been exposed, and their true character demonstrated—it may safely be affirmed that these cases are without parallel in the judicial history of this country....
>
> It is no slight satisfaction to feel that the evidence has been such as to leave nothing to inference, suspicion, or conjecture, but that the proofs of fraud are as conclusive and irresistible as the attempted fraud itself has been flagrant and audacious.[55]

[54] *Ibid.*
[55] Johnson, *José Yves Limantour v. The United States*, 1.

CHAPTER NINE

Back in the Saddle Again

ONCE MORE, in April, 1856, J. Ross Browne turned his attention to cattle. To recheck on the overland trade from Mexico to California, he set out to see if the duties collected could pay the expenses of collection. (He was almost certain before he left that this could not be the case.) Collector Milton S. Latham, at Browne's request, detailed two reliable inspectors from the San Francisco Customs House to accompany him. Browne paid them out of his allowance and hired a guide, at $50 plus expenses, out of his own pocket. Burning to see new country, as ever, Browne hurried ahead with his expedition on April 20 after reminding Guthrie that he would carry it out at no additional expense to the government over the normal situation.

His route of march lay through the Santa Clara Valley, which he called the San José Valley, south of San Francisco, thence via the west side of it through Castro Valley and Amador Valley to the great San Joaquin Valley by means of Livermore Pass over the Diablo Range. He crossed the San Joaquin River to Stockton, continued further up the Central Valley for twenty-six miles on the west side and then for two hundred miles on the east side, passing Tulare Lake, the Kings River, Four Creeks, and Visalia. His route then lay along the foothills of the

Sierra Nevada as far as Fort Miller,[1] then back across the San Joaquin Valley again and over Pacheco Pass[2] in the Diablo Range to San Juan Bautista, Santa Clara, and San Francisco. Browne was twenty-nine days in the field. He covered at least six hundred miles of country and visited all of the cattle ranges of the San Joaquin Valley.

Browne's journey was an eventful one. As he wrote Guthrie, "At Visalia we found that a war[3] had broken out between the whites and the Southern Indians, extending from the Four Creeks [the present area of Woodsville] to the Tejon. Great alarm existed throughout the Valley and it was found necessary to send out troops from Fort Miller and Fort Tejon. All trade was at an end for the present." Browne became frankly alarmist; he added: "The probability is that the war will be general from Puget's Sound to San Diego." (This was one time when Browne was quite wrong: it did not spread; it was all over in six weeks.) "Fifteen Valley Indians were killed within a few miles of our camp and the white families have sought refuge in a mill at Visalia whilst the men are preparing for a vigorous defense. It is impossible to predict what the result will be, but I fear from the lawless character of the white settlers and their determination to have a war and exterminate the Indians that

[1] The Indian uprising in the Sierra foothills in 1851 which brought about Jim Savage's countermeasures and the Mariposa War led to the establishment of Fort Miller, first called Camp Barbour. It was the sole army bastion guarding the San Joaquin Valley and foothills until Fort Tejon was set up in August, 1854. Fort Miller was the post to which Captain Harry Love of the California Rangers brought the head of arch-outlaw Joaquin Murieta for Surgeon William F. Edgar to pickle in a barrel of whisky. The town which grew up around it, Millerton (nee Rootville), became the seat of Fresno County when it was created in 1856, the year the army post was abandoned and the year Browne visited it. The fort was re-established during the Civil War, then reabandoned. The area is now covered by Friant Dam's Lake Millerton, but one of the old structures was moved to Fresno where it may still be seen in Roeding Park.

[2] Pacheco Pass has been a trans–Coast Range route since ancient Indian times. In 1856 and 1857, about the time Browne used the pass, A. D. Firebaugh was improving it for a toll road. In 1858 the Butterfield Overland Mail stages took it, and, slightly relocated, it is a major automobile link between the Salinas and San Joaquin valleys.

[3] The Tule River Indian War of 1856 broke out after Indians stole some horses on the stream. Hotheaded settlers made up a punitive expedition under Nathan Dillon and others. After a few skirmishes, regulars from Fort Miller reinforced the local minutemen and defeated the Indians at Battle Mountain. Kings River Indian Subagent William Campbell brought them to terms a short time later.

there will be much trouble and that the prosperity of the Indian reservations will be greatly impeded."[4]

As for the cattle trade, Browne once again verified his belief that all stock was entering the state via Fort Yuma. It was being bought in small lots after entry, but before the longhorns reached Los Angeles. It was thus quite impossible to determine either the identity of the original owners or whether duty had been paid on the stock or not. Said Browne: "I do not think it will ever be possible in a country like this, where the frontier is remote and thinly settled, and where all are interested alike in defrauding the revenue[!], to collect a considerable amount of duties from this source, and I am still of the opinion that if stock were made free it would be better than any system of inspection that could be devised."[5]

Returning to San Francisco, Browne almost at once turned up more cases of politicking and outright thievery. He discovered that E. D. Hammond, a clerk in the Assistant Treasurer's office, had embezzled a neat $4,244.21 in his spare time—of which he had plenty.[6] Meanwhile, attempts were being made to remove the Chief Coiner of the Mint from his job by R. W. Slocumb, who was after the position. The Coiner, John Echfeldt, not only swore before a notary that he had always been a good Democrat and never a Know-Nothing as accused, but he even sent the affidavit to J. Ross Browne to bolster his reputation.[7]

Next, Browne took on a bit of General Land Office business in the interior. He reported on it to Washington in September. His digging uncovered improper expenditures in Marysville by Register Charles S. Fairfax and Receiver John A. Paxton of the United States Land Office there. These were prominent men; Fairfax was a descendant of Lord Fairfax and, within a year, he would be clerk of the state Supreme Court. In 1854 he had served as speaker of the Assembly. Late in his career he would be chairman of the California delegation to the Democratic National Convention (1868) in New York. But he did not awe Browne, nor did Paxton. The latter was a Virginian who would later be eulogized for his luck in business:

[4] N. A. 177-1-345.
[6] N. A. 177-1-349.

[5] *Ibid.*
[7] N. A. 177-1-354a.

Like many an early pioneer, he owes his financial success to the adjust-
ment of affairs which rewards prudence, energy and sagacity. . . . Mr.
Paxton's versatility of talent, together with his practical business knowledge, enabled him to engage in many different enterprises in his chosen
locality. His business operations . . . were attended, in a remarkable degree,
with uniform success . . . [thanks to his] persistent endeavor to pursue
an honest and blameless career in all his business relations with his
fellow-men.[8]

Browne felt that Paxton's success was a little too remarkable; perhaps
he had adjusted the government's affairs as well as his own. Democrats
of the Sacramento Valley, among them a prominent citizen named
Charles Lindley, were after Paxton's scalp. They wanted him removed.
But to Browne's disgust, if not his surprise, it was not because of swindling. The hatchet men were out to "get" Paxton solely for failing to
contribute anything to promote the success of the Democratic party
after his appointment. According to these men, Paxton had devoted
himself to speculations, peculations, and financial intrigues to the detriment of pork-barreling, political intrigues, and the spoils system. Paxton,
who was treasurer of Yuba County, had an associate or partner in his
machinations, Mark Brumorgen. The latter was city treasurer of Marysville. The two had a marvelous arrangement, Browne discovered. While
Paxton speculated in city scrip, his banker pal traded off by handling
the former's county scrip. Browne was reluctant to bring charges against
the well-liked Fairfax. He was popular in both the political and personal
sense. In any case, the agent doubted that Fairfax was a party to deliberate
fraud and guessed that his entanglement with Paxton and Brumorgen
was the result of his being careless and intemperate.[9]

The Mint still plagued Browne, too. In September and October he was
kept busy by the scandal-wracked institution. It was forced to close to
depositors when it ran out of acid again. Once more an expected shipment of nitrate of soda, used in making the acid, failed to arrive by ship
from Valparaíso. The ship, 140 days out, was long overdue on the
Embarcadero and feared lost.[10] After the Mint had suspended operations

---

[8] Phelps, *Contemporary Biography of California's Representative Men*, II, 358–60.

[9] N. A. 177-1-369.   [10] N. A. 177-1-372.

for five weeks, Browne learned to his dismay that there was a Chilean brig, the *Jenny Lind*, loafing off the heads, loaded with nitrate. It had been doing so for five days before one of Browne's contacts leaked the information to him. Private parties were interested in delaying her arrival, wishing, for business reasons, to keep the Mint's operations suspended as long as possible. It was a thoroughly disgusted and exasperated Browne who hurriedly hired a steam tug to bring in the *Jenny Lind*.[11]

Browne had the misfortune to be plunked down in San Francisco in the midst of one of its periodic crime and graft waves, the one which culminated in the formation of the Second Committee of Vigilance, in 1856. The second time of crisis followed hard on the heels of the first one, of 1849–51, when criminals—the "Hounds" and others—grew so powerful that they all but took over the city and necessitated the formation of such units as the First California Guard, a city militia unit, and the First Vigilance Committee of 1851. A prominent member of the First California Guard was Edward H. Harrison, James Collier's predecessor as collector of the port of San Francisco. (Collier is usually thought of as the first collector, but Governor Mason appointed Edward Gilbert in 1849. He declined the post, and Harrison accepted when it was offered to him. It proved to be a lucrative position, and it was said that he was a near millionaire in a few months.)

The crisis of 1856 was detonated by James King of Williams' muckraking editorials in the *Bulletin*. When he reminded the public that James P. Casey was not only a ballot-box stuffer but also an alumnus of Sing Sing, that gentleman shot him down. Casey soon "swung" for his deed at the hands of the new Vigilance Commitee. Josiah Royce, who called the Vigilantes' actions of '56 "the Business Man's Revolution," described King of William well when he wrote: "His courage was of a quality touching desperation. . . . He acted like a man with nothing to lose . . . [when] he determined to break up the iniquitous nest of political pimps and murderous demagogues which infested the place."[12]

There was much more to the Vigilante troubles than met the eye. It

---

11 N. A. 177-1-376.

12 Richard H. Dillon, "Rejoice Ye Thieves and Harlots," *California Historical Society Quarterly*, Vol. XXXVII, No. 2 (June, 1958), 142.

was not, alas, a simple case of "good guys" versus "bad guys." There was a great deal of politics involved in the strife. The contemporary minority view was that Vigilantism contained a lot of Know-Nothingism and anti–Democratic party feeling. This view has not yet been fully explored. Ned McGowan, one of the politicians who had to flee town in fear of being lynched after being accused of complicity in the murder of King of William, differed wtih Josiah Royce in evaluating the martyr-editor: "Day after day this self-created censor fulminated his abuse indiscriminately on the innocent and the guilty, making shuttlecocks of the reputations of some of the best and most enterprising men in the state till, emboldened by impunity, his apparent zeal in the cause of reformation ran into the wildest fanaticism."[13]

Browne was not as anti–Vigilance Committee as the fleeing McGowan, of course, but as a good Democrat—a "charter member" of the party in California, being elected one of four secretaries chosen at the first meeting of the political sect on October 25, 1849[14]—he was glad to see the Vigilance movement dwindling by September 20, 1856. On that day he wrote to Secretary Guthrie: "The Vigilance Committee question is all quiet now and if reckless and foolish people will only try as hard to avoid bloodshed as they do to bring it about, there will be no further difficulty."[15]

He also had a pithy comment on the darling of the Republicans, John C. Frémont. Of the erstwhile "Pathfinder" and prominent leader of the Black Republicans, he wrote: "Fremont is very unpopular in this state personally, but the Republican forces are strong and the battle will be hard."[16]

Once again in his October letters Browne revealed the wear and tear on his constitution, the erosion of his health, which his heavy duties as confidential agent entailed. He still stuck to his original interpretation of his duties—"To examine into every branch of public business connected with the collection of the revenue and the disbursement of the public

[13] *Ibid.*

[14] Frank Soulé, John M. Gibson, and James Nisbet, *Annals of San Francisco* (New York, Appleton and Company, 1855), 142.

[15] N. A. 177–1–374.

[16] *Ibid.*

moneys"—but when Guthrie suggested opportunities for further government work after completing his current tour of duty, Browne's answer was not enthusiastic. He wrote:

> In reference to your last suggestion as to a change in position. I am free to confess my hopes have been growing rather shadowy for some time past. Hard labor, constant wear and tear of mind, the ceaseless struggle against my fellow man, have almost worn me out at last, and if it were not for my family I would sell out my lease of life for a small consideration. For three years past I have been working uphill, to attain one single object— the means to visit foreign countries. Defeat has attended my every effort, with all its depressing effects. I am now no better able to travel than when I started. . . . Yet, firmly believing that no man who is true to himself *can* fail in his object, I have never despaired of final success.[17]

The one job which appealed to Browne in his funk was an appointment as a roving agent. This globe-trotting position would automatically provide him with the travel for which he ached. It would be a job similar to his San Francisco post but one charged with the visiting and inspecting of all American consuls and consulates in the Pacific, the Orient, and, indeed, throughout the world.[18] But, of course, such an ideal post for Browne never came to pass.

Special Agent Browne was grudgingly forced to change his mind on Agoston Haraszthy, the brilliant Magyar of the Mint, at this time. His agonizing reappraisal resulted in a recommendation of October 2, 1856, that the Hungarian be fired. He explained to Guthrie:

> He is a very efficient officer, but of late has been engaged a great deal in his private affairs. When he came here it was supposed that he was very poor. It is now generally believed that he is worth some thirty or forty thousand dollars, owns a large ranch, etc. From these and other reports which have reached me, as well as from his attempt to obtain the Mint sweeps [i.e, sweepings],[19] I consider him an unsafe man and would

[17] N. A. 177–1–378.

[18] *Ibid.*

[19] An investigation by Browne turned up gold dust not only in the Mint's sweepings but on its roof, on near-by roofs, and in the chimney. This explained some of the Mint's losses. N. A. 177–1–380–382.

recommend his removal. Having my confidence in public officers so often shaken of late, I scarcely know what to do about suggesting the name of a suitable person to fill his job.[20]

Although Browne abhorred politicking, he was occasionally forced by circumstances to engage in party politics himself. In October he did so in retrieving the commission of Conrad Wiegand, assayer of the Mint. Wiegand had insisted on publishing anti-administration essays over a pseudonym (W. Carroll) in what Browne described as a Black Republican newspaper. Wiegand then loudly defended the Vigilance Committee in a public lecture, even though the Agent had briefed him on the views of the Secretary of the Treasury and the President of the United States— that no government employees were to engage in any connection with, or co-operation with, the extra-legal Committee of Vigilance. This lecture was, to Browne, an open defiance of the government and sufficient cause for the dismissal of Wiegand.[21]

By mid-December, Browne was reporting that the outbound steamers were crowded with loyal Democrats heading for Washington and a helping of the spoils. This was the case even though Browne personally refused all requests for leaves of absence by political hacks and would-be office seekers who were in government employ in San Francisco. He told them that deserting their posts to rush east to an El Dorado of spoils meant that they were immediately stamping themselves as unfit for any government office. Browne was not critical of higher-ups who avidly sought office. This was part of the game of politics. He had a good word for Latham at this time, and he predicted a fierce struggle among Gwin, Broderick, and the Collector for the Senate vacancies.[22]

On December 4, Browne asked Guthrie to get in touch with the Commissioner of Indian Affairs, who had offered him a job in his department. The Treasury Agent was inclined to accept in order to carry out the task, which intrigued him, of investigating Indian affairs in Oregon and Washington. (He eventually took the job.) But first he wanted the Commissioner to know that he could not possibly accomplish it in the

[20] N. A. 177–1–378.
[21] N. A. 177–1–380.
[22] N. A. 177–1–388.

time prescribed by someone in Washington, D.C., who did not realize how slow travel was in the wilderness of the Northwest Corner. He ended his note: "The duty is one that I am really desirous to perform, but it should be done faithfully and thoroughly, or not at all."[23]

By the summer of 1857, Browne was reporting to a new chief, for Howell Cobb[24] had succeeded James Guthrie as Secretary of the Treasury. On May 4, 1857, Browne informed Cobb that he was investigating a smuggling case on the southern California coast. He had been alerted to it by the Vice-Consul in Mazatlán, Mexico. The latter accused the French bark *Phoque* of evading customs. Captain James Alden of the Coast Survey spoke the bark off Santa Barbara and had his officers board her. But they found nothing suspicious, reporting her to be a whaler, although she was more likely a sealer since her name, *phoque*, meant "seal" in French. The boarding officers were told by her master that she had put into Santa Barbara for fresh meat and vegetables. A little later, when Alden passed out of the Santa Barbara Channel, he spied a school of whales. He relayed word to the captain of the *Phoque* but he, to Alden's surprise, made no effort to capture them. This most decided lack of interest in a sea hunt led Alden and the Vice-Consul to suggest that the *Phoque* was a smuggler. The latter alerted Browne. Cobb's agent was inclined to discount the possibility of the Frenchman's being a contrabandist. He thought that the vessel was probably engaged in the taking of seals and sea lions along the coast for their oil. But he ventured no reason for the Frenchman's unwillingness to go after bigger game and oil in more quantity in the school of cetaceans. Browne explained his reluctance to accept the smuggling idea:

> I have visited every portion of the Southern California coast and think it scarcely possible that the vessel could have been engaged in smuggling. There are but few places where she could have landed a cargo of liquors.

[23] N. A. 177-1-394.

[24] Cobb was a former Congressman from Georgia who was instrumental in securing the nomination and election of James Buchanan, his close personal friend. Buchanan repaid him by making him Secretary of the Treasury in 1857. Cool toward slavery, and a Southern Unionist, Cobb, nevertheless, aligned with the seceding states, was considered a possibility for the Presidency of the Confederacy, served as a general in the Confederate Army, and was a relentless foe of postwar Reconstruction. *Dictionary of American Biography*, II, 241–43.

At San Luis Obispo, Santa Barbara, San Buenaventura, San Pedro and San Diego there are revenue officers within immediate reach and no case of smuggling could occur without their connivance. The entire coast is abrupt and rockbound, with these exceptions, and it would be almost impossible to land with boats or otherwise at other points except in the calmest weather, and even then with great difficulty. Besides, the back country for some distance from the coast is composed almost wholly of sterile mountains, inhabited only by a few Spaniards and Indians. . . . If there is any smuggling done on this coast, it is at San Francisco where there are inducements and not in sparsely inhabited and impoverished districts where there is neither means to purchase nor inhabitants to consume luxuries that would be worth importing from Bordeaux. On my next visit south, I will make special inquiry into this case.[25]

Once again in the summer of 1857, for perhaps the last time, Haraszthy and the Mint returned to haunt Browne. The latter reported to Cobb on a large deficit in the returns of the Hungarian Melter and Refiner—$135,000, to be exact. The latter's explanation was that much gold was passing up the chimney in the updraft. Browne had already found this to be true, by personal investigation. But he was not ready to believe that $135,000 had taken that route out of the building, even though a zinc flue belatedly installed by Haraszthy in the chimney did trap eight hundred ounces of gold. Browne gave the Magyar his choice. He could either submit to arrest on charges of embezzlement or surrender all his property, including deeds, mortgages, his famous twenty thousand grapevines, and so forth. This property would be placed in trust subject to execution by the government upon a court judgment against him. Haraszthy's attorney advised him to submit to arrest, but he declined and the Melter-Refiner accepted Browne's alternative course. He turned over to the hard-boiled Special Agent property which, in his estimate, was worth $215,000 and which, in Browne's view, was of $150,000 value.[26]

In the last extant document of the Confidential Treasury Agent's file, J. Ross Browne reported to Cobb:

It would be unjust in the present stages of the investigation to hazard an opinion of his [Haraszthy's] guilt. The deficit may have occurred from

25 N. A. 177–1–400.   26 N. A. 177–1–406.

natural causes or from malfeasance on the part of his subordinates. . . . In conclusion [however], I trust the Department will bear in mind that I recommended the removal of Mr. Haraszthy a year ago or more . . . on grounds of suspicion as to his integrity based on facts communicated, and expressed apprehension that the escape of gold through the chimney, which was a fact demonstrated to some extent, would be made use of as an excuse for indefinite loss.[27]

Shortly after this time, Browne found himself to be, increasingly, a political *persona non grata*. He was much more of an honest man than he was a party man; he stepped on too many loyal Democratic toes along with those of other political coloration. When he continued the kind of reporting he had done for the Treasury Department in his new assignment, the Indian problem in Washington and Oregon, he was committing political hara-kiri. But the hardheaded muckraker continued to expose the chicanery and swindling which went on beneath the surface on the West's westernmost frontier. He could be fired, but he could not be intimidated and he could not be bought.

[27] *Ibid.*

CHAPTER TEN

The Coast Rangers

THE LAST DOCUMENT of J. Ross Browne's tour of inspection for the Treasury Department is dated June 5, 1857. Less than a month later he was on the Redwood Coast of California's Mendocino County, far from the cares of office and enjoying himself hugely as a member of an organization called the Coast Rangers. San Francisco has always been famous for elite clubs formed by blithe spirits, clubs whose exclusiveness is in reverse ratio to their formality. The Bohemian Club, E Clampus Vitus, and the Roxburghe Club spring to mind.

Colonel Jack Hays, whom Browne had met when Hays was United States surveyor general in 1854, began the organization, unwittingly, in 1852 when he and James Tobin decided to take an outing in the wild Coast Range mountains near Clear Lake. Colonel Hays enjoyed the hunting and fishing and respite from office work so completely that he determined to repeat the treatment ever summer thereafter. He and a friend, John A. Freaner, dubbed the informal group the Mendocino and Clear Lake Hunting Club.

After their joint excursion in the Central Valley in 1854, J. Ross Browne and Jack Hays became fast friends. The following summer Browne was not only welcomed to membership but was voted the hunting club's official historian, by acclaim. His first act in office was to junk the club's cumbersome handle and rename the group the Coast Rangers.

In July, 1857, Browne was tired and apprehensive of his future. He had inklings galore that his honest and critical reports from the West had made him politically expendable in Washington. The trip which Hays was making that summer was just what the doctor ordered. The Texan and his fifteen or so cronies took a small steamboat across San Francisco Bay and San Pablo Bay, up Petaluma Creek past Midshipman Point, Black Point, and Lakeville to the town of Petaluma. At this agricultural center they switched to mules and horses and rode northward through the Santa Rosa, Russian River, Ukiah, Matomka, Little Lake, and Sherwood valleys until they reached the wilderness area of the Noyo River. The party descended this still-picturesque stream to the sea at Fort Bragg. The Coast Rangers continued their leisurely ride along the rugged coast, often riding on the very beach itself, dodging their mounts in and out of the pounding surf. Sometimes they scattered naked Digger Indian men and women with crude, cornucopia-shaped traps in the waves, taking surf fish. Descending Strawberry Valley to the small but deep and fordless Ten Mile River, the amateur outdoorsmen, like Browne, found themselves floundering in a dangerous, tide-deepened stream mouth. They finally found some Indians whom they could hire to ferry them across the river, bringing their roped horses across in tow. Jack Hays was a real frontiersman, however, who was not going to pay a redskin to get him across a California creek. He left his companions and rode upstream a mere hundred yards until he found a place where the current was slowed by the terrain to allow banks less steep than at the mouth. He stripped, tied his clothes in a bundle, which he held high over his head with his rifle, and eased his horse into the river. He crossed without incident. When the wet and dejected Rangers straggled into the new camp Hays had selected for them, they found the former Texas Ranger awaiting them with the butchered carcass of a fine buck he had killed to pass the time of waiting.

Browne, as historiographer of the Coast Rangers, lampooned his companions unmercifully. His fellow Rangers included such men as General John E. Addison, commander of the San Francisco militia, and Judge

Ogden Hoffman, his erstwhile antagonist in the coolie ship controversy but now his friend. But there was one exception. He admired and respected Colonel Jack Hays too much to joke about him. One did not poke fun at a man one idolized. Browne noted:

> It is refreshing to find a man in the full enjoyment of a national reputation who can afford to be perfectly natural and unsophisticated; a genuine hero, modest to the verge of bashfulness, yet brave and steadfast as a true gentleman and a hero should be.[1]

Of Hays, whom he termed "the noblest Roman of them all," J. Ross Browne wrote:

> What can I say of him in the brief space of a few pages that will convey an adequate idea of his remarkable history and character? I would tell you of the beautiful prairies of Texas and the blue seas of clover between the Nueces and the Rio Grande; of the mottes of woody islands that loom up in the distance; of the wild spring flowers and the balmy and odorous atmosphere that never was equalled in any other country; of the wild mustangs that prance along the horizon, occasionally charging up toward you and sweeping off again till they are lost to the eye; of the deer and the antelope that course over these broad seas of flowers, and the flocks of wild turkeys that range along the watercourses—all these I would endeavor to picture to your mind so that you might understand the fascination of frontier life in Texas. I would then tell you of the Mexican invasions and the fierce and bloody contest of the Texans in defense of their country; of the struggles of the settlers with the wild hordes of savage Comanches and Lipans who roamed over these beautiful prairies; of the white women that were carried into captivity and cruelly treated; of the children that were snatched from the doorsteps of cabins and never heard of again; or only after the lapse of years; of the midnight massacres that struck a gloom in the minds of men; and all the horrors of Indian warfare.
>
> And then, in the midst of these scenes of suffering and distress, how a young stranger of gentle manners but firm and determined aspect came among the people with his rifle and powder flask and joined in their defense. I would follow that youth, for there is a fascination in his presence and point him out to you as he stands with unblenched features and eagle

---

[1] J. Ross Browne, *The Coast Rangers* (Balboa Island, Calif., Paisano Press, 1959), 30.

eye in the midst of dangers; often separated from his comrades for days, and compelled to fight his way alone through bands of savage Comanches; always foremost wherever death seemed inevitable, yet of a happy and cheerful disposition, placing a fair estimate upon the value of life and determined to make the most of it. I would tell of the strong and daring spirits that instinctively gathered around him; how he was chosen leader of a company whose career on the borders of Texas for many years has rarely been paralleled in the annals of frontier life for deeds of chivalrous and romantic daring. In a country where such qualities are by no means rare, it is wonderful how devotedly these men clung to their leader, and what a pride they felt in his growing fame, for soon his exploits were the theme of every tongue and the whole country echoed with his praises. Amidst all, from first to last, he was brave, gentle and true; devoted to his friends; everywhere beloved, yet shrinking from all demonstrations of applause with a timidity almost feminine; seeking no reward save to render some service to his country. Since that period he has occupied several high posts of honor and trust. . . .

As he sits yonder by the fire, cooking a rabbit, you would never take him for a hero. He is the very plainnest and most unsophisticated of mortals— is actually unconscious of the difference between a great man and a common man, treats us with equal simplicity and kindness, and likes the whole world so well that he is constantly trying to do somebody a service. I have no doubt you and I will enjoy the benefit of that rabbit. He would give you an entire ox if he had one cooked and then seem mortified that it was not an elephant or a whale. . . .

There is such an overflow of genial simplicity about him, such an unconscious power of winning our sympathies and respect, such an entire absence of egotism, and so much that is true, generous and reliable in his whole nature and character that you are completely charmed.[2]

Browne can be forgiven for his eulogistic enthusiasm and his pride in possessing the friendship of Colonel Jack Hays. After three years of dealing with grafters, con men, and loafers, Hays, in Browne's eyes, loomed like a giant among pygmies. A slight case of hero worship was only one of the many after-effects of his Treasury Department tour of duty in the Far West.

[2] *Ibid.*, 29–30.

But Browne had no qualms about teasing Hays's cronies. Jim Tobin, though cofounder of the hunting club with the Colonel, was still, in 1857, a most inept woodsman. Browne delighted in detailing his misadventures, all in good humor. Tobin, whom J. Ross Browne called "Captain Toby," was "a wild Irishman by birth and an Indian by instinct. . . . His home is in the saddle, his bedroom under the trees," said Browne.

I say the Captain is eminently qualified by nature to be a guide. In making that assertion I do not mean to intimate that he was ever known to find the right trail or to avoid losing himself and the entire party committed to his charge before the expiration of each day's travel. The special quality in which he excels is in the art of persuading everybody that he is familiar with every stick and stone of the route. . . . In fact, that he was the original discoverer of the particular range in question. . . . The predominating talent of the Captain is his wonderful capacity for finding bad trails. If there is an impracticable mountain within ten miles of the direct route, or a cañon out of which no white man was ever before known to make his exit on muleback, Toby is sure to find it. . . . To oblige a tired man he will make a mole hill out of the most formidable mountain, and assert in the most positive manner that it is only three miles to the camping ground when it is at least ten. If the day's travel happens to be unusually rough, he calls the trail "a little gulchy," but promises that it will be "all easy work tomorrow." For those who give out, and protest they cannot go an inch farther, he carries a large pewter flask which usually hangs from his saddle. What it is I am entirely unable to say, but it always has the desired effect. He calls it "nourishment" and says it is "good for man or beast."[3]

One of the most delightful campsites of the Coast Rangers was Bear Harbor, a ghost town almost on the Mendocino-Humboldt County line, today inhabited by two people. After Browne's visit it became a doghole port for lumber schooners, acquired a railroad, a pier, and a scattering of buildings as well as a satellite town, Needle Rock (now also "ghastly") to the north. Bear Harbor suggested lonely Gardiner, the farcical "port" he had investigated on the Oregon Coast three years earlier. In any case,

[3] *Ibid.*, 27–28.

Browne used Bear Harbor as a port of entry for a mythical customs collection district in an article on the Coast Rangers which appeared in *Harper's New Monthly Magazine,* in order to lash the customs service with a bit of barbed satire.

He wrote:

I was lying on my back, at a little distance from the fire, looking up at the stars. The discussion between Phil Wilkins and the Judge fell pleasantly on my ear but my thoughts were on the great future of Bear Harbor. What might be made of such a place in ten years—nay, in five! Here we were, a small party, surrounded by a wilderness of mountains, rocks and roaring breakers, with nothing but our mother earth to sleep on and the broad heavens for our canopy. It was easy and natural to picture the change that time might produce when it would be a populous and thriving community, with public buildings, offices, hotels, warehouses, and all accompaniments of civilization.

Taking into view the remarkable progress of California, it certainly is not anticipating too much to look forward to the day when Bear Harbor will be a great emporium of commerce and industry. At present, it is true, there is no way of reaching this favored locality except over Captain Toby's trails, which, as I have already stated, must have been originally intended for wild goats. Yet I do not regard that as an insuperable obstacle. Wherever goats can travel, so can public funds. The only difference is that the latter are a good deal harder to catch after they once get loose from the Treasury. All that is needed is an appropriation from Congress.

Access to Bear Harbor by means of water would be easy enough if there was any harbor there. Vessels might then anchor when they arrived. Unfortunately, it is an open roadstead filled with rocks and presenting altogether a most frightful aspect in bad weather. It derives its name not so much from its natural commercial facilities as from the number of bears that come down the various cañons at night in search of mussels and dead fish. Still, this cannot be regarded as any serious objection to Federal enterprise. Have we not breakwaters in many places on our Atlantic coast where nature never intended commerce to exist and where, accordingly, none does and can never exist? If not there, we certainly have a sufficient number of precedents in the line of internal improvements.

But if Bear Harbor is eligibly located for any purpose in the world it is for a port of entry and customs house, and I had in imagination drawn a complete picture of this national establishment, with collector and deputy collectors, surveyors, clerks and inspectors, all busily engaged in the duties of their office when I was startled by the cry—"A grizzly in camp! Run for your lives!"[4]

Browne's fireside musings were unhappily interrupted by the un-invited visitor to camp, *Ursus horribilis*, but he was able to continue them at a later date and incorporated them in the format of a fictitious letter to the Secretary of the Treasury in his collection of essays and adventures titled *Crusoe's Island*:

If Bear Harbor is eligible for any purpose in the world it is for a port of entry and a customs house. Not that there are any inhabitants there at present, or in the vicinity, except Indians, bears, elk, deer and wildcats; not that any vessels ever come in there, or ever will, perhaps, but as a guard against smuggling. You know, sir, from the experience of collectors from Passamaquoddy Bay to Point Isabel, and from San Diego to the Straits of Fuca, that smuggling must be going on somewhere, else why is the Treasury Department flooded with applications for an increase of in-spectors? Even senators and members of Congress unite in the opinion that a great deal of smuggling is perpetrated on remote and isolated parts of our coast, for they are always recommending some friend in whom they have confidence to keep a guard upon the revenue at such places. One would think that smugglers would rather pay duties and take their wares into a good market than put them ashore where there are no inhabitants and transport them at double the risk and cost to some place where they are wanted. If they must enjoy the pleasure of violating the law at all, would it not pay better to smuggle their wares directly into the principal cities as New York or San Francisco, for example? I know that in the former place they incur some risk of detection from night inspectors who are supposed to be always on the lookout about the wharves after dark; but in San Francisco the night inspectors have been abolished on account of the soporific effects of the climate. Several of them fell asleep directly after receiving their appointments and never woke up, except on pay day, during the entire term of their service.

4 *Ibid.*, 60–62.

For some years, at least, one collector of customs could perform all the duties that might be required of him at Bear Harbor. No doubt the dullest and laziest politician in the entire state could be hired to occupy the position at three thousand dollars per annum. The collector at the city of Gardiner, which consists of two small frame shanties and a pigpen, situated at the mouth of the Umpqua River—where shipwreck is almost certain in case a vessel attempts to enter—receives only a thousand dollars per annum. Sir, it cannot be expected that a gentleman more than ordinarily gifted with valuable traits of character can be obtained for so small a sum. Government is compelled to pay for the services of active and intelligent collectors at the ports of Benicia, Sacramento, Stockton, Monterey, San Pedro and San Diego, three thousand dollars a year, each. If they were at all conspicuous for idleness, it is impossible to conjecture what it would cost to obtain their services; but the amount of labor performed by these gentlemen (who, by the way, are excellent persons and for whom I entertain a great personal respect) is almost incredible. At Benicia the duties of the office are absolutely onerous. From one to two vessels a year enter that port with coals from Cardiff, which are deposited at the depot of the Pacific [Mail] Steamship Company. Upon these coals the duties have to be computed and accounts rendered to the Department, besides which he is compelled to keep an accurate account of his own salary. For all this he is allowed only the occasional services of one inspector, whereas he ought to be allowed three. If they were gentlemen of a lively temperament they would, at least, give something of vitality to the present deserted appearance of the port. I have known a smaller number than that to produce a considerable sensation in the public streets of other cities. A great deal of trouble to the Benicia Collector might be saved if the two Cardiff vessels per annum were permitted to enter at San Francisco on their way up.

At Sacramento, the duties of the Collector are still more arduous. Indeed, it is a matter of surprise that any man can be found to undertake them at three thousand dollars a year. A vessel with foreign goods entered this port in 1849, since which some six or eight consecutive collectors have been anxiously awaiting the arrival of another. The most remarkable part of it is that the other vessel has never yet arrived. Upon a review of the facts, I think that any person of a less sanguine temperament than a collector of customs would have long since given up the hope of obtaining any public revenue from this source. Somehow, all the vessels have a habit of stopping at San Francisco, paying their duties there, discharging their cargoes for interior transportation and going about their business, which must be a constant subject of mortification to the Sacramento collectors. I have known respectable gentlemen who occupied this position to be denied over twenty-five dollars a month for office rent, after it had ranged for years at two or three hundred—even denied the services of a deputy or clerk, and actually compelled to make out their own pay accounts!

And yet these officers are required to attend at primary meetings, conventions, and legislative assemblages, and keep the party all right, when there may be a complication of difficulties between the various aspirants for the Senate of the United States, utterly impossible to settle except by electing them all.

At Stockton, the case is still harder. I never knew a collector there to have anything at all to do, except to keep the run of his office rent and salary which, in justice, it must be said is a branch of public duty always faithfully performed. Yet this officer is expected to pass the time agreeably year after year on a miserable pittance of three thousand dollars, without even the hope of ever seeing dutiable cargo landed upon the wharves of the city. I do not believe that the most sanguine gentleman that ever held that position aspired to anything of greater commercial value than a flock of sheep supposed to be on the way from Mexico, and for the capture and confiscation of which two inspectors were for many years stationed at the Tejon Pass, about three hundred miles from Stockton. But even the hope of seizing these sheep or their descendants has been blasted since Congress abolished the duties on stock; and now the Collector, to protect the revenue, must fail unless he succeeds in getting hold of a box of contraband articles that it is supposed certain parties in San Francisco are awaiting an opportunity to send up, either by the steam navigation line or some of the small sailing craft that ply on this route. As this box of goods has been expected ever since 1852, the prospect of its appearance and seizure is becoming more favorable every year. If there was a surveyor stationed at the mouth of the San Joaquin—say, in the city called "The New York of the Pacific," —the chances of seizure would be greatly augmented. There is a surveyor of customs at Nisqually, in the Territory of Washington, and another at Santa Barbara, who might render some aid by the transmission of secret information. I do not know what has become of the surveyor at Pacific City, near the mouth of the Columbia. The last time I saw him he was engaged in the performance of his official functions in the tin business at Oregon City, the City of Pacific having been discontinued about two years previous in consequence of a lack of inhabitants.

At Monterey the amount of hardship endured by the Collector is absolutely incredible. Not only is he furnished with an indifferent government house to live in, which costs an annual outlay of several hundred dollars to keep it from falling to pieces, and thereby crushing himself and assistants beneath the ruins, but he is required to look after two inspectors who are appointed to aid him in protecting the coast from the nefarious operations of smugglers. Besides this, it is supposed that a mysterious vessel has been hovering the Bay of Monterey ever since 1852, with an assorted cargo of bar fixtures, boots, bowie knives and revolvers, upon a considerable portion of which duties have never been paid. This vessel is no doubt awaiting an opportunity to land these articles in violation of law and to the great detriment of the Treasury. The Collector is expected to be present or within reach of a telegraphic dispatch whenever she makes her appearance; and it is further expected that he will not flinch from his duty even should she prove to be the Flying Dutchman or the Wizard of the Seas.

At San Pedro the coasting steamer *Senator* touches for grapes and passengers some half a dozen times a month, and the Collector is expected to keep a record of that vessel's arrivals and departures; also the range of Captain Banning's paddle-wheeled steam skiff *Medora*, six scows, and several fishing smacks. In addition to these onerous duties, it devolves upon him to keep his own pay account and see that the light does not stop burning of nights in the public lighthouse on Point Conception, without any money to pay the keeper and assistant except such casual remittances as maybe made once or twice in the course of as many years. I knew one lighthouse keeper who stood by the light manfully for a whole year and finally had to sell his chance of pay for the means of subsistence. Some of the lighthouse keepers, indeed, are supposed to live on whale oil, the Board in Washington being evidently under the impression that oil is a light article of diet, upon which men will not be apt to go to sleep. Another reason, perhaps, for the remissness with which their salaries generally arrive is that their stations are generally not densely populated with voters or, in fact, with anything but sheep and rabbits. I have a person in my eye whom I would like to recommend for the collectorship at San Pedro whenever the present incumbent may think proper to resign. By the way, the latter is a very clever and estimable gentleman, to whom I intend not the slightest disrespect in thus referring to his office; but there are peculiar qualifications for every position in life, and the individual to whom I refer possesses some very remarkable advantages over the generality of custom-house officers; that is to say, he can sleep at his desk in the midst of the direst confusion; is never known to be in a hurry; thinks no more of time than he does of eternity, or anything else; and invariably postpones till tomorrow what most people would deem of vital importance to be done today. His work is generally in arrears, but will be right—[*en*] *poco tiempo*!

At San Diego the same burdensome and oppressive state of things exists. The Customs House is an old military building, with a roof that falls to pieces every winter and a set of doors and windows through which both wind and rain have free access. The only article of public property about the premises that yet sticks together is a tremendous iron safe, in which the revenue is going to be kept—as soon as it is collected. Even this is getting rusty from want of use. The books have an ancient and fishlike aspect; and a public shovel, that is used to clear the mud away from the door when-ever a vessel is seen in the offing, is going away year after year and will eventually be reduced to a broken handle. This office is inaccessible by means of a boat, though in bad weather the deputy prefers to reside in an old hulk that lies at anchor in the bay. The building is eligibly located in a chapparal of prickly pears, without about five miles of Old Town or, properly speaking, the beautiful city of San Diego. Mexican stock were formerly imported into this district but, having been made free by act of Congress, the Collector is left destitute of occupation and is compelled to seek business and society in various parts of the state. Now and then, how-ever, he is supposed to take a look at his pay account and see that the public lighthouse on the Point [Loma] keeps burning of nights, notwithstanding the roof has blown off. As Government refuses to furnish him rain water to drink, he is compelled whenever his official duties call him to the port of entry, to hitch up his buggy and travel five miles to the city of San Diego every time he is thirsty. Indeed, so parsimonious is the Department becom-ing of late that it will not even allow him a deputy or clerk at public ex-pense, although there has been one there for years. I look upon this as a very severe course of discipline to impose upon any gentleman whose services are presumed to be worth three thousand dollars per annum, and would recommend that he should at least be allowed a bottle of whiskey.

All these are examples of the manner in which executive patronage may be enlarged without inconvenience to commerce or obstruction to navigation. If it were not for the collectorships, what would the delegation in Congress have to make up the complement of their indebtedness to partisan politicians? And, if one delegation were denied this privilege, how could accounts be settled with fellow members similarly situated in other states? An inspector of customs at a compensation of five hundred dollars a year (for there is nothing to do), would of course answer the requirements of commerce at any of these ports; but then, what sort of an officer would that be to the owner of one or more members of the Legislature? It would be especially severe at Bear Harbor, where there will be no coffee houses, billiard saloons, or other places of amusement for some time.

In view of these suggestions being urged upon Congress by the heads of the departments, I would mention that, in the temporary absence of Government buildings at Bear Harbor, a number of chapadans, or brush tents, at present occupied by Indians, can be leased for a term of years at a rate not exceeding from five hundred to a thousand dollars each per month. The very best of them can be had for less than the rent paid for the Union Street bonded warehouse in San Francisco, toward the building of which Government loaned seventy-two thousand dollars as an advance of rent and paid, by way of interest on the capital, for four years, two hundred and eighty-eight thousand dollars; after which, upon the united representation of twenty influential merchants, a collector and deputy collector of customs, and a special agent, that the premises were worth only about fourteen thousand per annum, it paid one hundred and ten thousand more to abrogate the contract and as a solemn warning to all private individuals and public officers not to attempt such a speculation as that again. The chapadan of the chief Digger, To-No-Wauka, could be purchased in fee simple for less than twenty-eight thousand dollars which was the exact amount annually expended for the rent of the United States Courtrooms at San Francisco until my friend, Yorick, the Government Agent, reduced it to ten thousand, after which, of course, he was removed.

As an additional protection to the revenue, I would suggest that a revenue cutter be stationed at Bear Harbor, modeled after the fashion of a large washtub, which would be but a slight improvement upon the sailing capacity of the three cutters now stationed on the Pacific coast. The masts might be constructed out of large tin dippers, inverted, in the bowls of which marines could be stationed to keep a lookout for smugglers. Spare blankets would answer for the sails, and a large carving knife run out at the stern would serve admirably to steer by. In order that there might be no danger of missing the way during dark nights from any variation in the compass, it would be well, perhaps, to abandon the compass altogether and send a boat ahead with a light, to point out where the rocks and smugglers might be found. There being no vessels to catch at Bear Harbor, no inconvenience would result from the fact that such a cutter would be as well calculated to lie at anchor as the cutter *Marcy* at San Francisco which has been known to pursue several vessels for infractions of the revenue laws, but never to catch any of them. I attribute this not to any want of zeal on the part of the officers but partly to the superior speed of the runaway vessels, and partly to the fact that the *Marcy* is obliged to lie at anchor for six months in the Bay of San Francisco, for want of other occupation. The remaining six months she necessarily spends in the Straits of Carquinez near Benicia, in order to get rid of the barnacles that accumulate on her bottom during the term of her sedentary career below.

If exception should be taken to this precedent on the ground that a revenue cutter may sometimes really be wanted at a port of entry where there is some commerce, surely none will be taken to the cutter *Lane*, stationed within the mouth of the Columbia River. For the officers of this cutter I entertain the most sincere respect; but if she has ever been known to chase anything larger than wild ducks, the fact must have been hushed up from motives of public policy. It has certainly not been a matter of general comment. About one vessel with dutiable merchandise enters the Columbia in the course of half a dozen years, and certainly all sailing vessels have difficulty enough in getting in, without attempting to run away after they come to anchor. Indeed, I don't know where they would run to unless it might be over the Cascades and through the Dalles to Walla Walla, or up to Oregon City on the Willamette River, where the flour mills of Abernethy & Co. would soon grind them to pieces.

To suppose that they would undertake to run away before they get over the bar is to suppose that they might just as well stay away altogether and thereby avoid the risk of shipwreck in addition to the remote possibility of being captured by a revenue cutter. The officers condemned to this station have my most ardent sympathies. It generally rains at Astoria between two hundred and three hundred days every year, the consequence of which is that the whole country and everything in it has a mildewed appearance. Already I can fancy that barnacles are growing on the beards of these gentlemen; that their skin is becoming slippery and green; their eyes sharkish in expression, from a constant habit of looking out for smugglers that never can be within five hundred miles; that the habit of pulling ashore in boats and back again; "making it so" when four and eight bells are announced; looking up at the masthead and then down again; going below and reading the same old newspaper and coming up again; turning in and taking a nap, and turning out when the nap is ended; exercising their quadrants by an occasional peep at the heavenly bodies; eating three scanty and melancholy meals a day; doing all this and never doing anything else, unless it may be to superintend the patching of an old sail which has rotted to pieces, or the splicing of an old rope to keep the blocks from falling down on their heads, will eventually so wear upon their mental and physical resources as to drive them all mad. Should it ever be the misfortune of any suspicious character to fall into the hands of these gentlemen, I have no doubt he will have reason to regret it during the brief period of his existence; for they will certainly cut him to pieces with their swords, or blow him to fragments out of one of the public guns, on the general principle that, being paid for doing something, they ought to do it as soon as possible.

The revenue cutter at Puget's Sound, familiarly known as the "*Jeff Davis*," finds occasional occupation in chasing porpoises and wild Indians. It is to be regretted that but little revenue has yet been derived from either of these sources; but should she persist in her efforts, there is hope that at no distant day she may overhaul a canoe containing a keg of British brandy —that is to say, in case the paddles are lost and the Indians have no means of propelling it out of the way.

These vessels, in addition to their original cost, which was not cheap, considering their quality and sailing capacity, require an expenditure of some forty or fifty thousand dollars a year for repairs, rigging, pay for officers and men, subsistence, etc., as also for powder to enable the officers to kill ducks and salute distinguished people in these remote regions. Now and then they run on the rocks in trying to find their way from one anchorage to another, in which event they require extra repairs. As this is for the benefit of navigation, it should not be included in the account. They generally avoid running on the same rock and endeavor to find out a new one not laid down upon the charts—unless, perhaps, by some reckless fly—in order that other vessels may enjoy the advantages of additional experience. The beauty of Bear Harbor in this respect is, that a cutter could run on a new rock every day of the year so that, by designating its exact location on the chart, there would be three hundred and sixty-five rocks per annum to be avoided by vessels entering the harbor.

Some military protection would probably be required there for several years to come in order to protect the citizens from the attacks of grizzly bears. I would suggest that a post be established on some eligible point and comfortable quarters erected for the officers and soldiers. While these quarters are in progress of erection, it might be well to station a large rooster in the top of a neighboring tree to give warning of the approach of the enemy. As Rome was saved in one way, so might Bear Harbor be saved in another. Should it become necessary to abandon them, the citizens will no doubt be willing to purchase them at public auction.

I do not know what the military quarters at Fort Miller are going to do, but the last time I saw them they looked very sorry they had ever been built. The same may be said of the quarters at Benicia, Fort Tejon and San Diego, which goes to prove the transitory character of military operations. So long as our army goes about the country dropping down beautiful little cities we in the line of civil life can certainly have no objection. As expense is no object, perhaps, to the War Department, I would suggest that there is a very rugged point of rocks near the entrance of Bear Harbor, upon which a friend of mine has located a claim that he is willing to sell for military purposes for the sum of one hundred and fifty thousand dollars. It commands a fine view of the ocean, and abounds in mussels and albacore; besides which, it is cheaper and uglier than Lime Point at the entrance of the Golden Gate and would not require near so much writing to make the purchase satisfactory to the public.

For a few years, during the infancy of the community, it may be necessary for some enterprising citizen to borrow from Government one hundred thousand dollars at six percent per annum, in consequence of the high rates of interest in California. There will be no difficulty in doing this, I apprehend, if he have influence at court. A precedent may be found in the case of the Folsom estate, against which judgments had been obtained and an execution placed in the hands of the marshal. Private parties found it to their advantage to step in, purchase a portion of the property, pay a portion of the debt, and upon giving satisfactory security, assume the remainder, amounting to a hundred thousand dollars at six percent. It may be a little irregular to favor particular parties in this way, but then, public money had better be bringing in six percent than lying idle in the Treasury; and besides, when it is found necessary to issue Treasury notes in order to carry on the government, they bring a premium, and there is a gain to that extent over the ready cash. If all the public money was loaned out at six percent and all the private money that might be necessary borrowed at five, of course the financial condition of the Treasury would be one percent better per annum.

After these things were done and the business of Bear Harbor placed upon a permanent footing, private instructions might be issued to the Collector of Customs to go out and stump the state in behalf of the great principles of national economy. Experience would enable him to stand firmly upon the broad platform of public integrity and when he addressed the multitude he could dwell, feelingly, on the sublime doctrine of earlier days—"Millions for defense, but not a cent for tribute!"—He could put his hand upon his brow and solemnly declare that, so long as he was gifted with the light of intellect to comprehend the sound doctrines of public policy bequeathed to us by our forefathers, he would stand by the law and the Constitution. He could put his hand upon his heart and call upon the people to witness that he, for one, had ever remained true to his first principles. He could put his hand upon his stomach and avow from the bottom of his soul that he conscientiously indorsed the measures of the prevailing party. He could put his hand upon his pocket and affirm in all sincerity that he went heart and hand with the reigning powers on all the questions of the day.[5]

Browne dropped back into the happy-go-lucky routine of camp after getting some of his satire committed to paper. He joined the others on their last evening in camp in a mighty binge in which all sang and danced to the tune of "Oh, we won't go home until morning!" And the next morning they did start for home—and for new adventures for Washington's Confidential Agent in the West.

[5] *Pages*, 256–69.

CHAPTER ELEVEN

Indian Wars

CALIFORNIA HAD HAD PRIOR EXPERIENCE with secret government agents—starting with Thomas Oliver Larkin, first and only United States consul in Mexican California, who was a confidential agent and spy for Secretary of State James Buchanan before the Mexican War. Even so, California could not swallow such a reformer as J. Ross Browne, who found San Francisco to be as corrupted as Hadleyburg itself. Small wonder then that the unsophisticated areas of Oregon and Washington found him a bitter governmental pill as he poked and pried into the easy money, corruption, greed, double-dealing, opportunism, and expediency which marked public affairs in those territories during their swaddling years. Browne became anathema to the piratical pioneers of the Northwest Coast.

In 1857 he began his survey of the Indian troubles in Washington and Oregon and, incidentally, an inquiry into the Catholic versus Protestant wrangle which had added complications to the uneasy situation resulting from a series of Indian wars and forays.

Browne's northernmost tour of duty had two immediate results: He was soon out of a job; two of his letters were printed as powerful and influential Congressional documents which, in time, worked for the betterment of Indian relations. The two communiqués were combined into a House document entitled *The Indian War in Oregon and Washington*. This report, published in Washington in 1858, was the self-administered *coup de grâce* for Browne as a civil servant. It appeared that he was bent on political suicide, and he was not reappointed to any government investigating post as he had hoped, if not expected, that he might be. This was not the last that the government would see or hear of Browne but when he went out this time, temporarily, it was with a considerable bang, one which echoed most loudly in the corridors of the Office of Indian Affairs.

On January 25, 1858, the House of Representatives, in compliance with its own resolution of the fifteenth of the month, asked for and received the report of the special agent investigating the condition of the Indians in Oregon and Washington Territory. The document was referred to the Committee on Military Affairs and then ordered to be printed. Jacob Thompson of Mississippi, Secretary of the Interior, had passed the Browne letters along to Speaker of the House James L. Orr after having received them, in turn, from Charles E. Mix, the acting commissioner of the Office of Indian Affairs.

The letter which became *House Executive Document Number 38* of the First Session of the Thirty-fifth Congress was a letter which Browne had written in San Francisco on December 4, 1857; *House Executive Document Number 39* he had penned in the same city a little earlier, on November 17. In these communications he reminded James W. Denver, commissioner of Indian Affairs, for whom Mix was substituting, that he had carried out his tour of inspection under the Commissioner's instructions of May 1, 1857.

Denver's special agent felt that the information which he had obtained would have an important bearing on future Indian policy and the future prospects of the two Pacific Coast territories. After his arrival in Oregon he had conferred with all the leading citizens and federal officers of the country and had traveled widely in the area. He had found a complete unanimity on but one subject—a general denial of allegations that the settlers had commenced hostilities with the Indians for the purposes of speculation. Browne began:

From previous acquaintance with the people of Oregon, I had formed the opinion that they were peaceable, honest and industrious. It seemed to me scarcely possible that they could be guilty of so great a crime as that charged against them. In view of the fact, however, that objection might be made to any testimony coming from the citizens of the Territories, and believing also that it is the duty of a public agent to present, as far as practicable, unprejudiced statements, I did not permit myself to be governed by any representations unsupported by reliable historical data.[1]

J. Ross Browne came to the conclusion that the feud between the Commanding Officer of the Department of the Pacific and the citizens of the sister territories—out of which the charges of speculation had sprung up and bloomed—was actually of little importance, at least nationally. Browne was sure that it was just a personal and political quarrel, an undignified and unstatesmanlike and unsoldierly fight, to be sure, but a mere side show of the Indian war, for all the confusion it bred. Speculation on the public treasury had not triggered the Indian war. Denver's agent stated flatly:

The origin of the war is no different from that of any other Indian war. It is the natural result of emigration and settlement; and whether the Governors of the Territories, public officers and citizens generally committed an error in not placing themselves under the control and direction of General Wool,[2] who came up after the war had commenced, or whether the part taken by him was best calculated to preserve and maintain peace, is not the question now to be decided.[3]

A war took place—an expensive and disastrous war—from the effects of which the Territories will suffer for many years. Neither the commanding officer of the military department nor the citizens of the Territories, in my opinion, could have prevented it. . . . It was a war of destiny—bound to take place whenever the causes reached their culminating point. . . . The history of our Indian wars will show that the primary cause is the progress

---

[1] *H.R. Exec. Doc. No. 38*, 35 Cong., 1 sess. (1858), 1.

[2] John E. Wool, a New Yorker, entered the United States Army in 1812, became inspector general in 1821, and was made a brigadier general in 1841. He won distinction in the Mexican War and in 1854 was appointed commander of the army's Department of the Pacific. *Lippincott's Pronouncing Biographical Dictionary*, II, 2494.

[3] *H.R. Exec. Doc. No. 38*, 35 Cong., 1 sess. (1858), 2.

of civilization, to which the inferior races, from their habits and instincts, are naturally opposed. From the time of the landing of the Pilgrims on Plymouth Rock to the present day, we have had wars with the Indians, and they have all had a beginning. It matters little whether an individual act of agression or a general movement becomes the signal for hostilities— a prior cause must exist.[4]

Contributing to the erosion of peace in Oregon and Washington was the sectarian strife between Protestants and Catholics. Browne found little to choose between the two missionizing groups. The Protestants, especially Rev. H. H. Spalding, claimed that the murder of Dr. Marcus Whitman in the fall of 1847 was done not only with the knowledge but with the connivance of the Roman Catholic missionaries. Father J. B. A. Brouillet, vicar-general of Walla Walla, made a refutation of the charges, and this document Browne submitted to the government as part of his report. But, he warned Denver:

> A perusal of the pamphlet will abundantly show the bitterness of feeling existing between the different sects, and its evil effects upon the Indians. It will readily be seen that as little dependence can be placed upon the statements made by one side as by the other and that, instead of Christianizing the Indians, these different sects were engaged in quarrels among each other, thereby showing a very bad example to the races with whom they chose to reside.[5]

The Treasury-agent-turned-Indian-expert returned to the prevailing theme of his paper, explaining both the murder of Whitman and the outbreak of war upon the seizure of Indian land by white squatters— his natural law or destiny of encroachment by a superior race on an inferior race. Browne pointed out that Washington, D.C., had responded to the exhortations of the late Senators Thomas Hart Benton and Lewis F. Linn of Missouri, and of Oregon Territorial Delegate Samuel R. Thurston, by encouraging the pre-emption of Indians lands by white settlers with a donation law giving individuals 320 acres of the public domain and married couples 640 acres. The land was granted in fee simple upon actual residence of four years by the homesteaders. The

[4] *Ibid.*, 2–3. [5] *Ibid.*, 3.

donation law did not except from settlement lands upon which the Indian title had not been extinguished. Explained Browne:

> This has been a fruitful cause of difficulty. It was unwise and impolitic to encourage settlers to take away the lands of the Indians. It was well understood from experience with the Indians of other states that they always claimed a right to the lands upon which they resided. They could never be taught to comprehend that subtle species of argument by which another race could come among them, put them aside, ignore their claims, and assume possession on the ground of being a superior people. Ever since the Ordinance of 1787 it had been the practice of Government to recognize in them a possessory right, which could only be extinguished by purchase or mutual agreement. . . .[6]

> Of course, as the terms are always dictated and enforced on the one side, whether the other party was satisfied or not, this compulsory process cannot properly be dignified by the title of treaty. None of the so-called treaties with the Indians are more than forced agreements which the stronger power can violate or reject at pleasure, and of which privilege it has availed itself in all the treaties made with the Indians of Oregon.[7]

Browne was no wooly-minded theoretician who thought that the tide of Manifest Destiny could be turned back, however. He wrote:

> Civilization cannot be held back upon grounds of priority of possession. The question is simply one of public policy. When it becomes necessary to remove the aboriginal races to some more convenient location, they must be removed. But the stronger power, from motives of humanity, concedes to the weaker certain rights which it is bound in honor to respect.[8]

Tracing the background of Pacific Northwest redskin troubles, Browne described the Indian Commission, appointed by the President, which met at Champoeg in March, 1851, to negotiate treaties with various tribes of the Willamette. Reservations were set up and Indians herded onto them but, unfortunately, they were located on lands already claimed by whites so neither race was happy with this bit of diplomacy. The settlers held protest meetings. They were hardly necessary. The treaties were never ratified, and the Indians never received the promised considera-

---

[6] *Ibid.*, 4. [7] *Ibid.* [8] *Ibid.*, 5.

tions for their removal to the reservations. The special agent could not help noting that "between private individuals, this would be regarded as obtaining property under false pretenses."[9]

The Indians had been pushed as far as they could go. The result was war, as Browne reminded his superior:

> The Rogue River War of 1853 will not soon be forgotten. . . . Had they [the Indians] chosen to hold out and take to the mountain fastnesses of their country, it might have taken ten years to subdue them. It was not only through the determination and gallantry of General Lane[10] who led the volunteer forces in this war, but his thorough knowledge of Indian character, his skill in that sort of diplomacy, his general sagacity and prudence, that it was brought to a close. The most enlightened of the chiefs knew him personally and respected him both in war and peace. But they either misunderstood the terms of the treaty, or the inducements held out to them to stop the war were such as it was not afterwards practicable to fulfill.[11]

The immediate provocation of the more recent war in Oregon was the ousting of the powerful Klikitats from the Willamette lands which they had long before conquered from other tribes. They were removed by the Superintendent of Indian Affairs in the spring of 1855 to their original lands north of the Columbia. The Klikitats were particularly bitter since they were the most powerful tribe of the area and they had been friends, even allies, of the whites during the Rogue River War. As Browne remarked, the transported Klikitats charged the whites with bad faith and fraud. They denounced all whites as cheats and swore to get satisfaction.

In Washington Territory, the key people were the Yakimas. The Yakima tribe had long been under British and Hudson's Bay Company

[9] *Ibid.*, 6.

[10] Joseph Lane was one of the most colorful—as well as honest—public figures in the Far West. Born in Buncombe County, North Carolina, he was a Mexican War veteran whom Polk appointed governor of Oregon Territory in 1848. He took over the government of the Territory in 1849, ended the Rogue River War with the Treaty of Table Rock in September, 1853, and went on to be delegate and United States Senator from Oregon. *Dictionary of American Biography*, V, 579–80.

[11] *H.R. Exec. Doc. No. 38*, 35 Cong., 1 sess. (1858), 6.

influence. Their minds had been poisoned by British agents; they had never felt the power of the American government; they had little respect for Yankees. But they were not unaware that these men, so pale of face, were taking away land from their Indian neighbors to the east. In the British-American boundary dispute over Oregon Territory, the Yakimas naturally sided with the "King George men." The tribe was even further predispositioned to hostility by the astonishing animosity toward the Americans of one of the Yakima chiefs, Kamiakin. According to Browne, he "as early as 1853 projected a war of extermination against the whole race of Americans."[12]

Kamiakin sought a power coalition of Yakimas, Cayuses, Nez Percés, and Walla Wallas against the Yanks. Father Pandosy, a priest at Atahnam Mission, reported to Father Mesplie at the Dalles that both the Nez Percé and Cayuse tribes were holding war feasts in April, 1853. The word was forwarded to Major Benjamin Alvord, who reported it to General Ethan A. Hitchcock, then commanding the Department of the Pacific. The result? Both Alvord and Pandosy were censured by their superiors as alarmists. Browne emphasized these preparations for war by the redmen in refuting the rumors and claims that the white settlers had gotten up the war for speculative purposes.

The Nisqually Indians of Puget Sound were also pro-British and anti-American. (The British, fewer in numbers and less aggressive, posed less of a threat to the Indians than the "Boston men" who swarmed like ants.) Governor Isaac Stevens had tried to treat with them but with scant success. And Browne was not surprised.

> Under the circumstances of difficulty attending the making of these treaties, I am satisfied no public officer could have done better. The treaties were not the cause of the war. I have already shown that the war had been determined upon long before. If Governor Stevens is to blame because he did not so frame the treaties as to stop the war, or stop it by not making treaties at all, then that charge should be specifically brought against him. My own opinion is that he had no more control over the course of events than the Secretary of War in Washington [D.C.].[13]

12 *Ibid.*, 10.
13 *Ibid.*, 11.

Like Kamiakin of the Yakimas, [Leschi, Chief of the Nisqually] nation, was very hostile to Americans. He traveled and preached a fanatic doctrine, just as the Yakima did, painting a frightful picture of the land of darkness—"*polakly illeha*"—of foul, muddied streams, deadly insects, and general death and torture—in short, a first-rate Nisqually hell—to which the whites wished to drag the Indians.

Browne had to repeat to the government a common belief in the Northwest, that the Mormons were aiding the Indians. The proof was largely the ammunition and powder of Mormon origin which a Captain Shaw of the Walla Walla Volunteers had found in Indian hands, and the claims of Mormon complicity by George B. Simpson, an interpreter at the Cascades.

The Washington and Oregon Indians managed to go on the warpath in concert in the summer of 1855, but their plans and alliances had not had time to mature. The first victims of their wrath were two unsuspecting miners from Maine who were en route to the new Colville diggings. They were murdered by the Yakimas. When Indian Agent Bolen heard of the killings, he rushed from the Dalles to see Kamiakin. The latter was absent and another chief, Ouahi, received him and heard his remonstrances. Riding homeward, Bolen was overtaken by two or three "friendly" Yakimas who rode along with him for a time. Then one lagged behind, and while the other two kept the brave—or rash—Indian agent's attention engaged, the laggard shot him in the back. The cowardly trio then dragged him from his mount, scalped him, and burned his corpse.

By October, 1855, it was a hot war. Indians were slaughtering whites indiscriminately, including women and children. For this reason alone —a surely foreseeable result of frontier warfare—Browne felt that he could label the charges of speculation and concocted war as absurd and monstrous:

> No compensation that Government could make would atone for the murder of families, the stoppage of labor everywhere, the loss of time, the suspension of emigration, and the numerous evils resulting from the disastrous conflict.[14]

14 *Ibid.*, 13.

If his letter contained in *House Executive Document Number 38* was an explanation of the causes of the Indian war, *Document Number 39* was a detailing of his activity in the two territories, and from it one can reconstruct his tour of reconnaissance. He had hired former Captain C. J. Sprague of the United States Army, a veteran of the Mexican War, to assist him in the complicated and laborious details of the investigation. In his report to Denver, he paid tribute to the services of Sprague, from whose experience in frontiersmanship Browne had profited in his earlier explorations of California.

The two men arrived at Rainier, on the Columbia, on August 19, 1857, just as Governor Stevens' message concerning Colonel Isaac N. Ebey reached that point. Former Collector of Customs Ebey had been murdered by Indians at his Whidby Island home. Rumors flooded the little town as did some authentic reports, such as the one that some settlers were fleeing the Port Townsend area. In view of the state of alarm prevailing among the settlers, Browne decided to hurry to Olympia via the Cowlitz River to ascertain the true condition of affairs. He soon saw symptoms of Indian war—nervousness and alarm at Cowlitz Landing, some thirty miles from the river's mouth. Local people told him that Indians of the vicinity had left the area to visit the tribes of the upper Cowlitz. A number of whites took these moves as attempts by the local redmen to ally themselves with the Yakimas prior to falling on the whites. But Browne pooh-poohed these fears; he was well aware that the Indians were accustomed to make these social calls during the summer.

Browne was of the opinion that there was no real connection between the murder and beheading of Ebey and the condition of the Territory's tribes. And yet:

> It was painfully apparent . . . that the disastrous results of the late war had engendered a feeling of suspicion and insecurity greatly militating against any friendly relations between the settlers and the Indians throughout the Territory. . . . So great was the shock produced by this tragic event that the most trivial occurrences were at once magnified into premonitions of further bloodshed.[15]

15 *H.R. Exec. Doc. No. 39*, 35 Cong., 1 sess. (1858), 2.

On his way from Cowlitz Landing to the capital, J. Ross Browne passed through country which he had traversed in 1854. He was shocked by the obvious effects of the Indian troubles. Even though there had been no collisions with the redskins in the immediate area, the fine farms and luxuriant grainfields and herds of butterball-fat stock were no more. The region looked like many other parts of the Territory, now. He wrote:

> All along the road, houses are deserted and going to ruin; fences are cast down and in a state of decay; fields, once waving with luxuriant crops of wheat, are desolate; and but little if any stock is to be seen on the broad prairies that formerly bore such inspiring evidences of life. The few families that remained, either from necessity or inclination, were forced to erect rude blockhouses for their defense, into which they gathered by night during the hostilities, in constant apprehension of attack.[16]

Browne explained why he had to describe this area:

> I mention the facts with a view of showing that so far, at least, the "war speculation" charged upon the settlers of Washington Territory presents an unprofitable appearance.[17]

Within two miles of Olympia, Browne and Sprague encountered the wagons of the Pettigrew and Hastings families, fleeing to Oregon. At noon of August 22, the trail-weary men entered Olympia. Browne was disappointed to find that Governor Stevens was still in Oregon and that Acting Governor Mason was away with the Indian Agent, Captain M. T. Simmons, on a canoe trip to Port Townsend to investigate the murder of Ebey and to take measures to protect the citizenry. There were no canoes left at Olympia, and it looked as if Browne would have to continue his investigation by land. But by a stroke of luck, Captain Hyde of the United State revenue cutter *Jefferson Davis* had just arrived from Port Steilacoom with prisoners from Port Townsend. Hyde invited the Interior Agent to make use of the cutter, which was lying at anchor in Port Steilacoom. So, on the morning of August 24, Browne and Sprague started out on horseback over the twenty-two miles of trail meandering through a thick, almost impassable forest. They made the

[16] *Ibid.*, 3.
[17] *Ibid.*

port by noon, although in passing through the bleak area, constantly clouded with smoke from forest fires, they had not been able to see more than a mile or two in any direction.

The officers of Fort Steilacoom, on the edge of a fine prairie a mile from the harbor, suggested that Browne make his headquarters there. He gratefully agreed. Colonel Silas Casey had abandoned the army post at Muckleshoot about twenty-five miles inland, where three hundred of the more troublesome Puyallups, Nooscopes, and Green River Indians were interned, for the new site. The Indians were still at Muckleshoot, but Colonel Casey did not consider a post and a force to be necessary there. He suggested to Browne that the Indian Department take over the comfortable buildings erected there by Lieutenant David B. McKibbin. Browne thought that this was a splendid idea and said as much to Denver:

> The valley of the Muckleshoot is admirably situated for a local agency. The Indians of the valley were amongst the number concerned in the Green and White River massacres at the beginning of the war, and unless some supervision is kept over them, they may, from their proximity to the Yakimas and Klickitats, produce great trouble in future.[18]

(The only irritant to Browne was the presence of two squatters who had taken out two claims when the post was established. They were bought off by the army, but the two speculators had returned after the camp was abandoned by the military.)

On August 25, after a ten-mile ride from Fort Steilacoom on a rough trail through a dense stand of timber, Browne reached a sawmill at the head of Commencement Bay. There he hoped to cross by water to the Puyallup Reservation, but, the tide being out, he and Sprague had to tie up their horses and hike for five miles on a foot trail. He found the Reservation, set up by the Treaty of Medicine Creek, to be situated on low and marshy land along the Puyallup River, with a few open prairie patches of value for grazing. Only about fifty Indians were there when he arrived, together with the Indian Agent and a blacksmith. The remainder—four hundred or so—were out fishing and gathering berries,

[18] *Ibid.*, 4.

he was told. The Special Agent made an inspection of the dozen rough two-apartment houses built for the Indians at a cost of $215 each and the employees' house, a six-room building costing $680. Browne was disappointed to find that only two or three Indian families had taken up residence in the houses built for them. "It has not been practicable to induce the Indians to live in these houses. . . . They prefer temporary wigwams which they can move about at pleasure. Their chief objection to houses," he went on to say, "is the vermin which, from their filthy habits, soon become such a nuisance as to render the houses uninhabitable." But he was still optimistic. "It is hoped, however, that during the rainy season, when this nuisance becomes abated, they will avail themselves of the shelter afforded by good and substantial buildings."[19]

Browne thought that the government had received its money's worth from the builders, what with the difficulties of securing labor on the remote frontier and especially since the contractors had not yet been paid and there seemed little chance of their getting their money for some years to come.

There was no lack of good food on the Puyallup Reservation. Fish were plentiful in the river, and inexhaustible quantities of berries grew in the adjoining woods. Browne looked over the patch of good, fenced bottom land where the Indians were raising eighteen acres of peas, potatoes, cabbages, beets, and carrots. He found that some of the reservation Indians hired out to settlers for one dollar a day and that a crew of them, superintended by the Agent, had cut seventy tons of hay and sold it at a good price.

Browne investigated the claims of would-be squatters to the reservation land which they occupied under, as they claimed, the provisions of the donation and pre-emption laws. His conclusion was that they had, in most cases, abandoned their claims there and taken up others, elsewhere, before the Reservation was established. He also found that the donation claims were not defined as to boundaries and that other provisions of the donation act—which required actual residence on the site and improvements upon it—had not been complied with. In any case, reported Browne, all the 160 claims were null and void because the government,

[19] *Ibid.*, 4–5.

by the Pre-emption Law of September 4, 1841, reserved to itself the control of all public lands to which Indian title had not been extinguished.

Leaving the Puyallup Reservation, Browne visited the Nisqually Reservation, only twelve miles away, on August 26. He found rough but well-built houses there too. But, unlike the garden patch which was Puyallup, Nisqually Reservation boasted one little fenced plot of twenty acres. The combination of poor land and poor weather (drought) had conspired to create a crop failure. Only nine acres of peas were raised; the remaining eleven acres were plowed for the sowing of seed in the fall. There were also some ten acres planted to potatoes in the river bottom, but the reservation land was mostly gravelly prairie, too poor even for grazing. "Nothing can ever be done to make this profitable as an Indian farm," Browne reported to his chief. "We found no more than five or six families of Indians on this reservation."[20] Browne also found them to be lazy and, as he put it, "entirely insensible to kindness." The men were not out picking berries; they lay under the trees, gambling. The Agent confessed to Browne that he could do absolutely nothing with them. "Any coercion on his part would be followed by desertion; once in the woods it is impossible to capture them."[21]

Without venturing his own opinion of their philosophy, Browne passed on the Indian Agent's summation of it. "They cannot be made to understand why Government should take their country away from them and then compel them to work for a living. They say Government deprived them of their national heritage; now let it support them." It was not surprising that Browne was unimpressed with the two sites. "I do not anticipate any beneficial results either from this or the Puyallup Reservation."[22]

He was even less impressed with the results of the temporary small agencies, called "reservations" locally, out of convenience, and which resembled some of California's tiny rancherias. Such a one was the Fort Kitsap Agency of Indian Agent George A. Page. The Fort Kitsap reservation lay at the head of Port Madison Bay, sixty miles from Steilacoom.

[20] *Ibid.,* 6.
[21] *Ibid.*
[22] *Ibid.*

The cutter had a difficult time getting Browne there, being delayed two days en route by calms and head tides. Few Indians were to be seen at Kitsap. The peaceful natives of Puget Sound had scattered into hiding in various creeks and inlets upon the news of the depredations of the northern Indians. Of the 440 Squawmish and Dwamish Indians supposed to be headquartered at Kitsap, he found only 30. Page and his assistants, H. O. Briant for the Squawmishes, and J. H. Goudy for the Dwamishes, had built fifteen frame shanties at $100 each on the beach for their charges. But there was no sign of land under cultivation; no sign of any other improvements. In fact, as far as Browne could see, no work of any kind whatsoever was being done by the Indians. He was relieved to learn that they were not on the government dole. They lived by fishing and berry-gathering as they had done since time immemorial. The sick and the aged, only, received a little coffee and flour, now and then, and blankets. The employees, of course, lived at public expense—and they did no work, either, he was quick to note. "I can see no permanent good likely to result from the expenses incident to this system of partial supervision." His recommendations were clear. "All the Indians should be concentrated, as far as practicable, at some principal reservation and compelled to work; and all white employees not actually engaged in active labor should be discontinued."[23]

By the thirtieth of the month, Browne was at the Port Townsend Agency, conferring with Thomas J. Hanna, the local Indian agent. Another nominal agency like Kitsap, no government relief was being extended to the Indians of the district. They were Dungeness and Clallam tribesmen, numbering 1,100 in all, of whom only 100 were resident at Port Townsend, the others being scattered all along the shore of Port Townsend Bay and Dungeness Point and Hood's Canal. At the time of the inspector's visit, most of them were at the latter point, digging clams and catching and curing fish. They had been driven from their potato patches on Whidbey Island by the northern raiders. According to Browne, the latter liked to "make a practice of robbing and murdering the Sound Indians whenever they catch them."[24]

[23] Ibid., 7.
[24] Ibid.

It was at this time that the San Franciscan met the Duke of York, the once-powerful chief of the Clallams, who, by 1857, was much debased by alcoholism. Browne's description of his visit to the Duke of York and the Duke's eye-blackened favorite, Jenny Lind, in his works *The Coast Rangers* and *Crusoe's Island*, was a devastating commentary on frontier viciousness and earned him many enemies in Washington. In his official report to Denver, Browne did not abuse the Port Townsendites as much as in his more popular writings. He was content to observe:

> From what I saw during my stay there, I formed the opinion that the Duke of York and his amiable family were not below the average of the white citizens residing at that benighted place. With very few exceptions, it would be difficult to find a worse class of population in any part of the world. No less than six murders have occurred there during the past year. It is notorious as a resort for beachcombers and outlaws of every description.[25]

The military post five miles away Browne found unimpressive. Major Granville O. Haller had his hands full with the settlers in town who encouraged his soldiers to desert. Browne thought the post useless. In an area so thick with trees and undergrowth that even the Indians had to travel by water, soldiers were of little use in their fort. Browne felt it might just as well be fifty miles out of town as five. There could be no forced marches, no gallant charges, no dragoons galloping to the rescue in that country. "Before the soldiers from the fort could reach Port Townsend, the town might be in ashes, and every inhabitant murdered. One war canoe of 60 northern Indians could do it in half an hour."[26]

The *Jefferson Davis* (finally) made a good run, carrying Browne from Port Townsend on September 1 to the Tom-Whik-Son Agency of Colonel E. C. Fitzhugh, near the coal mines of Bellingham. She dropped her hook only six hours after weighing it. Fitzhugh supervised 540 Lummas and 300 Samishes, the two tribes usually lumped as Salt Chucks, or fishermen—salt-water Indians. There were also 412 Nootsaks living ninety-six miles from Bellingham Bay at the foot of Mount Baker, and a

[25] *Ibid.*, 8.
[26] *Ibid.*

few other scattered bands which berried or raised potatoes for subsistence and were, supposedly, under Fitzhugh's direction.

Browne thought that this agency should be continued since its Indians were both peaceable and self-supporting. Also, he was impressed by the Indian Agent and Commanding Officer of the small army post near by. The former, Colonel Fitzhugh, was very well acquainted with all of the Indians north of Port Townsend, spoke their languages, and commanded their confidence and respect even though the warring northerners, in bravado, had sent word that they intended to take his blockhouse and his head. Fitzhugh had only six or seven men, coal miners, under his command and, besides muskets, only a single howitzer at the blockhouse. His great source of protection, if it could be called that, was his Indian colony. The peaceful Puget Sound Indians would give him notice of the approach of any war party. He also had a doughty ally in the commandant of the little picket post established in August, 1856, on Bellingham Bay, about five miles from Whatcom. This officer was Colonel George E. Pickett, the hero of Pickett's Charge at Gettysburg six years after Browne met him.[27]

Browne was impressed by the little fort's blockhouse, by the kind and hospitable Pickett, and by the neatness and order of his post. "He is determined to give the northern Indians some trouble in carrying into effect a threat recently made by them—that, having carefully examined his fort, they meant to have it and, at the same time, his head."[28]

Denver's agent described the marauding northerners, who meant every word of their threat. (After killing Ebey they had cut off his head, and it was not recovered for two years after the murder.) Indians of Nootka Sound and Prince Edward Island, accustomed to committing petty depredations upon both Indians and whites of Puget Sound for years, were joined by some from as far away as Sitka, Alaska. These Apaches of the North came in great, seagoing war canoes. Browne

[27] Pickett became famous first in Washington for his strong stand against the British in the trouble over ownership of San Juan Island just two years after Browne left him. When ordered off by the British, he announced he would fire on any landing force, saying, "I am here by virtue of an order from my government, and shall remain till recalled by the same authority." *Dictionary of American Biography, XIV*, 570.

[28] *H.R. Exec. Doc. No. 39*, 35 Cong., 1 sess. (1858), 10.

described these craft as being capable of speeds of seven to twelve miles per hour, with each one bearing an arms chest of muskets and ammunition, all in prime condition.

The Confidential Agent visited Ebey's Landing and Whidbey Island on September 3. He laid the murder of the former Collector to the outlaw beachcombers—white squawmen and worthless Indians—who had drifted south to the area. (Actually, the foul deed was done by 200 Kakes or Haidas from the north, stealing up on the landing in their war canoes.) "The crime was the more atrocious as he had never, in any manner, molested or offended them but, on the contrary, from a naturally kind disposition, had been in the habit of giving them food and clothing whenever they applied to him."[29]

Inspecting the murder site, Browne found Ebey's house, a small log hut, thoroughly ransacked. All of the furniture had been taken away by the Colonel's relatives, and the place was an utter wreck. The depressing scene made a deep impression on him, and Browne finally, in his own mind, fixed the real blame for Ebey's sad death on the U.S.S. *Massachussetts*. (He wrote Captain David Farragut and told him so, too.) Two years earlier the navy ship had killed five or six Indians with her cannon and then abruptly departed the scene. Wrote Browne:

> There can be no doubt that the immediate cause of this murder was the act of the steamer *Massachussetts*. That a vessel of the United States should kill a party of Indians, knowing that it is the custom of this race never to forget an injury, and immediately after take its departure, and leave the settlers to bear the consequences, evinces either a want of regard for the common principles of humanity or unpardonable lack of judgment. For what purpose, it may be asked, are vessels of the U.S. stationed on the Pacific Coast? Is it that they may lie rotting at Mare Island, where they are of no use, or that they may be used to protect the lives of the settlers on the remote shores of our frontier?[30]

Browne wondered if hostiles could be pursued into British or Russian territorial waters by American vessels. He suggested that the cutter *Jefferson Davis* be used in the Sound to pacify the Indians—although she

[29] *Ibid.*, 11.
[30] *Ibid.*, 12.

needed four days to reach Steilacoom from Port Townsend (only ninety miles), he claimed, and sometimes took ten days. He dismissed the idea of the mail steamer *Constitution*'s being used as a Puget Sound police-man. He derisively pointed out:

> An unseaworthy, unarmed hulk . . . she makes but six miles per hour, under a heavy press of steam whereas a northern war canoe can easily make ten, and thus run around her. . . . She has no guns, men or munitions of war. . . . She is, in short, no more use in the waters of Puget Sound as a protection to the settlers than the loose lumber that lies around the saw-mills.[31]

The Confidential Agent had plenty to say on the subject of chastizing the Indians:

> The British Hudson's Bay Company have had no difficulty in main-taining their supremacy over these races; but they pursue a different course. Whenever one of their subjects is murdered they pursue the murderers, compel them to surrender, and execute them on the spot. The Indians well understand that no matter where they may go they will be followed and captured and so sure as they deserve it, will suffer death. Our Government adopts a different policy. It sends up a war steamer to the Sound; this vessel drives out a few Indians, fires several rounds of ammunition into the trees back of Seattle, causes a general reverberation of large and small guns around the shores of the Sound, winds up by killing some four or five Indians, informs the settlers that there is no use in staying any longer, as the enemy have all left, gets up a head of steam and paddles back to Mare Island, where she rests from her labors for the space of one or two years.[32]

But then, military posts are established; pickets and blockhouses are erected; officers' and soldiers' quarters are constructed; daily parades take place. All this is done without doubt. But the country is impassable; the woods and undergrowth form a barrier to land operations along the shores of the Sound more impregnable than the great Chinese Wall.

I consider, therefore, that so far as any beneficial result is concerned, this expensive system of operations is worse than useless. One war steamer, of

31 *Ibid.*
32 *Ibid.*

suitable size and well-armed and equipped, would do more good than the whole military force united, as it is now situated.

I trust the attention of the War Department will be called to the subject.[33]

On September 3, Browne proceeded on foot from Ebey's Landing to Coop's Landing, a pleasant two miles away, past abandoned settlements. He thought the land very rich and the finest agricultural area that he had seen in all of Washington Territory. Some of the families of Whidbey Island had fled to the blockhouse at Coop's, on the east side of the Isle, where a sergeant and ten or twelve soldiers from Fort Steilacoom guarded them against Indian raiders. From Coop's, Browne proceeded to the Penn Cove Indian Agency, six miles further by water. There had been no braves at Coop's to paddle him over, but Coop had assured him that women could handle a canoe as well as their men so Browne set out with a couple of Indian women paddlers. They not only got him to the Agency with dispatch, but they accompanied their paddling with songs. At Penn Cove Landing he talked to Robert C. Fay, agent for the 1,340 Skagit Indians there. The latter had received no government provisions for some time, but his charges grew potatoes—1,500 bushels of them, in fact. He told Browne that the Skagits were much afflicted with sickness—tuberculosis, venereal disease, and influenza.

Once again Browne applauded Governor Stevens' plan of concentrating the Indians of the Sound in one location, say Puyallup, instead of having them scattered from Olympia to Bellingham under hardly nominal "control" in which they made not even the most halting progress toward civilization.

> At every place where they are in the habit of resorting, trading posts are established by a depraved class of white men who furnish them with whiskey. Boatloads of whiskey follow them wherever they go. The agents have really little or no control over them and the result is, they are descending from the level of Indians to that of the depraved whites with whom they associate.

Browne was no romantic Rousseau; he would brook no nonsense about "the noble red man." But he did sympathize with their plight. He laid his recommendations on the line:

33 *Ibid.*, 13.

It can hardly be expected that these numerous tribes shall continue to have the unrestricted range of Puget Sound. Some provision must be made for them consistent with the progress of immigration and settlement. The best mode of decreasing the expenses of the Territory will be to encourage population and the formation of a state. But so long as large bands of Indians, in a condition worse than pure barbarism, are permitted to roam at large, committing petty depredations wherever they can, lounging idly about the farms, consuming the substance of the settlers, affording a profitable trade to the worst possible class of whites that can infest any country, there will be little hope for the Territory of Washington.

I submit these views with a sincere conviction that the large appropriations made for the relief of the Indians in that Territory are resulting in no practical good either to the Indians or to that class of settlers whose presence is desirable. Nor is the lust for office, which is engendered by the large number of employees in the district more advantageous to the unhappy race whose welfare it is the object of the Government to subserve, than to the interests of the Territory.[34]

September 5 saw Browne back at Port Townsend, where he was fortunate enough to meet the mail steamer *Constitution*—an "old hulk," he had called her. She was up from San Francisco. He took passage in her to Olympia via Seattle and Dwamish Agency, where J. H. Goudy had his 420 wards. The tireless investigator reached Olympia at 8:00 P.M. He was in a canoe en route to the Squaxon Reservation the next morning. The reservation lay about ten miles from Olympia on Klackemin Island, at the entrance to Budd's Inlet. Special Agent W. B. Gosnell and Quincy A. Brooks, a schoolteacher, provided Browne with company on the three-hour canoe trip. He found only 12 men and a few old women and young children of the 350 to 370 Squaxons who should have been at the reservation. But the others were out gathering supplies for winter. Besides the usual frame buildings, this reservation boasted a blacksmithy run by Truman Hack. Brooks, finding it impossible to round up the Indian children for school, was acting as a clerk, keeping all the accounts and correspondence of the Indian reservation. Little land was fenced or cultivated, and Browne, in his report, pronounced it barren and unfit

[34] *Ibid.*, 15.

for cultivation, the expense of fencing and plowing it unlikely to be returned in crops.

The Confidential Agent found Gosnell intelligent and efficient but helpless. Browne observed the practice of the whisky trader only a few miles from the Indian agency. Whenever he got a new supply of spirits, he would descend to the beach and blow a horn, "at which signal they paddle off in their canoes and enjoy a general debauch, which only ends when the whiskey gives out. In this way, their blankets, clothes and earnings are sacrificed, and they return, naked, sick and dispirited."[35] But Browne could not blame Gosnell. "In stating the actual conditions of the agencies," he told Denver, "it will be understood that the blame does not necessarily fall upon the agents. Great difficulties have been experienced here which are scarcely known in more settled countries, and the evils are frequently beyond the control of the officers in charge."[36]

The investigator's next task was to look over the accounts of M. P. Simmons, the principal agent for the Puget Sound District. Browne lauded him and his clerk, C. H. Armstrong, as well:

> Mr. Simmons is necessarily absent most of his time on official visits to the various points of the Sound. His long experience of Indian affairs and thorough acquaintance with the Indians render his services of inestimable value. He was one of the first settlers in the Territory of Washington and has been personally acquainted with all the Indian chiefs of the past fifteen years. Owing to his friendly relations with them, it would be difficult to find a more suitable person to conduct the affairs of the Agency.[37]

Governor Stevens had made five treaties with the Indians, at Medicine Creek, Point Elliott, Neah Bay, Olympia, and Point No Point. But only the first had been ratified. The breaking out of hostilities had prevented ratification of the others. Browne was aware of the criticism of Stevens, and after hearing all kinds of testimony, rumor, and gossip, he reported that, to the best of his knowledge, the Governor had acted conscientiously and with regard for the public interest. The treaty provisions did not ignite the war since, as he had already pointed out, the true causes existed

[35] *Ibid.*, 16.
[36] *Ibid.*, 17.
[37] *Ibid.*

long before Stevens. Browne admitted that the Territorial administration had made many errors but claimed that the conditions in Washington were anomalous:

> No parallel can be found in any territory of the United States, no terri-torial government was ever conducted under circumstances so disadvan-tageous, or where difficulties so formidably existed. Tribes of Indians with whom no previous relations of friendship had been established had to be brought within the restrictions of laws of which they had never heard; a white population, composed of adventurers from all parts of the Union, had to be restrained from acts of retaliation where aggressions were com-mitted upon them; the jealousies of political and military cliques had to be encountered at every step, and every species of annoyance, privation and suffering endured under relentless opposition, the bitterness of which can only be accounted for by the indomitable energy and manliness with which it was resisted.[38]

The provisions of the Treaty of Medicine Creek were only partially carried into effect. In the years 1855 to 1857, Congress appropriated $16,500, $7,500, and $7,500. The visiting agent prowled through the com-plicated maze of accounts. He found that $6,125.46 was still due the Indians from the first appropriation. Nothing of the second sum had been disbursed, and none of the third had even been received. Said Browne:

> I freely confess my inability to understand the details of the expenditures made in Washington Territory, except upon the general principle that the Superintendent took the responsibility of applying the moneys transmitted to him in such manner as he deemed most advantageous to the Indians, without regard to funds, forms, or instructions.[39]

But Browne reminded Denver that even Stevens' bitterest enemies had not charged him with putting public money to his own personal use, or with any kind of pecuniary speculation.

On September 7, Browne found the house of Sydney S. Ford, local agent for the Chehalis District, on the bank of the Chehalis River. Like

[38] *Ibid.*, 18–19.
[39] *Ibid.*, 19.

Simmons, Ford was an old-timer in the Territory, familiar with the Indians and well fitted for his post. He had in his care Chehalis, Cowlitz, and Chinook Indians. They seemed a sorry lot to Browne, except for the 75 or so of the Upper Cowlitz tribe, a nearly wild group on an upstream prairie. (The more "civilized" Upper Chehalis were a cut above the rest, too.) Their kin, the Lower Cowlitz, some 250 in all, lived between Cowlitz Landing and the mouth of the Chehalis. They no longer hunted, having been deprived of all their firearms during the Indian war. Although expert canoemen, they were generally idle. Browne ruefully remarked, "Whiskey has nearly destroyed them. They are all diseased and cannot exist more than a few years longer."[40]

The 200 or more Chinooks living along the Columbia River near the mouth of the Cowlitz he found to be "a feeble and degraded race known as 'Fish Eaters.'" Only the Upper Chehalis Indians appeared active and intelligent to the Secret Agent. They were good salmon fishermen. Like the Cowlitzes, they were allowed no guns or powder but they remained good hunters. They were directly under Ford's supervision, but, except for occasional coffee and sugar for the aged and infirm, they neither asked nor were given government provisions. They appeared to thrive on Oregon grapes, salal, raspberries, blackberries, and whortleberries. Still, they were not a warlike race.

There was also a handful of tribes, minor nations, which Browne accounted for to his superior—the Satsops, Queets, Quinnoyaths, and Quilloyaths. Then he described the Indians beyond, toward Cape Flattery, as wild and unacquainted with white men.

The Grande Ronde Reservation, which Browne reached on September 16, after a pleasant thirty-mile journey from Salem, boasted a military post commanded by Captain David A. Russell on an eminence overlooking what the Californian called the *"rancherías,"* and about two miles from the headquarters of Agent J. F. Miller. The officers and 20 men occupied a neat and substantial military outpost. Miller had taken charge of 1,925 Indians on November 25, 1856, about 909 of them either Rogue Rivers or Shastas. They were a sickly group, decimated by consumption and venereal disease. They had frequent and bloody quarrels,

[40] *Ibid.*, 21.

blamed their many deaths on the new environment, and made it impossible for the Agent to help them. In May, before Browne's arrival, most of the Rogue Rivers were removed to the Siletz, burning their sixty-dollar shanties as they left, according to their custom but to the shock of the Agent. Only old Chief Sam and about 58 men of the tribe, with their families, remained on the Grande Ronde. Sam liked to boast that he and his people had never gone to war against the whites. He apparently expected to be rewarded handsomely for his neutrality if not for his loyalty. Browne sized the Chief up as wily, avaricious, and unscrupulous.

Intelligent and industrious were the Umpquas, and the Calapooyas, of the Grande Ronde Reservation. They had suffered much sickness, but the health of the band of 262 appeared to be improving at the time of Browne's visit. Not warlike, they abstained from any hostilities against the whites and were rewarded in traditional frontier fashion by being rounded up, dispossessed of all their property, and moved to the Grande Ronde from their homes. Browne suggested that they be indemnified by the government for their property losses, about $3,000.

The once-powerful Willamettes were poor and powerless in 1857. There were 660 of them but they were divided into many small bands under subchiefs. They had remained in the Willamette Valley during the 1855 war, seeking only to save their lives. But the whites had continued the process of reduction of this tribe which had been begun by the marauding Klikitats. Explained Browne:

> Since 1843, when emigrants began to fill up the Valley, they have been dwindling away and are now a degenerate remnant, suffering from disease and addicted to all the evil habits of the whites. They have worked a good deal among the settlers and when not in reach of whiskey are docile and expert in all kinds of farming operations.[41]

The Special Agent's visit to the Grande Ronde hospital showed him that little had been done to reduce sickness among the Indians, but not because of any fault of the doctors. It was mainly the superstition and lack of self-care of the Indians. Browne looked at the record for August,

[41] *Ibid.*, 23–24.

1857, and found the doctor reporting 168 Indians sick in camp and 30 in the hospital. Browne guessed that there were five times 168 actually sick in camp during his inspection, and yet he found only 3 patients in the hospital.

The school was, so far, a failure, too. The Indian children had attended only when it was a novelty. Even the food, clothing, and presents given young scholars in order to bribe their parents into keeping them in attendance proved to be insufficient as lures. Moreover, Browne felt that they unlearned at night, around the campfires, what they had picked up at school during the day. He thought that the young students should be completely separated from *all* Indian influences before any beneficial results could be seen—an interesting, if shocking, example of an early exposition of the idea of brainwashing as practiced in the twentieth century by dictatorships.

The day after he arrived at Grande Ronde, the Special Indian Agent made a general but detailed reconnaissance. He found 2,320 acres under cultivation, of which well over 1,000 acres were fenced. This fenced acreage—some 1,663 acres—was divided into about six plots; 91 acres were in peas, 11 in turnips, 125 in potatoes. Some 316 acres were sown in wheat, and 380 in oats. The final 740-acre tract was pasture for the Reservation's stock. To Browne's eye, the soil was barren, cold, and clayey. He was, therefore, not surprised to find that, for all the energetic effort of the Grande Ronde people, the crops failed almost entirely. The wheat was cut but was too poor to thresh, yielding, at best, only 10 bushels to the acre. Oats were poor, as were potatoes, and only the peas and turnips did well. An unseasonal dryness plus a late planting contrived to ruin Agent Miller's hopes.

None of the Indians would work unless paid. About forty, mostly Willamettes, Calapooyas, and Umpquas, did all the farm work of the Reservation for $30 each per month in credit at the Reservation store. "They say, very justly," reported Browne, "that whilst they are willing to work for themselves, they do not want to raise crops to feed the lazy Indians of other tribes, who would rather starve than work."[42]

The Reservation embodied quite a complex of buildings, mostly log

42 *Ibid.*, 25.

huts of white settlers who had sold their claims to the government. But there was a good two-story Agency House, begun by Superintendent Palmer and finished by Miller, in which the latter resided with his family. There was also the schoolhouse, slaughterhouse, hospital, storehouse, boardinghouse for the working Indians, and buildings for the blacksmith, the carpenter, and other mechanics. An expensive tin shop was a failure. Said Browne of it: "Tin ware can be bought and delivered at the Reservation at less than it will cost to manufacture it. I have to recommend that it be discontinued."[43]

The sawmill had proved more practical. He found it in operation. The gristmill lay unfinished, a monument to the change-over in Superintendents. It was begun by the administration prior to that of J. F. Miller, but the Superintendent, Sawyer, got only the framework and roof up before he was replaced. Commented Browne: "It seems a pity that so good a piece of work, upon which so much labor has been expended, should now go to ruin. It is estimated that it will cost $5,000 to complete it. I am clearly of opinion that it would be better economy to complete it than to suffer it to remain in its present condition."[44]

At Grande Ronde a fine community of 190 board houses had been built. But only a few were occupied, usually by chiefs and headmen and their families. The Indian aversion to living in the white man's style which Browne had noticed earlier was most apparent on the Grande Ronde. To make matters worse, once-occupied houses were quitted upon the death of an inhabitant and, as he explained to Denver: "When a member of any family dies, the house is abandoned and never again occupied. It is supposed to contain 'bad medicine' or evil spirits and no persuasion can induce the Indians to go back into it."[45]

Grande Ronde was an impressive Indian reservation, but it was also an expensive one. Browne quickly determined the reasons. It was in an area of bald hills, destitute of game and even of berries. Crop failure there was a crisis rather than an annoyance. Rations of beef, every four days, and flour, once a week, had to be issued the government's wards

43 *Ibid.*, 26.
44 *Ibid.*
45 *Ibid.*

regularly, and the Special Agent warned: "If the supplies were stopped for a single week, they would all starve or abandon the Reservation." Again, Browne could not help but be abashed at the thoughtlessness of the Indians: "By wastefulness they contrive to get rid of the abundant supplies furnished them in about half the allotted time, in consequence of which they suffer partial starvation during the intervening period. Neither advice nor the pangs of hunger can change these improvident habits. Repletion and starvation are prolific sources of disease among them."[46]

Browne found a clerk employed by the Indian Agent without authorization but reported that he had done good work and, in fact, indispensable work which the Agent had not had time to do. He urged that the man be kept on. "If he [Agent Miller] is not allowed a clerk, he must detail some other employee under a different name. I am unable to see what advantage is gained to Government by any deception of this kind. What one agent cannot do, it will not be practicable for another to do, so that the removal of an agent for this cause will not obviate the difficulty."[47] Browne brought his obstinate honesty to bear on the many-tentacled red-tapeworm of bureaucracy which fattened off the Indian Bureau. But he was eager to fire only incompetents and thieves, not hard-working clericals.

In order to check his own assessment of the situation, Browne decided that he should call a *wa-wa*, or powwow, with the Indians of Grande Ronde. He asked the Agent to inform the Indians and Miller did so. On the following day, they were all assembled. There was also a sprinkling of whites in attendance, including General Joe Lane, Territorial delegate to Congress, and James W. Nesmith, superintendent of Indian affairs in Oregon.

Special Agent Browne explained his mission to the Indians with great care. He had come in order to hear them out. He urged that they speak their minds freely in order that the President might learn from their own mouths what their hearts were.

First to speak was Sam, chief of the Rogue Rivers. He spoke with such marvelous frontier elegance that one suspects the fine editorial hand of

[46] *Ibid.*
[47] *Ibid.*

Browne in the printed version of his *wa-wa*. If not, then Sam is an unsung Logan of the Far West. He began:

> Before we came to the Reservation, myself and my people were promised cattle, horses, clothing, &c. We were to have coffee and white sugar. We were to have, each, a piece of land to cultivate. What we raised by our own labor was to be ours, to do as we pleased with.
>
> Now we have not had any of these things. The Government—Uncle Sam—has not complied with these promises. We have waited and waited because the Agents told us to be patient, that it would be all right bye-and-bye. We are tired of this. We believe Uncle Sam intends to cheat us. Sometimes we are told that there is one Great Chief and sometimes another. One Superintendent tells us one thing and the Great Chief removes him. Then another Superintendent tells us another thing, and another Great Chief removes him. Who are we to believe? Who is your Great Chief, and who is to tell us the truth? We don't understand the way you act. With us, we are born chiefs; once a chief, we are a chief for life. But you are only common men, and we never know how long you will hold your authority, or how soon the Great Chief may degrade you, or how soon he may be turned out, himself. We want to know the true Head, that we may state our conditions to him. Let him come here, himself, and see us. So many lies have been told him that we think he never hears the truth, or he would not compel us to suffer as we do.
>
> Captain Smith, U.S.A., Palmer, Metcalf, and others, promised us that as soon as the war was over we would be permitted to return to our country. Now the war is over. Why are we kept here still? This is a bad country. It is cold and sickly. There is no game on the hills. My people are all dying. There will soon be none left. The graves of my people cover the valleys. We are told that if we go back, we will be killed. Let us go, then, for we might as well be killed as die here.
>
> The Table Rock Reservation was made under the Treaty of September 10, 1853. We made it with Generals [Joe] Lane and [Joel] Palmer. When the last war broke out we were driven away from there. We never sold Uncle Sam that land. General Lane is now here. He knows what was told us; that we would have to leave it for a while. But we never sold it. If Uncle Sam intends to keep it from us, then let him pay us for it.[48]

48 *Ibid.*, 27–28.

Several other chiefs spoke, making the same general points as Rogue River Sam, but none matched his eloquence.

After his powwow, Browne visited Salem, the capital of Oregon Territory, to examine the Superintendent's office. Nesmith was now entirely responsible for the Indians of both territories, for the Washington Superintendency had been discontinued. The Confidential Agent suggested to Denver that it would take only a glance at the map to show the utter impracticality of trying to control both of the large Territories from Salem. To support his position, he jotted down a table of distances from headquarters to various agencies. From Salem to Cowlitz was 135 miles; to Port Townsend, 296 miles; to Walla Walla, 335; to the Pend d'Oreilles, 550 miles. No superintendent, even if he traveled every day of the year, could visit all the agencies, and Browne felt that the personal visits of the Indian Office's men were absolutely indispensable to the success of the reservation system. Moreover, added Browne: "A portion of the route lies through the Snake country, where hostilities are constantly to be apprehended. Even to Walla Walla, a military escort is now necessary."[49]

Agent Browne suggested that the great extent of territory be carved into three superintendencies—one to be Oregon west of the Cascades; the second to embrace the land in Washington between the Columbia River and the northern boundary, the Cascades and the coast; and the third to cover the territory of both Oregon and Washington which lay east of the Cascades, to the summit of the Rocky Mountains. Browne was not overstating the case when he assured Denver that "this would surely give ample occupation to three of the best men that could be selected." He went on:

> But, when it is taken into consideration that all of these duties now devolve upon one superintendent, that he must audit and transmit to the Department all the accounts of the agents, make out his own reports, and conduct his own correspondence with the agents and the Department, keep the books of his office, make contracts for supplies, turn over the monies transmitted to him for disbursement, make his estimates for expenditures during each quarter, and supervise the conduct of the various employees, as well as the wants and necessities of the Indians, that it

[49] *Ibid.*, 29.

devolves upon him to maintain friendly relations between the settlers and the tribes under his control, that he is not even allowed the assistance of a clerk or messenger, it will, at once, be seen that it is not practicable to find a person of the requisite qualifications to fill such an office at a salary of $2,500 per annum, or, in fact, at any compensation whatsoever.[50]

Browne called his Chief's attention particularly to the pressing need for a superintendent east of the Cascades, where wandering bands of red men were committing depredations on emigrant trains and retarding the settlement of the fine Columbia River cattle ranges and the riparian farm lands of the Walla Walla country. He reminded his superior of the richness of this area which was becoming a no-man's land:

> Previous to the late war, many settlers had taken up claims between the Dalles and Fort Walla Walla which they were compelled to abandon in consequence of Indian hostilities. If the treaties made by Governor Stevens are considered objectionable, let others be made; and, if practicable, this fine region opened by emigration. Thousand of hardy adventurers on the Western frontier of the Atlantic states are ready to pour into it and, by means of their stock and labor, give it an intrinsic value greatly exceeding the expense of opening it to settlement.[51]

Proof that Browne was a child of his times was his hostility toward the much-suspected Mormons. He warned the government of what he considered to be the nefarious effects of the Latter-day Saints in the area east of the Cascades.

> The necessity of some such action on the part of Government becomes still more apparent in view of the Mormon influences which are now rapidly extending thoroughout that region. Already have Mormon settlements been made on several of the tributaries of the Columbia, and it is a well-ascertained fact that the disaffection of the Indians arises, in great part, from the teachings of the Mormon leaders, who are constantly instigating them to acts of aggression. Is it well, then, to suffer this fine country to fall into the hands of a renegade and debased people, from whom nothing but evil can come to the inhabitants of the adjoining territories?[52]

[50] *Ibid.*, 29–30.
[51] *Ibid.*
[52] *Ibid.*, 30.

Had more than a token few of Browne's salient points been taken to heart in both Washington Territory and Washington, D.C., not to mention Oregon, the tragic pattern of Indian versus white strife which has so stained the history of the Far West might have been lessened in the northwesternmost corner of the United States. Just one of the Confidential Agent's points was that the Indians simply could not form an abstract idea of (unseen) authority:

> I consider it indispensable to the success of any system which may be devised that the Superintendent should visit, in person, all the tribes under his control. To maintain friendly relations with them, it is absolutely essential that he should see them at frequent intervals, inquire into their condition, listen to their complaints, give them advice and counsel, make them occasional presents in token of his good will, and otherwise let them know practically, that he is their friend. They can form no abstract ideas of unseen authority; they must see and know the ruling power.[53]

This simple rule—that Indians had to see power to know authority—should have been an absolutely essential maxim of the government on the Western frontier. No pacification of the Indians was possible without their being, at once, shown the power and the friendship of the Great Chief. But Browne's advice was ignored or, at least, not implemented. The result was seen in bloody skirmishes and battles from Beecher's Island and the Little Bighorn to Tule Lake and the Modoc Lava Beds. Browne, in urging on the government this simple rule, predicted the results of its inactivation when he said:

> It is better, in my opinion, to prevent bloodshed than to indulge in subsequent controversies about the authorship of it, and, in the end, incur war debts amounting to millions of dollars, which always, sooner or later, fall upon the Government.[54]

While at Salem, Browne went over the books of Superintendent Nesmith and former Superintendent Stevens, item by item. He probed into such minutiae as the vouchers or claims of traders and stock drovers. But there was a lot of fiscal badlands and even *terra incognita* in the

[53] *Ibid.*, 29.
[54] *Ibid.*, 30.

Office's papers, since Superintendents Palmer, Hedges, Stevens, and Nesmith had all failed to specify payments to the satisfaction of the Commissioner of Indian Affairs. Therefore, Browne tried to explain to him some of the peculiarities which had resulted in tangled accounts— expenses of following and capturing runaways; losses of supplies by shipwreck; impassable roads. In the latter case, the rainy season turned the rude roads into intermittent stream beds and, if goods were trans- ported over them in that condition instead of being stored on the reser- vations, "the cost of transportation, admitting that pack mules can occasionally be used, almost equals the value of the supplies."[55]

Finally, Denver's Confidential Agent grappled with the problem of technically "excessive" distribution of annuities or treaty goods to the Indians. He made an explanation which would have been completely satisfactory to someone on the Pacific Slope but which, alas, would not be to a desk dragoon in Washington, D.C. He wrote:

> Living on the same reservation, governed by the same agents, knowing no reason why any partiality should be shown to one tribe above another, it is not within the power of the Superintendent to preserve order among them and, at the same time, carry into effect the provisions of the existing treaties. The delivery of annuity goods to one tribe, and the non-delivery to another, would be a signal for an outbreak which no force at his com- mand could suppress. Nor is this at all unreasonable. The whites are unable to justify any favoritism, and the Indians are fully aware of the fact, for they are sufficiently sagacious to understand the general principles of justice. It has been found necessary, therefore, to make presents to all the Indians, as far as practicable at the same time, under the heads of different funds. This has given rise to the inextricable confusion in the accounts.[56]

The last Indian agency which J. Ross Browne visited and reported upon to Denver in his tour of duty as confidential Interior Department agent was the Siletz Reservation, to which he came just before the autumnal equinox. On September 21 he found the Reservation, seated in the Coast Range but embracing an area of variegated topography. The

[55] *Ibid.*, 36.
[56] *Ibid.*, 37.

northern portion was heavily wooded, and it abounded with game. The southern sector, on the other hand, was rather barren. Siletz lay about sixty miles from Salem via Fort Hoskins. This military post lay about midway between the two sites and marked the end of a good wagon road from the capital and the beginning of a rough path to Siletz.

The prospects of the Siletz Reservation delighted Browne, particularly the lush meadows:

> The first prairie lies 15 miles from the source of the Siletz River. A series of prairies extends from that point west towards the ocean, bounded by strips of woodland along the river, the meanderings of which form very distinct boundaries to each prairie. These various spots of land are estimated to contain altogether about five thousand acres. The soil is a rich, warm loam, easily worked, and remarkably productive. I have seen nothing to surpass these prairies in any part of Oregon in position or quality, being thoroughly irrigated and fenced in by natural boundaries, almost dispensing with the necessity of wooden fences.[57]

Denver's reporter was quick to scotch the tales spread by the military that the Siletz Agency was badly located. He attributed this talk to the unfortunate disposition of the army to deprecate the Indian Department. Browne pointed out that the original location of the blockhouse—six miles from the agency—was unfortunate. It was too far to afford the reservation employees any real protection. But the new site, Fort Hoskins, thirty miles away in a branch of the Willamette River Valley called King's Valley, might as well have been on the moon. Browne tried, hard as he might, to puzzle out the reasoning of the military in moving the post farther away from the agency. He told Denver:

> It has been suggested that the settlers of the Willamette were apprehensive of danger in case of an outbreak and, for this reason, the post was located in King's Valley. I have made diligent inquiry of the principal settlers and find, without exception, that they regard it as a nuisance and are opposed to its continuance there. They say it is a detriment to them instead of a benefit. As to any practical protection, they consider such an idea simply preposterous.

[57] *Ibid.*, 39.

Expensive quarters for the officers and men are now being built near the present site, which is upon a private claim. I beg most earnestly, in behalf of common sense, that this unnecessary expense may be discontinued, if it be in any way designed to benefit the Indian Reservation. Every soul at the Agency might be murdered a week before the tidings could reach Fort Hoskins. What is to prevent the Indians from cutting off all communication? If they commit a general massacre, they will take good care that news of it shall not reach Fort Hoskins until they are several days on their journey towards the mountains of the Umpqua, the only direction in which they ever try to escape.[58]

The wheat crop at Siletz, because of a late planting, had been a total failure. But the thirty acres put into oats had responded nobly, bringing forth forty bushels to the acre. Potatoes and peas were doing well at the time of Browne's equinoctial visit, but the Indians had looted most of the tubers from their subterranean nests before they came to maturity, in what Browne considered to be the time-honored tradition of Indian improvidence.

R. B. Metcalfe, Indian agent at the Siletz Reservation, was not on the best of terms with his opposite numbers of the military in the Northwest. Lieutenant Philip Sheridan, in fact, preferred charges against him for violent and improper conduct toward the Indians—a case of the pot calling the kettle black, if Little Phil's later career in the Indian wars is considered. Sheridan notified the Superintendent of Indian Affairs via the War Department of Metcalfe's acts. Browne investigated the collision between the two and found it to be just another round in the interminable slugging match between civil and military authority on the Western frontier:

> The whole quarrel seems to have arisen from a prevailing jealousy between the civil and military authorities as to control of the Reservation. The agents being responsible for the maintenance of peace among the Indians under their charge and the security of the lives of the employees, I consider that the officers of the Army have no right to interfere, unless called upon, and I can see nothing to disapprove in the course pursued. As to the various charges of insolent and improper language, exciting threats,

[58] *Ibid.*

etc., it is no doubt true Mr. Metcalfe has a way of his own of talking to Indians; but they appear to like him, nevertheless, and his wonderful control over them during the trying ordeals of the past winter shows that he thoroughly understands their character. As an example of this remarkable supremacy, I need only refer to an incident which recently occurred and which is attested to by all the employees. The murderers of Benjamin Wright, late an Indian Agent on the Coast, had brought with them to the Reservation his scalp, over which they held nightly dances. Mr. Metcalfe regarded this as an outrage and demanded the scalp. Upon their refusal to deliver it up, he took the murderers, two in number, dragged them into his office in the face of 200 Indians, and there told them that unless the scalp was delivered in fifteen minutes, he would kill them both. One of them was then set at liberty. The Indians continued to gather and there seemed to be a general determination to kill the Agent and the few employees who stood by him. Before the expiration of the allotted time, however, the scalp was delivered and peace restored.[59]

The facts of the quarrel between the gutty Metcalfe and the equally doughty Phil Sheridan were these, according to J. Ross Browne:

Lt. Sheridan had undertaken to move certain tribes of Indians to the Reservation. As they were somewhat averse to going and were in a disaffected condition, he deemed it expedient to disarm them, but promised that, upon their arrival at the Reservation, their arms would be returned to them. They were well provided with muskets, of which they well understood the use. A number of them, however, retained their arms; and, as soon as they came upon the Reservation, they demanded the return of those which had been taken from them. At this time the condition of the various tribes was so threatening that Mr. Metcalfe did not think it safe or proper to comply with their demand. On the contrary, he felt constrained to compel them to turn over the arms which they still retained. The employees gave him notice that unless this was done they would be forced, in self-preservation, to quit the premises. The Indians refused to surrender their muskets. Mr. Metcalfe then armed himself and a party of four employees and, in defiance of their threats, took the muskets away from them. Lt. Sheridan regarded this as a break of faith towards them and so reported to his commanding officer.[60]

[59] *Ibid.*, 47–48.
[60] *Ibid.*, 47.

There was no doubt from the tenor of Browne's reports that he esteemed Metcalfe highly. (The canny Agent had averted a real clash when he recovered the arms from the braves by bribing them. He presented them with thirty horses. The crisis then blew over.) Browne described the problems which afflicted Siletz during the severe, rainy winter of 1856–57 and Metcalfe's valiant efforts to overcome them:

Great difficulties and hardships were experienced and but for the extraordinary firmness and energy of Agent Metcalfe, the Indians would have abandoned the Reservation. I consider that great credit is due him, too, for the manner in which he preserved order among these wild and warlike tribes under so many disadvantageous circumstances; and it is a matter of surprise how they ever got through the winter. When Mr. Metcalfe reached the Reservation, there were neither tents nor buildings of any kind upon it. There was no provision to support the large bands of Indians soon after congregated there. Dense floods of rain were pouring down, day after day, without cessation. The whole country was deluged with water. The Indians, naturally averse to being taken away from their homes, not knowing what was going to be done with them, strangers to the arts of civilization, disappointed in the fulfillment of nearly all the treaty stipulations, and suffering from cold and partial starvation, were in a disaffected and dangerous condition. To add to these sources of trouble, a schooner laden with a cargo of flour was wrecked on the 9th of December at the mouth of the Siletz River. In this was centered all their hopes of relief. The flour was packed ashore and carried up on the beach, thirty feet above the high-water mark. It was piled up there ready to be carried to the Reservation, which [chore] they were in the act of commencing when another storm arose and drove up the waters of the ocean to such a height that nearly all the whole amount saved from the wreck was washed away and lost. In this way, 55,000 pounds of flour, one ton of potatoes, and other substantial stores for winter use were destroyed at this inopportune crisis. . . . To prevent absolute starvation, the Agent, in the meantime, contracted for a supply at the King's Valley mills, distant thirty miles over the mountains. It was impossible to deliver it by means of wagons, and even for pack mules the mountains were then impassable. On the summits there was from two to four feet of snow. Bands of the strongest and most reliable of the Indians were engaged to cross the mountains and pack this flour to the Reservation, which they succeeded in doing after the most incredible hardships. They packed upon their backs, in this way, 20,000 pounds of flour. . . .

Having no funds to pay for this timely supply, the Agent had to make such terms as he could, and the prices charged were, of course, very much beyond the cash rates. . . . On the 7th of April, another cargo of flour reached the Yaquima. What had been received from King's Valley was consumed and, by this last arrival, it was hoped that further suffering would be prevented. Upon examination, however, it was found that the supposed flour was an inferior article of shorts and sweeps, ground over, and, of course, only fit for cattle. The contract was for a good article of fine flour, to be delivered at ten cents per pound or twenty dollars per barrel, a price sufficiently high to insure the delivery of the best quality. Flour at Portland was then worth eight dollars a barrel. Allowing $2 a barrel for transportation, it will be seen that even if good flour had been delivered, its cost to the Government would have been exactly double its market value. But to deliver ground shorts and sweeps at this rate was a fraud of the most palpable and enormous character. The Agent, however, had no choice but to receive it. The Indians were in a state of starvation. In a few days more, they would have been driven by the laws of self-preservation to abandon the Reservation and seek relief by attacking the settlements. The flour was taken, with a protest against the fraud. . . . The cargo of April 1st was carried up to the Agency where it was dealt out under the regulations as long as it lasted. But, owing to its inferior quality, it made many of the Indians sick. They got the idea that the whites had poisoned it and it was with the utmost difficulty that the Agent pacified them. He ate freely of the flour, himself, in their presence. . . . On the 29th of April a cargo of 31,000 pounds arrived. This was even worse than the other . . . conclusive evidence of wilful fraud; such a fraud, too, as, under the circumstances, must be regarded as evincing cruelty as well as avarice, and is deserving of the severest penalties of the law.[61]

In May still another load arrived and, again, on September 23, a fourth shipment. This, Browne had to see for himself. He went down to the warehouse with Agent Metcalfe and General Lane to inspect it. "I made an examination of each sack as it was delivered at the warehouse," reported Browne, "and found more than half of it to consist of shorts and

[61] *Ibid.*, 40–41.

sweeps, and the remainder a poor quality of flour, worth about $5.00 a barrel in Portland."[62] He recommended that it not be accepted but left to lie there at the contractor's risk until he should take it away. He also urged that no payment be made for the bad flour foisted upon Metcalfe and his starving Indians. "My opinion is that, upon a suit against them (Agent and Superintendent) by the contractor, it can be shown that there was an absolute breach of contract and that no jury of common honesty would award more than the actual value of the article furnished."[63] (Later, in Portland, Browne followed through by looking up the contractor personally. The latter swore that he, too, had been swindled. He placed the blame on the mill of former Governor George Abernethy and was agreeable to a fair arbitration of the value of the flour delivered.)

Before he wound up his trouble-shooting tour of the Pacific Northwest, Browne tried his hand at powwowing again. He asked Metcalfe to arrange for another *wa-wa* with the principal chiefs and headmen quartered at Siletz. He let it be known that he wanted to receive the Indians' views of the government's policy toward them, particularly. On the appointed day, a large group gathered at the storehouse. Among them were John, chief of the Shastas; Joshua, chief of the Lower Rogue Rivers; Jackson; Lympy; George; and other southern Oregon chieftains.

First off, Browne had his interpreter tell them that the President was puzzled by the conflicting reports on the Indian war and, since his heart was good toward them and since he tried to do much for them, he was pained to hear they were dissatisfied. "He had thought it best," said the interpreter, to send an agent to talk with them and take down what they said in writing, in order that he might hear, as with his own ears, how they were disposed towards him and why they were dissatisfied." The chiefs heard him out then spoke their feelings. Joshua led off, saying:

> It is very good of the President to do this. We are glad to see a messenger from him come among us, that we may state our wants and have our talk sent to him direct. I want to say for my people, that we have not been dealt with in good faith. When we made the treaty, General Palmer told us we

[62] *Ibid.*, 42.
[63] *Ibid.*

were to have a horse apiece; that we were to have nets to fish with; cooking utensils, sugar and coffee, when we came to the Reservation. That we were to have a mill to grind our wheat and make lumber to build our houses; that we were to have everything we wanted for ten years; that we would have a white doctor and plenty of medicines, and none of us would die. That all of these things were to be given up in payment for our lands. That we would not have to work for them, but had a right to them under the treaty. The Agents treat us well—except George at the Yaquima. I do not like him. He troubles our women, he beats them. This is all I have to say.[64]

John rose next and spoke directly to Browne, ignoring the interpreter:

It is well that you should understand what little I have to say. I never saw you before, but expect you came here for a good purpose. It is good of the President to send you to know what our hearts are. For my own part, my heart is sick; many of my people have died since they came here; many are still dying. There will soon be none left of us. Here the mountains are covered with great forests. It is hard to get through them. We have no game. We are sick at heart. We are sad when we look at the graves of our families.

A long time ago, we made a treaty with Palmer. There was a piece of land at Table Rock that was ours. He said it should remain ours but that, for the sake of peace, as the white settlers were bad, we should leave it for a while. When we signed the paper, that was our understanding. We now want to go back to that country.

I am glad I can now send my talk to the President. During the war my heart was bad. Last winter, when the rain came, and we were all starving, it was still bad. Now it is good. I will consent to live here one year more. After that, I must go home. My people are dying off. I am unable to go to war, but I want to go home to my country.[65]

George next took the floor:

I also want to tell you what my heart is. What the white chiefs have said to me. I have not forgotten. When Palmer was buying our lands, we sold him all our country except two small tracts, one at Evans Creek and one at Table Rock. That portion was reserved for our own use. We did not

[64] *Ibid.*, 44–45.
[65] *Ibid.*, 45.

sell it, and such was the understanding when we signed the treaty. I would ask, am I and my people the only ones who have fought against the whites that we should be removed so far from our country? It is not so great a hardship to those who have always lived near here. But to us it is a great evil. If we could be even on the borders of our native land, where we could sometimes see it, we would be satisfied. I have kept silent until now. The time has come when I can talk out. I want the President to know how we feel about it. I am carried further away from my country than anybody else. My heart is not bad, it is sick. Palmer told us, when he bought our country, that we could live at Table Rock and Evans's Creek for five years. I told Palmer we would never consent to sell him those lands. We wanted them to live upon. We could always fish and hunt there. We only wanted the mountains, which were of no use to the whites.

I am told the President is our Great Father. Why, then, should he compel us to suffer here? Does he not know it is against our will? If he cannot fulfill the promises made to us through his agents, why does he not let us go back to our homes? Does he like to see his children unhappy? We are told that, if we go back, the white people will kill us all—that their hearts are bad towards us. But the President is powerful. Let him send a paper to the whites and tell them not to trouble us. If he is powerful, they will obey him. We are sad now. We pine for our native country. Let us go back to our homes and our hearts will be bright again like the sun. Before I end my talk, I would ask what has become of our guns. Palmer took them from us on pretence that he would return them as soon as we reached the Reservation. We have never seen them since. Has he stolen them?[66]

John indicated that he wished to be heard again and Browne let him speak:

I have a word more to say and then I am done. My heart is for peace. When there was war we fought like brave men. But there were many of us, then. Now, there are few. I saw, after we had fought for our country, that it was no use—that we could not stand it long. I was the first to make peace. My people were dwindling away before the white men. All the tribes that were united with us were fighting in different parts of the country, but they were badly provided with arms. The whites were numerous and rich. They had muskets and ammunition. My son-in-law went

[66] *Ibid.*, 45–46.

200

to the Dalles to live with the Yakimas and Klickitats. I made peace and sent word to him to tell them that I had made peace and it was no use to fight any more. For this, I think we deserve well of the President. He ought to let us go home and not compel us to remain here, where we are all dying.[67]

Jim, Chief of the Kootenays, was last to speak:

My talk shall be short. I think we have been here long enough. We come from the mouth of Rogue River. There, we had plenty of fish. It is a good country. We want to go back to our old fishing and hunting grounds. What George has said is our heart. We have long been wishing to see this *tyee* [chief] sent here by the President to know our condition. This *tyee* is writing our names on paper. We hope that paper will be sent back to us. We are afraid to have our names on it. If it should be lost, we will all die.[68]

Browne smoothed away a smile at this superstition of the Indians, in the midst of their eloquent pathos, and promised to pass every word of the paper safely on to the President in Washington, D.C. He explained that the Great Chief could not stop all the whites who came from the east to overrun Indian lands. But he could ask his Grand Council to pay the Indians for their land, at least, and give them a place in which to live apart from whites and, particularly, from bad whites.

Then Browne, who knew better, had to lapse into the litany of the professional agent, asking, first, of his audience why they desired to go home when they were fed and clothed, given beans, flour, and good blankets, and sheltered from the rain and cold. He meant it to be a rhetorical question, of course, and hurried on without waiting for an answer. "Soon, you will have fields of your own. But you must work. All white people have to work. The shirts and blankets you wear were made by white men's labor. Are you better than white men that you should live without working?" If General Palmer had deceived them, Browne promised to represent the case to the President. But they could not go home. Their lands were being filled up with settlers, and the deer and the elk were leaving. Browne repeated that he felt that they should be

---

[67] *Ibid.*, 46.
[68] *Ibid.*

paid for their lands and that he would tell the President this. But then he had to muster a stern look and intone: "In the meantime, however, you must remain quietly on the Reservation. If you undertake to go back to your homes, you will be shot down. And then the President's heart will be sad, because he can no longer protect you."[69]

[69] *Ibid.*, 47.

Epilogue

T
HE GADFLY OF THE TREASURY AND INTERIOR DEPARTMENTS
was tired as the fifties came to a close. Too, as *Harper's Weekly* later put
it, "before the close of the Buchanan Administration he got himself into
trouble with the powers at Washington for exposing the frauds committed in the public service."[1] He therefore began to lay plans for the
time when he and his family would be without the comfort of a government salary. Browne sent Lucy and his six children to Washington,
D.C., via the Isthmus during September, 1859. He stayed behind to sell
off his Oakland property in order to raise funds to get his family and
himself to Europe. The trip was a long-fought-for goal; without it, the
muckraking Confidential Agent might have quit government service
after his first few brushes with the lust for office. Browne was unable to
sell the property but he was able to lease it.

All the while, he hung on grimly to the last shreds of his position—
and pay—as an Indian Department inspector. What might be considered
as the high light of his last official tour of duty in a confidential capacity
was his being stranded in Crescent City on Christmas Day after a
steamer trip. He wrote Lucy:

[1] "J. Ross Browne, Our Correspondent at Large," *Harper's Weekly*, Vol. VII, No. 321
(February 21, 1863), 125.

What I dreaded has come to pass. Tomorrow will be Christmas. . . .
[However,] it is not altogether unprofitable to be imprisoned for a week or
two in a miserable place like this one. One has such a pleasant sense of
martyrdom. . . . Old John Rogers, who suffered at the stake, sang hymns
and was happy. Why shouldn't a man be happy staked in Crescent City?[2]

Browne, like so many other Californians, succumbed at this time to
the pull of Washoe, the silver mines of Nevada's Comstock area on the
leeward slope of the Sierra. The year 1860 found him in the mines after
a rugged March hike across the Sierra Nevada. His experiences in
Nevada he recorded brilliantly in such works as "A Visit to Washoe"
and "Washoe Revisited," and they became his most popular writings
about the West. When he returned to San Francisco he wrote his wife,
"I made my expenses and $500 clear, which, if the truth were known, is
more than most people have made in Washoe."[3]

He sailed from San Francisco for the Atlantic states in May, 1860, bid-
ding the West farewell for a period of four years. He spent this time
wandering all over Europe and writing of his adventures. But Browne
was not done with the West—not by a long sight. By 1862 he was back
in New York, lecturing in the vain hope of raising enough money in this
horrid fashion to transport his brood home from Frankfurt. He hated
lecturing; he once said: "I would rather cultivate cabbages in Oakland,
a thousand to one." It turned out to be his fortunate friendship with
Robert Walker, not his lectures, which saved the day. He was given an
Indian Service commission again and used a salary advance to retrieve
his tribe of Brownes from the Teutons. They were all, safe and snug, in
the Oakland house by September, 1863, while Browne set out for Arizona
with Colonel Charles D. Poston and a military escort to visit the friendly
Indians, the Pimas and Yumas, in that Apache-ravaged territory. He
found them nearly starving but was able to afford them some relief.

The Arizona trip provided him with more grist for his bibliographic
mill, and in 1869 he saw his *Adventures in the Apache Country* published. But long before that, he was back in the San Francisco Bay area,
then to Washoe again where he found more work than he could handle.

2 *Muleback*, x.
3 *Ibid.*, xi–xii.

("All I need is a dozen heads and hands to make a fortune," he complained. He made up to $2,500 in a month with but one of the former and two of the latter.) But the hectic pace was hard on his health, which had never been 1–A for all his adventuring, so he came back to Oakland to rest. The next spring saw him investigating mines for investors in the Reese River Valley of Nevada and, in January, 1861, in Arizona. Illness forced him to return home. When he recovered, he made the mistake of going into lobbying in Washington for California vintners and miners. He found this work distasteful, and his words of earlier years (in regard to session-reporting in Congress) came back to haunt him:

> The hollowness of political distinction, the small trickery practiced in the struggle for power, the overbearing aristocracy of station and the heartless and selfish intrigues by which public men maintain their influence . . . I became thoroughly disgusted with so much hypocrisy and bombast. It required no sage minister to convince me that true patriotism does not prevail to a very astonishing extent in the hearts of those who make the most noise about it. The profession I had chosen enabled me to see behind the scenes, and study well the great machinery of government, and I cannot say that I saw a good deal to admire.

During the winter of 1866–67, Browne explored Baja California, and *Harper's* later (1869) published the cream of his observations as *A Sketch of the Settlement and Exploration of Lower California*.

In 1868 the highest honor of his life came to him when President Andrew Johnson appointed him United States minister to China. He was not long in office before his frank-as-usual reports on conditions had the hatchet men of Washington, D.C., closing in on him. He expressed ideas which were no less than ninety degrees removed from those of his predecessor, Anson S. Burlingame, and which conflicted with government policy in the form of the Burlingame Treaty. He was recalled and spent the year or so following, his darkest days, in his new home at Pagoda Hill, Oakland. When his high spirits returned he hied them, and himself, off to London on mining business, then sailed back to the States to settle down at Pagoda Hill to business matters and plans for a novel he had long wanted to write.

Returning to Oakland from his San Francisco office on the evening of December 9, 1875, J. Ross Browne was suddenly taken ill on the ferryboat, possibly with appendicitis. He was unable to reach his home so he put up, instead, at the house of a friend. He died there in the night, only fifty-four years old.

Browne's death was unexpected and widely mourned. But he had lived a jammed-full life during his fifty-four summers, much of it in the West which he had come to love. Twenty-six years before his fatal last ferry ride, he had written to his wife: "Life is uncertain . . . but I am in good health and hope to live many a long and happy year with you, yet. . . . There is a Providence that controls your destiny, shape it as we may."[4]

Just a few years before his death, Browne stood off to one side and looked at himself quizzically and satirically, particularly the Browne of Interior and Treasury Department confidential service:

> When public clamor called attention to these supposed abuses and it became necessary to make some effective demonstration of honesty, a special agent was directed to examine into the affairs of the [Government] Service and report the result. It was particularly enjoined upon him to investigate every complaint affecting the integrity of public officers, collect and transmit the proofs of malfeasance, with his own views in the premises, so that every abuse might be uprooted and cast out of the Service. Decency in official conduct must be respected and the public eye regarded! Peremptory measures would be taken to suppress all frauds upon the Treasury. It was the sincere desire of the Administration to preserve purity and integrity in the public service.
>
> From mail to mail, during a period of three years, the agent made his reports; piling up proof upon proof, and covering acres of valuable paper with protests and remonstrances against the policy pursued; racking his brains to do his duty faithfully; subjecting himself to newspaper abuse for neglecting it, because no beneficial result was perceptible, and making enemies as a matter of course. Reader, if you ever aspire to official honors, let the fate of that unfortunate agent be a warning to you. He did exactly what he was instructed to do, which was exactly what he was not wanted to do. In order to save time and expense, as well as further loss of money

4 *Muleback*, 42.

in the various branches of public service upon which he had reported, other agents were sent out to ascertain if he had told the truth; and when they were forced to admit that he had, there was a good deal of trouble in the wigwam of the Great Chief. Not only did poor Yorick incur the hostility of powerful senatorial influences, but, by persevering in his error and insisting that he had told the truth, the whole truth and nothing but the truth, he eventually lost the respect and confidence of the "powers that be," together with his official head.

I knew him well. He was a fellow of infinite jest. There was something so exquisitely comic in the idea of taking official instructions literally, and carrying them into effect, that he could not resist it.[5]

[5] *Crusoe's Island*, 299–300.

Postscript

ONE MORE MISSING PIECE from the mosaic of J. Ross Browne's career has turned up as this book goes to press. A document in the Henry E. Huntington Library's manuscripts collection, "Report in Relation to the Official Transactions of Willis A. Gorman, Governor and Ex-officio Superintendent of Indian Affairs of Minnesota," proves to be Browne's communiqué to Secretary of the Interior R. McClelland on his investigation of government affairs in Minnesota, and particularly of charges that Governor Gorman was both inefficient and corrupt. Browne's report (above) of April 6, 1855, that Gorman was innocent of the wild charges infuriated Illinois Senator Stephen A. Douglas and Minnesota Territorial Delegate Henry M. Rice. It led to an angry White House meeting between the conniving duo and President Franklin Pierce, but the latter felt obliged to retain Gorman in office after Browne's report. Gorman's political enemies managed to persuade the President that Browne had whitewashed Gorman, and Pierce sent a second agent, Sidney Webster, his own secretary, to Minnesota. Webster found that Browne had been scrupulously correct, of course, and Gorman was not removed from office.

While in Minnesota, J. Ross Browne also investigated Indian affairs and railroad speculations.

208

Index

J. Ross Browne is printed on paper bearing the University of Oklahoma Press watermark, and has an effective life of at least three hundred years. The text is set on the Linotype in 11-point Granjon, with two points of space between lines. Granjon was designed by George W. Jones, one of England's great printers, and meets the most exacting requirements for fine book work.

UNIVERSITY OF OKLAHOMA PRESS : NORMAN